**A Penny-wise Mom Shares Her Recipe
for Cutting Hundreds from
Your Monthly Food Bill**

Family Feasts for $75 a Week

Mary Ostyn

Oxmoor House®

Published by Oxmoor House, Inc.
Book Division of Southern Progress Corporation
P. O. Box 2262
Birmingham, Alabama 35201-2262

ISBN-13: 978-0-8487-3296-7
ISBN-10: 0-8487-3296-0
Library of Congress Control Number: 2009925693
Printed in the United States of America
First Printing 2009

Oxmoor House, Inc.
VP, Publishing Director: Jim Childs
Brand Manager: Allison Long Lowery
Managing Editor: L. Amanda Owens

Family Feasts for $75 a Week
Editor: Pam Hoenig
Project Editor: Vanessa Lynn Rusch
Senior Designer: Melissa Jones Clark
Production Manager: Theresa Beste-Farley

Contributors
Illustrator: Steven Salerno
Copy Editor: Jacqueline Giovanelli
Proofreader: Dolores Hydock
Indexer: Mary Ann Laurens
Editorial Intern: Emily Chappell

To order additional publications, call 1-800-765-6400.
For more books to enrich your life, visit **oxmoorhouse.com**

This book is dedicated to my Grandmother
Marie, whose legacy of frugality and loving hospitality
has carried on through the generations.

contents

acknowledgments

First of all, I thank my precious husband and children for showing patience and fortitude during six months of writing and recipe-testing. You pitched in, helped out, ate up, and made it possible for me to complete this enormous undertaking.

Thanks to Angela Miller, my awesome agent, who saw the potential in my idea and knew the right people with whom to discuss it.

Thanks to Pam Hoenig, my wonderful editor at Oxmoor House. Your skillful editing, clear vision, and gentle direction on this project made it better than I had first imagined.

Thanks to my wonderful readers and friends at *www.owlhaven.net,* whose enduring interest in affordable and delicious food let me know that there was a need for this book.

And finally, thanks to God, who gave His precious Son for me.

what would you do with an extra $100 a month?

Turn on the news any time day or night and you'll see stories about sky-rocketing food prices. Families everywhere are struggling to buy nutritious food for their children without going broke. They'd love to walk out of the grocery store without feeling fleeced. But they don't necessarily want to spend their lives clipping coupons, and they don't want to eat endless plates of beans.

Here's the good news: It's possible to cut back on your grocery costs, even in this tight economy. The ideas in this book can help the average family save

$100 to $200 or more at the grocery store every month. Even already-careful shoppers will find additional ways to save more. And it won't require deprivation. *So dream a little: What would you do with a couple hundred extra dollars every month?*

My husband and I have 10 children. Four arrived by birth and six via adoption. Thanks to many years of feeding our family on a moderate income, I've become a black-belt budget stretcher. Last year our income was $56,000, and most months our food budget for 12 people is $900 a month. That includes 10 people ages 10 and older, a large variety of healthy, delicious food, and a few meals out each month. (With 10 kids, "date night" is an essential for my hubby and me!)

To get a little perspective on our spending, the USDA March 2008 "thrifty food plan" estimate puts average food costs for a family of 12 at $1,548 a month. That's a full $600 more than I spend. An average dinner for my entire family costs $15 or less.

It took me years of shopping and cooking and experimenting to get this good at saving money. But you can do it too. This book will show you how. Tips in every chapter will help you sidestep common spending pitfalls at the store. Action points at the end of Chapters 1–4 will help you customize a savings plan for your own family. And the recipe chapters share a wide variety of mouthwatering, kid-tested, economical meals sure to make your family forget you're living on a budget.

The New Frugality: It's a Good Thing

Most people I talk with are interested in saving money on their food bill, but tell me they're afraid it will take endless slaving in the kitchen. They think it might require them to eat food they really don't like. And frankly, they like the convenience and taste of restaurant food, and they don't want to give it up.

I'm here to tell you that you can eat good, affordable food without a ton of effort. And—here's what many people don't consider—being careful with your food budget will greatly expand your choices in other areas of your life. Most of us only have so much money, so it's not rocket science to figure out that spending less on food frees us to do other things with that money.

One of the things that enriches my family's life is a vacation on the beach every year. That vacation costs us a couple thousand dollars. That's money we wouldn't have if we spent it at the grocery store.

Make a list of your dreams and goals and put that list in a prominent place.

At its heart, frugality isn't about deprivation. It's about taking control of your resources. It's about making the most of what you have. It's about making dreams happen. One take-out meal isn't going to derail your dreams. But take-out four days a week just might.

Dream a Little

What are your dreams? Maybe you picked up this book simply hoping to reduce your grocery bill a little. Perhaps you're trying to pay off a credit card or save for a trip. Or maybe you're longing to become an at-home mom. There are lots of great reasons to spend your grocery dollars more thoughtfully. The clearer your goals are, the easier it will be to resist calling for pizza delivery and instead get out flour, yeast, and pepperoni to make your own.

It's All in Your Head

Attitude is everything. If you're feeling put upon and sorry for yourself as you roll out that pizza dough, changes in your budget aren't likely to stick. But instead, if you're thinking happily about being $30 closer to your goal, you'll be much more likely to build habits that will help you realize your long-term dreams.

What would you do with a few hundred more dollars each month? Make a list of your dreams and goals and put that list in a prominent place. Whether you use the found money to pay down some debt or provide your daughter with ballet lessons or build up a savings account for the first time, you're making your life better.

Often when people think of cutting back on their food costs, they picture boring meals and endless hours in the kitchen. Cooking does take some time, but a thoughtfully planned menu can include succulent barbecued beef, cheesy enchiladas, biscuits and gravy, and many other satisfying family favorites, many of which you can prepare in 30 minutes or less.

When you're thinking about getting by on a lower grocery budget, remember that different solutions will work for different families. As you read, it's important to be realistic about your time constraints. If one parent is at home all day, homemade cornbread and a chili that takes two hours to cook may be very doable. However, throw-it-all-into-the-slow-cooker-in-the-morning recipes may work better for a family with two working parents and kids who have soccer practice at 6:30 p.m.

Don't feel bad if some strategies don't work for you. But do read with an open mind and a willingness to experiment. It took me a while to figure out which stores consistently had the best prices on meat, and which recipes I could whip out even on a soccer night. It took me even longer to realize that soccer practice nights are perfect times to run in and out of nearby grocery stores and "cherry-pick" their weekly bargains. Change often feels awkward at first. Eventually you'll get quicker and things will start to feel natural.

Eating Great on $75 a Week

You may have to experiment a bit to find the level of frugality that works best for you and your family. I spend about $75 per person per month, which, for a family of four, would add up to $300 a month, or $75 a week for the entire family. I could go a little lower, but this budget provides for a comfortable amount of convenience and choice while still being wise with our money.

If you're spending $100 a week for a family of four, you're most likely already making careful shopping choices, especially if you live in an area where the cost of living is higher. But know that you could go lower if you need—or want—to. *That is what this book is all about.*

finding the hidden costs

If you feel like you're running a tight ship when it comes to your food budget, but need to save even more, consider keeping a food-cost journal for a month or two. Record every single food item that you buy all month. Most likely you'll discover some leaks in your budgetary boat.

That $3 coffee you grab on the way into work in the morning? That adds up to $60 a month. Taking your family out for pizza every Friday? Another $80 a month or more, depending on the size of your family. Your husband's vending machine snack and cola every afternoon? Thirty dollars a month.

I'm not saying you can't do any of these things. You may decide to give each family member a budget to allow for occasional snacks or school lunches or coffee breaks. But if you're trying to reach your lowest possible grocery cost, you need to know where the money is going. And you need to weigh every purchase carefully. As a result, you may end up deciding that saving an hour on cooking each week isn't really worth the $80 a month that Pizza Hut is costing you.

I'm confident that the tips in this book can help almost any family save $100 or more every month fairly painlessly. That's not a bad return on a $20 book, right? If you need to save more than $100 a month, simply implement more of the ideas I suggest.

Chapters 2, 3, and 4 end with a list of ideas you can try to save more money on your food budget. For example, creating a price book will tell you at a glance which store has the best price for each item on your grocery list. Planning a weekly shopping rotation will prevent you from hitting more than one or two stores a week (just limiting shopping time can be a great money-saver!). Keeping your pantry stocked with ingredients for five quick meals will help you resist the call of take-out. Doubling just two recipes each week (and freezing the extra meal) will dramatically decrease your time in the kitchen and make these changes a lot easier to stick with. And throughout the 200 recipes I include, you'll find Super-Saver Ideas to cut your costs even more.

I suggest that you go through these lists twice. First, check off the things that you're not doing yet, but that sound fairly easy to implement. Then try to pick one or two other things that might push you just a little bit beyond your comfort zone. You might find that the extra effort is worth the savings!

Baby Steps Towards Big Savings

A word of warning: Don't take it too fast. If you change everything you do all at once, you'll wear yourself out, and the changes are less likely to stick. It's far better to try a few new things each week. If something turns out to be totally unreasonable for your family, ditch it and try something else. For example, shopping with coupons might make your right eye twitch, but buying spices in the bulk food department may work beautifully.

But if you need to make drastic changes in your budget quickly, you may find it possible to save $300 or more every month by trying nearly every trick in this book. Don't beat yourself up, though, if you find you need to drop a few of the strategies to maintain your sanity. *Here's my little secret: Even I don't consistently do everything I advocate in these pages.* I've discovered what works for me, which tactics fit into my lifestyle. For that reason, I don't feel guilty that I rarely bake my own bread, and that I sometimes feed my kids fish sticks, and that an occasional $10 goes towards a bottle of wine.

Frugality is Freedom

There's a verse in the Bible that says, "The borrower is the slave to the lender." It doesn't feel good to be in bondage to the bank, to have every paycheck spent before you even see it. Feeding your family in an affordable way can help you take charge of your life and move you closer to your dreams.

In my life frugality has given me options that indebtedness would never allow. I've been able to be home with our children full time since 1998. We've paid off every debt except our house. We've been able to adopt. We've taken our children on international trips that have broadened their view of the world. And here's a secret I discovered along the way: If you have the right attitude, frugal shopping and cooking can truly feel like an adventure.

action points:

action point #1:

Make a list of what you intend to do with the money you save.

Having dreams for the future makes it so much easier to stay motivated on a daily basis. How would your life be better if you had a little more money in the checking account at the end of each month? What would you do differently? Write out that list and put it on your fridge or the bathroom mirror or stick it in your checkbook so you'll always remember the big picture.

action point #2:

Figure out your current grocery spending.

You can do this in one of three ways:

1 If you're the ultra-organized type, just open Quicken or another money management computer program on your computer and glance through your spending habits for the past few months.

2 If you're not in the habit of watching your money quite that closely, you can look at your checkbook register or online banking records to figure out how much you spent on food last month. Walmart or Target shoppers may not get an accurate picture, though, especially if you're in the habit of picking up clothing and household items while grocery shopping. But give yourself a ballpark estimate.

3 The final option is to work on this project gradually, by saving and adding up your grocery receipts for the next month. This is a good exercise for anyone, as it will make you much more conscious of the money you're spending. A heap of receipts is also a simple way to start your very own price book—a gem of a tool that I'll discuss more in Chapter 3. Don't forget to add restaurant meals in with your other food costs!

If you're surprised to learn how much you really spend in a month, take heart. That just means you have more room for improvement—and more room to impress yourself as you get better at the shopping game.

action point #3:

Take the quiz on pages 14–15 to learn what may be contributing to food expenditures in your house.

action point #4:

Set your first savings goal.

Once you've added up your expenses and taken the quiz to discover the areas you could use the most work in, compare your expenses to your goals. How much money are you hoping to save each month? Most people can cut back 10% fairly easily. A 20% savings is going to cost you a little more effort. You should probably only aim for a 30% savings if you're certain your food budget is extremely bloated.

Don't worry if at this point you have no idea how you're going to save that money. In future chapters, I'll discuss dozens of different ways you can do it. This first step is just to clarify how big your goals are, and thus how extreme the changes in your life need to be.

One instant way that most people can shrink their food budget is to stop eating out so much. As I said earlier in the chapter, you need to add your restaurant meals into your total food cost each month. But for the purpose of goal-setting, you may find it helpful to separate your restaurant money from your grocery store money, since that is an almost-immediate way to save money.

For example, let's say you normally eat out twice a week and spend about $25 a meal, for a restaurant total of $200 a month. You also spend $800 in the grocery store each month. A reasonable goal might be to reduce your restaurant spending by 50% and your grocery expenses by 20%. That would net you a savings of $260 per month.

Or you could reduce your grocery expenses by 10% (saving $80) and cut out all but one dinner out per month (saving $175) for a total monthly savings of $255. Only you can decide what is doable for you. *(continued on page 16)*

tightwad...or

How Frugal Are You?

Why is there always more month than money? Take this quiz, then add up your score in each section to discover which parts of this book might benefit you the most.

Food: Where Do You Spend Your Money?
(my score:_____)

1 In the grocery store, I want to get in and get out. No comparison shopping for me!
0 Not true   2 Sometimes true   4 Always true

2 I don't feel like it's worth my time to visit several stores for the best prices.
0 Not true   2 Sometimes true   4 Always true

3 Family members eat out or get coffee during the workday three or more days a week.
0 Not true   2 Sometimes true   4 Always true

4 I serve ready-made entrées (such as pizza, canned soup, lasagna, fish sticks, or hot dogs) for three or more meals each week.
0 Not true   2 Sometimes true   4 Always true

The Time Crunch (my score:_____)

1 I'm lucky to get showered every day. Forget finding time to cook every night.
0 Not true   2 Sometimes true   4 Always true

2 I often grab fast food while ferrying kids to multiple activities in the evenings.
0 Not true   2 Sometimes true   4 Always true

3 I buy lots of deli, carry-out, and prepackaged food to keep meal prep simple at home.
0 Not true   2 Sometimes true   4 Always true

4 I don't have time to pack lunches, so my family eats school food and restaurant food a lot.
0 Not true   2 Sometimes true   4 Always true

.......spendthrift?

Got Skills? (my score:_____)

1 I'm not good at cooking and/or I don't enjoy it.
   0 Not true   2 Sometimes true   4 Always true

2 I know I should be planning our meals ahead of time, but I can't seem to get in the habit.
   0 Not true   2 Sometimes true   4 Always true

3 I'm always running out of stuff. I head to the store three or more times each week.
   0 Not true   2 Sometimes true   4 Always true

4 Restaurant food tastes better than my cooking.
   0 Not true   2 Sometimes true   4 Always true

People and Preferences (my score:_____)

1 My family prefers prepackaged or takeout food over my cooking.
   0 Not true   2 Sometimes true   4 Always true

2 I buy organic or specialized food due to preference or my children's food allergies.
   0 Not true   2 Sometimes true   4 Always true

3 I regularly cook different things at a meal to satisfy different family members.
   0 Not true   2 Sometimes true   4 Always true

4 We love to eat out; we go to sit-down restaurants two or more times a week.
   0 Not true   2 Sometimes true   4 Always true

Your Highest Score Was:_____

Quiz Area	Your Score	If you scored highest in this area, you may find the following section of the book most helpful.
Food	....	pages 17–37
Time	....	pages 20–52
Skills	....	pages 47–64
People	....	pages 59–78

Below are some goals that you might consider. At the top are the smallest goals and lower down are the more challenging ones. Certainly you may aim for a more dramatic cutback than what I've suggested, but remember, gradual changes are the easiest to stick with. You can always revisit your goals in a month or two and try to save even more once you've had success on a smaller scale.

As you try to decide which goal might be most realistic for your family, take the time to fill in the blanks and calculate just how much you could save with each one. Seeing the dollar figure can be very motivating. I've left one goal blank at the end so you can set your own if none of mine feel right for your family. Once you've picked a goal, come with me to Chapter 2, and we'll talk about achieving it.

Suggested Goals

☐ **Save $50 a month overall.** (It's OK to be a little chicken-hearted at first!)

☐ **Cut restaurant spending by 50%.** That would save you $_____/month.

☐ **Cut restaurant meals to one meal per month.** That would save you $_____/month.

☐ **Ten percent overall savings.** That would save you $_____/month.

☐ **Twenty percent overall savings.** That would save you $_____/month.

☐ **Twenty percent grocery savings plus 50% less eating out.** That would save you $_____/month.

☐ **Thirty percent overall savings.** That would save you $_____/month.

☐ **Thirty percent grocery savings plus 75% less eating out.** That would save you $_____/month.

☐ **Your own personal goal:** _____

_____

_____

chapter 2

come shopping with me

When I'm driving through neighborhoods after dark, my gaze is drawn toward houses where windows are lit and shades are up. I think everyone has some curiosity about the way others live. That's why I've decided to take you to the grocery store with me and do a little show and tell. I'll give you a peek into my thoughts as I shop and show you the kinds of decisions that keep our grocery costs down.

First, Avoid the Store

My family is like any other—we rarely go a day without running out of something. But unless the needed item is something crucial like toilet paper or coffee (the elixir of life), I wait until my list includes at least half a dozen items before I head for the grocery store. The less frequently I enter the store, the less I spend. I figure I avoid at least $30 of impulse buying each time I skip a trip. If I decrease the number of trips I make per month by three, I've saved nearly $100 on groceries, not to mention the savings in time and gas.

Here's another thing about waiting: It gets my head out of the instant gratification mode. It makes me remember that we can live just fine without a whole variety of things. I'm not a martyr—if I need something, I buy it. But allowing myself time to reflect on a purchase helps clarify the true importance of an item.

For example, I've discovered that cloth napkins are quite doable for us. I still keep a stash of paper in the pantry but when our cloth napkins are clean, we use them. In contrast, once I lived for a couple of weeks without coffee creamer, and decided, never again. I know, I know—I won't die without coffee creamer. But the point here is not a life of deprivation. The point is to stop wasting money on the froufrou that sucks up your bucks without adding to your quality of life. Different people have different "needs." One of mine is coffee creamer. Figure yours out, and you'll save a lot of money.

Make a List Before You Shop

I make a "big" trip to the grocery store a couple of times a month. We keep a running grocery list on the side of our fridge. The list is often scrawled with various writing implements and spellings with varying levels of proficiency. Sometimes oddball items like horses and video games mysteriously end up on the list. But at least I have a list.

Before I leave for the store, I plan menu ideas for the next two weeks, adding any needed items to my list as I plan. (I'll talk more about that later.) Then I walk around the kitchen checking my pantry staples and adding those to the list. I also query everyone within earshot about anything else we might need. I've discovered that the kids are great at remembering needed items.

Occasionally, even after spending a long time compiling my list, in the scurry to get out the door with kids and shoes and jackets and keys, I manage to leave the list at home. If some of the teenagers have opted to stay home, we're in luck. I just call home and have one of them read off the list on the fridge.

pantry staples

Recently, my oldest daughter got married and asked me to make her a list of essential ingredients to make her grocery dollars stretch as far as possible. I pulled together the following list of essential pantry items.

Your list of staples may look different from mine. I buy very few canned goods, because, in general, ready-made canned foods such as soup are not money-saving items, especially in the quantities I need for my family. But this list will give families the raw materials to make a large variety of frugal meals.

- Baking powder
- Baking soda
- Bananas
- Barley
- Canned pineapple
- Chocolate chips
- Coconut
- Coffee
- Cornmeal
- Cornstarch
- Creamer
- Flour
- Garlic
- Legumes: lentils, red beans, split peas
- Oils: olive, sesame, vegetable
- Onions
- Pastas: egg noodles, macaroni, spaghetti
- Peanut butter
- Potatoes
- Quick-cooking oats
- Raisins
- Ramen noodles
- Rice

- Seasonings: basil, chili powder, cumin, ginger, oregano, pepper, red pepper flakes, salt, sweet paprika
- Shortening
- Soy sauce
- Sugar: brown, confectioners', white
- Tomato paste
- Tomato sauce
- Tuna
- Unsweetened cocoa powder
- Vanilla extract
- Vinegar
- Yeast

Refrigerator/Freezer Staples
- Apples
- Butter
- Cabbage
- Carrots
- Cheeses: Cheddar, Parmesan, mozzarella

- Chicken breasts/thighs
- Cream cheese
- Eggs
- Flour tortillas
- Fresh ginger
- Frozen corn
- Frozen peas
- Ground beef
- Lettuce
- Milk
- Pepperoni
- Sour cream
- Salad dressings
- Salsa

If not, I get the fun of reconstructing the list in the car with help from my kids. "Who wrote stuff on the list this week?" I'll call to everyone in the car. "Do you remember what you wrote down?"

Kids call out items, while the designated scribe scribbles away. I'll then go through the list of things I want to cook for the next week or two, again taking comments from the peanut gallery. Lists made in this way are less complete than lists made thoughtfully at home. But they still help stave off the mental overload that can happen when you venture into the store without a list.

War at the Store

Later, I'll talk about the various stores at which I shop, and the advantages of each. But let's start by walking through the aisles of a fairly ordinary grocery store, which is where I do the bulk of my shopping. You'll notice pretty quickly that what I don't buy is every bit as important—perhaps more important—than what I actually pick up off the shelves.

The most affordable store in our area is a basic chain grocery store with an outstanding bulk food department and a "bag your own groceries" policy. Bagging your own groceries can be a bit of a hassle, but to me the lower prices at this store are worth the extra effort.

Just inside the doors you'll see a large display of "special deals." Retailers like to place impulse-type buys front and center while shoppers still feel like they have money. Sometimes things you find there are real bargains but not always. Since only one brand is featured here at a time, I shop warily.

If I'm not certain an item is well priced, I'll wait to pick it up in the aisle where it's grouped with other similar items so I can compare prices. My price book helps with this as well—more on that later in Chapter 3. If I spot a deal I know is excellent, like $1.25 for a box of corn flakes, I'll grab it. In fact, whenever I find cereal for $1.50 or less, I buy at least four boxes.

Getting Those Fruits and Veggies

Produce can take a big bite out of your budget. Over the years, I've learned which items provide the most value and which should be bought only in season or in small quantities. Everyday staples in my home include bananas, carrots, onions, potatoes, garlic, fresh ginger, and cabbage. These foods are versatile and affordable year-round. I buy apples and oranges as well, but usually in smaller quantities, especially when their prices are at the high end of the spectrum when they're not in season.

Other things that I buy occasionally and/or in moderation in the produce section include mushrooms, bagged lettuce (when our greenhouse isn't producing), grapes (if $1.25/pound or less), broccoli, egg roll wrappers, green peppers (if two for $1), green onions, lemons, limes, green beans, and cilantro.

The Incredible Shrinking Salad

Have you noticed that bagged salads are getting lighter and lighter? I used to be able to get a full pound of salad greens for $2. Now the same priced bag weighs only 12 ounces, which means I need at least a bag and a half for my family. Head lettuce is the cheaper way to go. I will often mix one head of iceberg lettuce with half a bag of baby spinach for added color and nutrition. Spinach tends to be cheaper than fancy types of leaf lettuce, but it's just as healthy. And many kids who won't tolerate cooked spinach will eat it without any problem in a salad. In fact, if you don't tell your kids it's spinach, they may not even realize it.

I often substitute fresh cabbage when making salads. I cut half a medium-size head of green cabbage into very thin shreds, grate a carrot into it, and toss it with either ⅓ cup bottled Italian dressing or my homemade Asian Ginger Dressing (page 268). Since cabbage is so densely packed, it goes a long way. Half a head of cabbage will make enough salad to feed my whole family. It's healthier than iceberg lettuce, and it's more affordable than bagged spinach and other greens. Cabbage also has a much longer fridge life than lettuce, which means it can still provide you with a fresh salad two weeks after your last trip to the store, something you can't say for spinach and other leafy greens.

What's in Season?

We're fortunate to have a large garden and as a result I do a lot of canning. Because of that we almost always have tomatoes, apples, lettuce, and corn on hand, in some form or another. This really cuts down on our produce spending. But anyone can save money in the produce section by aiming to buy foods that

when are fruits & vegetables cheaper?

Bananas, potatoes, carrots, cucumbers, onions, and celery are usually a good deal no matter the season. Here's when to buy other fruits and vegetables.

January
broccoli
cauliflower
grapefruit
leeks
lemons
oranges

February
broccoli
cauliflower
grapefruit
lemons
oranges
papayas

March
broccoli
lettuce
mangoes
pineapples

April
asparagus
broccoli
lettuce
mangoes

pineapples
rhubarb
spring peas

May
asparagus
broccoli
cherries
lettuce
pineapple
rhubarb
spring peas
zucchini

June
apricots
cantaloupe
cherries
corn
lettuce
peaches
strawberries
watermelon

July
apricots
blueberries
cantaloupe
green beans

peaches
raspberries
strawberries
watermelon

August
apricots
cantaloupe
corn
peaches
plums
raspberries
strawberries
summer squash
tomatoes
watermelon

September
apples
grapes
lettuce
pumpkins
spinach
tomatoes

October
apples
broccoli
cranberries

grapes
lettuce
pumpkins
spinach
sweet potatoes
winter squash

November
apples
broccoli
cranberries
mushrooms
oranges
pears
pumpkins
spinach
sweet potatoes
tangerines
winter squash

December
broccoli
cauliflower
grapefruit
oranges
pears
sweet potatoes
tangerines

are in season, and supplementing with fruits and vegetables that are well priced year-round.

Yes, that means no December watermelon, no matter how yummy it looks. But eating seasonally really lets you savor the changing seasons and the good things they offer. If my family ate watermelon year-round, they probably wouldn't appreciate it so much when it was in season.

Don't Pay for the Packaging

Grocery stores with bulk food departments greatly expand your shopping choices. *But watch out: Things aren't always cheaper in bulk.* My precious coffee creamer, for example, is cheaper in the coffee aisle. But many deals are excellent. Some of my most frequent buys in bulk include chocolate chips, coconut, barley, cornmeal, dried beans, and lentils. I can buy seasonings—as little or as much as I want—for a fraction of what they cost in the baking aisle. This comes in handy when I'm trying a new recipe that calls for something unusual that I'm not sure I'll use again.

One day recently I decided to buy a new spice. I was in a hurry and intended to grab it out of the baking aisle. But when I saw that it cost $8, I just couldn't do it. I took a quick trip back to bulk food, where I was able to buy 4 ounces for just $1, saving me $7 and getting me four times as much seasoning. That's an excellent return on my five-minute time investment.

Where's the Beef?

Choices made in the meat department can make or break your budget. Here's where it really pays to stock up whenever and wherever the prices are lowest, even if that means visiting a different store now and then. When hamburger goes on sale for less than $2/pound, I stock up. Occasionally a small grocery store near me sells 5-pound "logs" of ground beef for $1.25/pound. When this happens, I'll buy 20 or 30 pounds at a time. Ground beef, well wrapped, can be frozen for up to a year, so I don't worry about buying too much.

I sometimes buy thin-cut top round steak, but only when it's $2/pound or less. I use this in stir-fries. I also buy hot dogs now and then. In general I buy generic food without a thought, but I'm picky about my hot dogs—they've got to be Falls Brand Beef. Since that brand is pretty expensive, we only have hot dogs once a

lean or regular ground beef?

Occasionally I'm able to find lean ground beef for less than $2/pound, but usually I just buy regular ground beef. If we ate lots of meat, this might not be a good choice, but I'm feeding normal-weight growing children, and we treat meat more as a condiment than the centerpiece of a meal. When I make a casserole or a soup, I rarely use more than two pounds for 10 to 12 people. After I cook the meat, I drain off the obvious fat, then spoon the meat into a bowl lined with a paper towel, which blots up more fat. This method reduces the fat in the beef by several grams per 3-ounce serving.

If you want an even greater reduction in fat, try this method.

1. Cook broken-up ground beef in a skillet until brown, 8 to 10 minutes.
2. Remove it from the skillet and let drain in a bowl lined with three layers of paper towels.
3. Microwave 4 cups of water on High, until very hot.
4. Place the beef in a mesh strainer or colander and set it over a large sturdy bowl.
5. Pour hot water over the beef and let drain 5 minutes.

This method, according to the Canadian Beef Council, will make regular ground beef lower in fat than extra-lean ground beef. Since extra-lean beef can cost twice as much as regular, this can save you a lot of money.

month or so. We don't use a lot of lunchmeat, since it's rarely very affordable. But when I need it for a picnic lunch, I compare prices and look for the lowest per-ounce cost.

Another thing that I sometimes buy in the meat department is sausage, to go with eggs for breakfast. I've found the sausage "logs" that I slice into patties myself are the most affordable way to go. I also buy a few pounds of bacon every month or so. Occasionally we eat bacon for breakfast, usually when we're camping, or for a child's birthday breakfast (I take requests on birthdays!). More often I'll use half a pound of bacon at a time as a flavoring along with onions and garlic in an otherwise vegetarian dish such as Cheesy Corn and Potato Chowder (page 192) or Spaghetti Carbonara My Way (page 164).

Around the holidays you can sometimes buy bone-in hams for as low as 99¢/pound. The cheapest way I've found to buy boneless ham is in those shrink-wrap packs. Then ask the butcher to slice it thinly for you. This service is free, and your ham will cost a lot less than if you buy it in already-sliced packages. Make your request at the start of your shopping trip, and pick it up when you're nearly done, and it won't even take you any extra time.

I buy roasts when they're $1.50/pound or less. I love to cook pork roasts overnight in the slow cooker—they're fall-apart tender by dinnertime with no effort on my part. But we only do this once a month or so because we end up consuming a lot of meat in one meal that way.

Even if your family isn't large, you'll save both money and time by occasionally cooking a turkey and freezing the leftovers.

Fish and Shellfish

Salmon is one of the rare main-dish items for which I'm willing to pay more than $2/pound. I serve it only once a month or so, but it's easy, healthful, and delicious. I find it to be most affordable when bought in the freezer case. I also occasionally buy imitation crab, medium shrimp, and boxed frozen catfish or tilapia. Used in moderation, these items add a nice variety to our diet without breaking the bank.

Poultry

When buying chicken, I rarely buy anything with bones that costs more than $1.25/pound. When I find it for $1/pound, I buy a month's worth all at once. I try not to pay more than $2/pound for boneless, skinless chicken. Sometimes I buy fryer leg quarters in 10-pound bags for 79¢/pound. When I get home with a big packet of chicken like that, I usually cook it right away (see page 70 for more on that), then the kids and I pick the meat off the bones and freeze it in meal-size portions. I save the cooking liquid to use as my own homemade chicken broth. It adds a wonderful flavor to soup.

how to bone a chicken leg quarter

Often you can buy chicken leg quarters for a very reasonable price. Here's how you turn bone-in chicken into boneless.

❶ Use a sharp kitchen knife to slice through the joint where the thigh and drumstick meet. The cartilage at this joint is soft, so if you're cutting in the right place your knife should feel little resistance.

❷ Once you've separated the leg from the thigh, make an incision along the top of the bone. Deepen the incision by slicing into the thigh until your knife reaches bone. The bone will be visible through the incision; it will look white and very firm.

❸ Take hold of the partially disconnected bone and pull it up and away from the thigh so you can slice underneath the remaining bone. You'll feel the bone begin to loosen from the thigh. Make the necessary cuts to remove the bone completely from the thigh.

❹ Slice the meat away from the bone by making short cuts with your knife. As the meat comes free, use your fingers to pull it clear of the bone. Keep cutting until you have removed any unwanted bits of bone, sinew, and tendons. Follow this same procedure to debone legs.

Around the holidays is a great time to stock up on turkeys. Several times each winter, when there is a great sale, I'll buy a whole turkey and make a turkey dinner just for us. I love those turkey leftovers, and we can usually get three or four meals from one big turkey. Even if your family isn't large, you'll save both money and time by occasionally cooking a turkey and freezing the leftovers.

Dairy

I look for cheese that I can buy for $2.50/pound or less. My supermarket usually offers two or three kinds of block cheese for that price, as well as 5-pound bags of grated Cheddar. I pass up anything that is priced higher. Often I'll wait to buy cheese at my local warehouse club where I can get 5 pounds of grated Cheddar for $13 and mozzarella for $2/pound. Grated cheese freezes wonderfully (pages 54–55). Even if it took me 6 months to go through 5 pounds of grated cheese, I would still buy it in bulk just to benefit from the lower price.

Eggs are a must-have item at our house, but since prices have gone up, I've gotten more careful about where I buy them. When I see dozens for $1.50 or less, I buy several dozen. I often find 5-dozen packs for $5 or so. That many eggs take up a fair bit of real estate in your fridge, but if you've got space, you might consider it. Make sure to check the sell-by dates on the boxes before purchasing them.

Milk is another item that I watch the price on. When I can find it for $2.80/gallon or less, I buy extra, and freeze what we won't use within a week. You can freeze milk without any problem, as long as you pour out half a cup first, so there is room for expansion in the jug.

Our family doesn't drink huge quantities of milk. Some of us are allergic to milk and, the truth is, it's very possible to get the protein and calcium you need from foods other than milk. If your family drinks a lot of soy milk, consider buying a soy milk machine. The SoyaJoy is a good, durable brand. It's very easy to operate, and the beans are amazingly affordable compared to store-bought soy milk. You'll recoup your investment pretty quickly if you go through more than a gallon or two of soy milk each week.

location, location, location

If you buy your cheese in the grocery store, it can make a difference where in the store you buy it. When it comes to cheeses like Cheddar or Monterey Jack that you may be using to make quesadillas or macaroni and cheese, you can expect to pay a premium for it in the cheese section near the deli counter. But look for those cheeses in the dairy section in the same store, and the prices could be $3 or less per pound. Also, be on the alert for these cheeses going on sale at the deli counter; when they do, just ask the deli person to cut you off a chunk without slicing it.

The same can hold true for items like tortillas and corn chips. You may find them to be cheaper in the Hispanic foods section than in the refrigerated case or snack foods aisle.

We also buy light sour cream, margarine, and real butter for baking and cooking. If there is a good sale on yogurt, we'll occasionally buy a few cartons for the members of our family who regularly pack lunches. If I'm planning to make lasagna, I'll sometimes buy cottage cheese.

Breakfast Food

Breakfast cereal isn't an especially frugal meal, and if you want to get your budget to its lowest level, you might want to stop buying it. I'm a slow starter in the morning, so I prefer to have cereal on hand for the days when I don't feel like cooking. But I do keep my cereal dollars to a minimum, employing a variety of strategies. For starters, I try not to pay more than $1.50/box. Often that means I buy generic cereal, which, to our family, tastes as good as any.

If you want to get your budget to its lowest level, you might want to stop buying breakfast cereal.

Next, I make sure that I buy only the lower-sugar cereals, such as Raisin Bran, Cheerios, Corn Flakes, Rice Krispies, and occasionally Corn Chex. Sure, my kids beg for the junk. But they also eat twice as much of it, and it disappears twice as fast. I figure we all will be healthier with a little less sugar in our diet.

I also keep my eye out for coupons for cereals that I normally buy. In the cereal aisle, I also buy grits (similar to Cream of Wheat, but cheaper), and cornmeal. I skip single-serving oatmeal, instead buying my oats in 50-pound sacks and jazzing it up at home with butter, apples, sugar, and cinnamon. For another healthy choice on busy mornings, try making your own granola (page 82).

Baked Goods

There are times when I make bread, but we eat it in such large quantities that baking all my own bread would be a huge time drain. I purchase most of our bread at the day-old bread store, where I pay $1.25 for whole-grain loaves of bread. I buy enough to last a week or two at a time, and store it in the freezer.

Sometimes I buy bread in the frozen food section, which gives us the pleasure of home-baked bread without the effort. It's not true whole-grain bread, but the per-loaf price is a bit lower than our local bread store.

I also buy hot dog and hamburger buns. Flour tortillas are an excellent, cost-effective item to keep on hand for Mexican dishes and to use as wraps for quick lunches. Occasionally we splurge on bagels.

In general we bake cookies (page 240) or make fruit crisps (page 246) to satisfy our sweet cravings. We also make our own biscuits (pages 223–224) to accompany various meals. Once you've done it a few times, you can pull together biscuits in 15 minutes or less. And homemade biscuits beat those store-bought pop-apart cans any day.

Baking Aisle

Staples from the baking aisle include flour, sugar, raisins, oil, shortening, and sometimes syrup (about half the time I make my own syrup—see page 272). Everyone over the age of seven in my family knows how to check unit prices. As my kids and I scan the shelves, I can regularly be heard to say, "Here's seven and a half cents per ounce—can anyone beat that?" Sometimes I'll buy a cake mix with a coupon. Once or twice a year I'll buy pudding or Jell-O. Occasionally I'll spring for brownie mix, usually to take on a camping trip. Other than that, we bake most things from scratch. Check out my homemade baking mixes (pages 277 and 280).

Canned and Dry Goods

The rule in the canned food aisle, in general, is, if the item is an ingredient for cooking, we buy it, but if it's something ready-made in a can we probably do not buy it. That means we buy spaghetti noodles, but not Spaghetti-O's. Instead of premade chili, we buy dried beans and make our own. We buy ramen noodle packets, but not chicken noodle soup. We buy canned tuna, but not the little packets with the tuna and crackers all together. You get the idea.

We buy generic peanut butter, checking for unit prices. Sometimes the tiny jars are a better buy than the big ones. Salad dressing is generic (if the price is right) or homemade (pages 267–269). We buy lots of noodles of different types. I make homemade macaroni and cheese, along with spaghetti, so I keep these noodles in stock. For added interest, I keep my eyes open for sales on fun shapes. My dollar store often sells pasta for 75¢/pound. Occasionally I can get 2 pounds for just a dollar.

are dried beans really worth it?

Lots of people buy canned chili because they think cooking dried beans is a big hassle. When we're camping, I go for canned chili myself. But most of the beans we eat on a regular basis start out as dried. In our area a 16-ounce can of ready-made chili is $1.25. A 16-ounce can of red beans is about 60¢. An equivalent amount of dried red beans is about 20¢. Granted, you'll be adding your own seasonings and meat to the lower-cost items to get the same product but it's obvious that you can save a lot of money by cooking your own beans.

I sometimes cook my beans on the stovetop, which, depending on the type of bean, can take two to four hours (check out the Bean Cooking Times chart on page 74). But I've found that the easiest way to cook beans is in my slow cooker. Depending on my schedule, I might start the cooker right after breakfast and cook the beans on High all day, or I might fire up the beans the evening before and cook them overnight on Low. Either way, you end up with well-cooked beans with almost no active management during the cooking process. A great tactic for minimizing the hassle of dried beans is to cook up a huge pot of them every few weeks. Cool the beans and freeze several meals' worth in gallon bags for use at later meals.

If dried beans still seem like too much work, consider buying canned beans and adding in your own meat and seasonings. This still offers a considerable savings over premade chili.

If you're only feeding a person or two, a can of chili isn't going to break your budget. But with my family, it takes four or more cans for a single meal. That adds up. You have to know your own tolerances and needs. But if you're serious about shrinking your grocery bill, it's best to avoid prepackaged stuff the majority of the time.

Snack Food

The snack food aisle is another budget-wrecker. I almost always have taco chips around, because they're a versatile addition to a meal. Like tortillas, taco chips are often cheaper in the Hispanic foods aisle. In summer when camping we buy pretzels and potato chips to eat in the car. We also occasionally buy saltine crackers. But we don't keep chips or pretzels around otherwise. They offer little nutritional value and they disappear too quickly. Very occasionally I buy nuts, usually for baking. But in general I find that nuts make very expensive snack food.

For affordable snacking, you can't beat popcorn. Popcorn also makes a great substitute for croutons on top of a bowl of soup. But steer clear of the microwave packets. You can easily make your own popcorn with an air popper. Or, if you don't mind a little oil, cook it in a pot on the stove. Here's how: In a large pot place ¼ cup vegetable oil, ½ teaspoon salt, and ¾ cup popcorn. Cook over high heat, covered, shaking the pot frequently to keep the popcorn moving freely in the pot while cooking. Remove from the heat when the time between "pops" stretches to 2 seconds. Watch carefully and remove sooner rather than later; having a few "old maids" in the pot is a lot better than burning a batch.

For affordable snacking, you can't beat popcorn.

Drinks

The drinks aisle is another place where you want to proceed with caution. We rarely buy cola, but when we go camping in the summertime I buy juice boxes and generic cola. I sometimes purchase individual drinks for soccer team snacks. For birthday parties I buy either Kool-Aid or two-liter bottles of cola. I'd say that, on average, we drink sugary drinks two or three times a month.

Since dentists say cavities are mostly related to soda consumption these days, this strategy saves money at the store and at the dentist's office. If cutting out all cola seems too extreme, you might consider trying various generic brands or cutting back on your consumption to save some money. The point is to figure out what works for you.

We buy coffee in 5-pound cans at our local warehouse club. We occasionally buy boxes of herbal tea. Usually I make a whole pot of tea using just a couple of tea bags, which helps stretch the tea, especially for our large family.

wine in a box?

Boxed wine has been popular in Europe and Australia for years. Good varieties have recently become available in the United States as well. One box is equivalent to four 750-ml bottles, and will stay good for four to six weeks after opening. Black Box Wine (*www.black boxwines.com*) has distributors in every state. Their boxes run around $20. Some Target stores also sell boxed wine. You can often get a nice Shiraz or sangria for $16.

We don't buy bottled water. Each family member has a water bottle to fill and use on bike rides, at sports events and picnics, and on car trips. Running bottles through a hot dishwasher every week or two keeps bacteria from growing. It's also a good idea to choose only opaque plastic bottles. Clear plastic bottles have been shown to leach chemicals that some studies have shown to be harmful to your health.

When it comes to wine and beer, admittedly the best way to save money is to not buy it. But if alcohol is a part of your life, you can save by partaking moderately, and by being flexible about the brands you buy. Plenty of excellent wines run $8 to $10 a bottle. Some good ones even have screw tops, allowing you to easily seal partial bottles to enjoy another day. If beer is your drink of choice, shop around. You may find the best buys at a local beer distributor or at a warehouse club.

Frozen Food

Frozen convenience food is often more expensive per ounce than steak, and in general the nutritional benefits are low. If you can keep your purchases in this section to a minimum, you'll save money. *But I'm like anyone: I succumb to the temptation of convenience food now and then.* Once a month or so I buy a big bag of fish sticks or several 10-packs of frozen burritos. At $2.25 for 10 burritos, they're a hearty snack for my teenage boys. But the less often I serve my family premade food, the less money I spend at the store.

We're an ice cream family, so we usually have some on hand. But—sorry, Ben and Jerry—we buy ours by the gallon in round tubs. We drink calcium-fortified orange juice every morning for breakfast, so we keep that on hand as well. Frozen orange juice is more affordable than fresh, and if you remember to pull it out of the freezer the day before you need it, it's very quick to mix up. Frozen vegetables can be very affordable when bought generic, especially if you stick with basics like corn and peas. In general, more ingredients means higher cost. When I'm strapped for time, I buy generic Asian-style frozen veggies for stir-fries, since the time savings are significant and the cost is reasonable. In the past I've bought tater tots and French fries, but these days we make our own "home fries" from fresh potatoes (page 203).

Having some convenience food on hand can be a real sanity-saver, especially in the middle of soccer season or on a night when you have to work late. If an easy freezer meal is going to help you resist the siren's call of much more expensive restaurant food, then by all means keep some on hand. But you don't want to overdo it, because you'll pay dearly for that convenience.

Paper Goods

Whether you're interested in eco-friendly living or just want to decrease your spending, think hard about your purchases in the paper goods aisle. Switching to cloth dish towels instead of paper is a real money-saver. We keep paper around to wipe up oil and staining foods—I buy the kind that rip off in half-sheets, and are plain white, as those are the cheapest. We dry our hands and wipe counters with cloth, greatly reducing the amount of paper we buy and toss.

If an easy freezer meal is going to help you resist the siren's call of much more expensive restaurant food, then by all means keep some on hand.

We also have a big heap of cloth napkins that we use most of the time. I cut flour-sack dish towels into quarters to make mine. Napkins can also be made from an old flannel sheet if you aren't afraid of sewing. Or look for inexpensive 10-packs of colorful washcloths for a couple of dollars at Walmart.

dollar shopping on vacation

Recently, we were vacationing in Newport, Oregon, which is a typical tourist town right on the coast. Grocery store prices are astronomical there—most of the time I just have to bite my tongue and get what we need without thinking too much about prices. On this trip, we spotted a new dollar store. It was huge and busy and extremely, amazingly helpful. We found crafts and sand toys and kites and all sorts of reasonably priced food items, most of which would have been double or triple the price at the regular grocery stores. If you're on vacation and need to shop, don't forget to check out the dollar store.

To save on the cost of paper goods, some people use handkerchiefs instead of Kleenex. I haven't been able to wean myself off tissues in that department.

Toilet paper prices can be amazingly confusing. Until recently I bought whichever brand was cheapest per roll. But sizes of rolls vary tremendously. Recently, I had a coupon for Scott toilet paper and was amazed at how long one huge one-ply roll lasted. Since that experience I've been buying on-sale "double-roll" packs, and also use coupons as much as possible (more about savvy coupon shopping later).

When it comes to plastic wrap and foil, check unit prices. Don't assume the warehouse store prices are best. Often dollar stores win in this category. The very best way to save money is to use less. I store food in reusable plastic containers as much as possible. I try to use my casserole dishes with lids, instead of the ones without lids, to save on plastic wrap. I buy store-brand zip-top plastic bags, and rinse out the gallon- and quart-size ones a few times so they don't get tossed in the trash after just one use. At the grocery store I tie off produce bags loosely so I can easily open them at home and use them another time or two. I also reuse my bread bags. This helps both my pocketbook and the environment.

Cleaning Supplies

Liquid dish soap, hand soap, and generic glass cleaner can all be bought at the dollar store in large jugs. I use these containers to refill smaller pump-style containers that I save and reuse many times. *Windshield wiper fluid is often very affordable and can be used in place of glass cleaner as well.* Ajax and Comet are great scrubbing agents and a good buy for the money. For really stubborn stains, I usually use Barkeeper's Friend, an excellent scrubbing powder that costs a bit more than Comet, but is still much cheaper than products like Soft Scrub.

Dishwasher detergent is one thing I don't buy generic. We have hard water at our house, and Cascade Complete is the only thing I've found that really makes my dishes shine. I wince whenever I buy it, but the gleaming dishes are worth it to me. On the other hand, I've been very content with generic laundry detergent, as long as it contains bleach. Your decisions may be different than mine. But don't be afraid to try lower-cost alternatives at least once. They just might work for you.

Pet Food

In the pet food aisle, we don't buy generic brands, but we don't buy the most expensive brands either. At Walmart we have had good luck with Special Kitty cat food. Our dog food of choice is usually Atta Boy. We tried generic brands for a while, but our outdoor cats seemed to be more susceptible to ringworm and other skin issues when we did. Shop around and check prices. In our area, Walmart is the best place for guinea pig food; we buy pine shavings for bedding at the feed store.

Baby Items

Baby formula is hugely expensive. Check the prices at all the stores in your area, and buy where it's cheapest, even if that means a trip to a different store every few weeks to stock up. When it comes to baby bottles, avoid getting started on the kind with disposable liners, if at all possible, since they cost so much more than the reusable kind. But if you do use them, Walmart is usually the best place to buy them.

Do you want to save hundreds of dollars? Don't buy baby food. I know—lots of people think of baby food as essential, but it really isn't. I doubt if I've bought even 20 jars of baby food for all my kids combined. I bought boxes of rice cereal when the babies were first learning to eat. After they got the hang of rice cereal, mashed potatoes, and applesauce, we began feeding our babies bits of whatever we were eating. Vegetables and pasta can be smashed with a fork in seconds.

If you want the convenience of premashed food, try freezing pureed fruits and vegetables in ice-cube trays. Once they're frozen, you can pop them out of the tray and into gallon-size zip-top plastic bags, thawing out a cube at a time as you need it. And, of course, Cheerios are the perfect finger food for babies who are a little bit older.

In years of diapering many babies, I've gone back and forth between cloth and disposable diapers. Cloth diapers cost more initially and take a bit more work, but will pay for themselves in just a few months. These days they're adorable and extremely functional. Disposable diapers can't be beat when it comes to convenience, however. When I was using disposables, I usually bought them at my local warehouse club or with double coupons. Wipes, on the other hand, are cheaper at Walmart.

action points:

Look through this list and give yourself a pat on the back for every tactic you're already using. Put a check next to the things that you think you might be able to start doing. Then run through the list one more time and check off a couple of other changes you might be willing to consider, either now or a few weeks from now. The more you do, the more you'll save!

☐ **Keep a running grocery list** to minimize forgotten items at the store.

☐ **Skip one trip to the store this week.** Make a list of what you need, but wait a few days before going. Chances are you can survive for a few days without some things.

☐ **Check your dollar store for good prices** on cleaning supplies, paper goods, and pasta.

☐ **Watch ads for sales on meat.** If you find something with a really good price, buy as much as you can store in your freezer.

☐ **Drink half as much cola this month.** Or, if that seems too dramatic, decrease your usage by 25%.

☐ **Buy two fewer bags of chips this month.**

☐ **Next time you run out of a spice,** save the empty jar and refill it from the bulk food department.

☐ **Consider using cloth napkins** for at least one meal a day.

- ☐ **Keep a kitchen towel on a hook** right next to your paper towels to make it easy to use cloth in situations where it would work just as well as paper.
- ☐ **Use plastic storage containers** when possible instead of plastic wrap.
- ☐ **Wash out and reuse** a couple of gallon-size zip-top plastic bags each week (only if they haven't been used for raw meat).
- ☐ **Make one batch of cookies a week** from scratch instead of buying cookies.
- ☐ **Make a batch of biscuits** instead of buying store-bought once this week.
- ☐ **Try the generic brand of three items** that you usually buy name-brand. Start with items your family doesn't care too much about. If you expect resistance, toss the identifying bags/packages before serving the food.
- ☐ **If you drink wine, try a less expensive brand this week,** maybe even one in a box.
- ☐ **Buy one item in a larger size** instead of in small bags if the price is right. Lego bins or Rubbermaid containers make good long-term food storage bins.
- ☐ **If you have freezer space, buy two weeks' worth of bread** at the bread store and store it in the freezer.
- ☐ **Buy one less frozen or takeout pizza this month** and make your own, using frozen pizza dough or my homemade recipe (page 226). Enlist your kids to spread the sauce, sprinkle the cheese, and add the toppings. Your cost savings per pizza will be anywhere from $5 to $15.

· · · · · ◆ · · · ·

one final thought:

Try not to feel overwhelmed by the huge number of changes that you could be making in your shopping. The best way to approach this is to work at it gradually, first incorporating the most doable changes, then adding more after the first changes start feeling natural.

guerilla shopping

If you're like many people, you can probably tell me the best prices for milk or chicken breasts in your area. But what about coffee, flour, corn flakes, or any of the hundreds of other things you buy on a regular basis? To save the most money, you need to know more than a few prices. In fact, the more prices you know, the more money you'll save. And the best way to gain this knowledge is to make a price book. This invaluable tool will allow you to locate the lowest prices for every item you buy on a regular basis.

What is a Price Book?

A price book is simply a notebook used to track prices of all the various food items you usually buy. Confession: When I first read about this idea, I was skeptical. Maybe I was cocky, but I felt like I already knew where things were cheapest. And I knew I didn't have the time to write all sorts of prices down.

When I finally overcame my reservations about the idea and gave it a try, I was amazed. Sure, I did know where to buy some things. But in those early weeks of price-booking, I had a lot of jaw-dropping moments, too. I discovered I'd been buying many things at the wrong stores, and as a result I had been paying way too much.

Think about it: On an average shopping trip, you may buy 50 or 60 items. What if you're overpaying for 10 of them? Even if the price difference is only 50¢ an item, that's $5 you didn't really have to spend. Multiply that $5 by six times in a month and there's $30. If you're like most shoppers, chances are good you're overpaying on more than 10 items. And in many cases the price differential is measured in dollars per item, not cents.

A price book gives you the power to become a discriminating shopper. If you see a sale in a news flyer, you'll be able to compare it to the cost listed in your price book and easily tell whether it's time to fill the freezer or walk on by. A complete price book can save you hundreds of dollars a year.

A price book gives you the power to become a discriminating shopper.

Price Book for the Easily Intimidated

A good price book will usually list a hundred or more items and the unit prices for your preferred brands at three or four stores in your area. Does that sound like a huge job? Don't panic! I'll break it down into doable steps. And the awesome thing is that you can immediately start saving significant money even before your price book is complete.

Start with a Stack of Receipts and a Highlighter

Gather the receipts from two to four recent shopping trips. The receipts can be all from the same store, or from several different ones. *Circle the 20 most expensive items that you bought on those trips with your highlighter.*

but I don't buy a birthday cake every week!

If you're going through your grocery receipts with your highlighter and find something unusual on the list, like a birthday cake or a deli tray you bought for a Christmas party, you don't need to list that item among your top 20 items. The object of this initial foray into price-booking is to record 20 commonly bought items.

But do make a note of that expensive purchase. In many cases there is a lower-cost alternative. With 10 kids, I save a lot of money by making my own birthday cakes. If you have only one child, a store-bought birthday cake might be a splurge you decide to keep. But if you're truly looking for the biggest savings at the grocery store, scrutinize every purchase carefully.

If you're like most people, meat, dairy, and convenience food will show up on this list. Coffee, breakfast cereal, and cola-type drinks also tend to take up a fair bit of the grocery budget for many people. Your list may be different than mine. Just figure out which items are sucking up the biggest chunk of your money on a regular basis. Once you've got your top 20 items, set those receipts aside, and continue to save any new receipts. You'll need them again later.

Get a small spiral notebook and write down your items, one per page. Underneath each item, make the following column heads across the page: Store, Date Bought, Brand, Total Price, Size, Unit Price. From the receipts you currently have, fill in the information you have. Peek in your pantry if the receipt doesn't list the size. You'll need that bit of information to calculate the unit price.

Calculating Unit Prices

Unit prices are usually calculated in price per pound or price per ounce, and are a good way to compare items of different sizes at the grocery store. For example, say you're looking at a 12-ounce box of cereal that costs $2 and a 17-ounce box of cereal priced at $3.50. It may not be immediately obvious which is the better deal.

Let's calculate the unit price for each of those boxes: Divide the cost of each box by the number of ounces in it. For the first box you would divide 2 by 12 to get about 17¢/ounce. For the second box you would divide 3.50 by 17, to get about 21¢/ounce. Now you know that the smaller box is the better deal. (This happens more often than you might think, so check those prices!)

Usually in large stores the unit prices will be listed on the front edge of the store shelf, which makes comparison simple. As well, you can often find the unit price listed on bread and other baked goods. But when an item is on sale or in smaller stores, unit prices will not be easily visible. So it's good to know how to do the calculations yourself.

Below is an example of a price book entry, complete with the unit prices. In this example, note that I've listed the bulk price for this item, $1.93/pound. To get the unit price for it, which in this case is cost per ounce, I divided the number of ounces in a pound (16) into the price, $1.93.

Remember, your notebook should list only one item per page, so that you'll have space to record prices from various stores. Obviously

the ever-shrinking package

These days, manufacturers are all out to save money. One of the most recent tactics is package shrinkage. You may have already noticed it. Cereal boxes are thinner. Peanut butter jars have deep divots on their bottoms. Pasta packages that used to weigh a pound now weigh 12 ounces.

This makes a price book even more important. If you're looking at two different brands that are also two different sizes, it's not enough to compare the price of the two packages. You need to be able to compare unit prices. But it can be hard to remember the best unit prices from store to store. Your price book is the best way to combat price confusion.

price book entry for coffee creamer

Store	Date Bought	Brand	Total Price	Size	Unit Price cost/size
Win-Co	7-27-09	Store brand	$3.09	32 oz	9¢/oz
Win-Co	7-27-09	Bulk	$1.93/lb	--	12¢/oz
Albertsons	8-02-09	CoffeeMate	$4.58	32 oz	14¢/oz
Costco	8-07-09	CoffeeMate	$8.49	64 oz	13¢/oz

you'll begin by just having one price written down for each item you've bought. No problem. Even having one or two prices to compare against as you shop will help. You can add more prices over time.

As you visit various stores to compare costs, buy only what you need. But while you're there, do note the prices and sizes of the most affordable brands of each of your "top 20" items. You can calculate unit prices right there in the store if you have a calculator with you, or you can wait until you get home, whichever is easier. Usually I just write down prices and do my division at home where it's quieter.

Expanding the Price Book

Once you have set up the price book to reflect prices for the top 20 items on your list, aim to add 10 more items each week to it. You may find it useful to work in categories. For example, one week you could record prices of baking ingredients. Another week you can price condiments. The next week it could be frequently purchased canned goods.

The price book will save you the most money if it's fairly complete. But don't stress yourself trying to pull it together in a week or two. If you need a break after recording your first 20 items, that's fine. Work with what you've got, and you'll still save money.

In fact, once you see how much money a price book helps you save, you may get a burst of energy. Work on the book as you have the time, remembering to break it down into smaller tasks. For example, reasonable goals might include:

☐ **Begin with 20 items.**

☐ **Add 10 new items each week.**

☐ **Visit a different store each week.**

☐ **Spend 15 minutes a day** looking at ads and receipts and recording grocery costs.

You'll find that even 15 minutes a day will yield a very useful price book in just a few weeks' time. Then, let the savings begin!

Use Those Sales Flyers

Grocery store sales flyers are a great way to add more data points to your price book without driving all over town. Sales flyers obviously tend to list "best" prices for items. You won't be able to count on those prices all the time at that store. But for maximum savings, your eventual goal is to buy most items most of the time at the cheapest possible prices. It's important to know how low you can expect those prices to get.

After a few weeks of paying attention to sales flyers, you'll start to notice patterns. In my area, Albertsons has sales every couple of months where cereal prices are excellent. When I see boxes of cereal for $1.50 or less, I grab enough to last for a month or two. A smaller store has bone-in chicken breasts on sale for $1.29/pound every month or so. I wait until the prices get that low to stock my freezer, and I try to buy enough to last until the next sale.

Check Out Some New Stores

As you set up your price book, make a conscious decision to broaden your shopping horizons. If at all possible, make plans to visit a different grocery store every week for the next several weeks. Most people have several stores from which to choose. If a store is 25 miles away, it may not be practical to shop there every week. But one trip every month or two might be a reasonable time investment, especially if the savings are outstanding.

I have a favorite grocery store about 30 minutes away where I do my "big" shopping twice a month. On alternate weeks we usually stop by Walmart, the store closest to our home. We visit the bread store and the warehouse store once a month. Every few months I'll also visit a Korean market, the dollar store, and the grocery outlet store. Knowing each store's "best" priced items makes it easier to decide where to shop, how often to shop there, and how much of each item I need to last until I visit there again. The best way to decide what will work for you is to visit the various stores and check out their prices.

Do Warehouse Clubs Really Save Money?

Don't plunk down the dough for a yearly membership at your local warehouse club until you're sure you'll save enough money to offset the cost of the membership. Take an hour or so and do some serious price checking at your local club.

My price club has excellent prices on dairy products, some vegetables, and bulk baking items, which makes the cost worthwhile for us. Meat and cereal prices aren't so good.

Impulse buys at warehouse stores make bigger dings in the budget than impulse buys at regular stores.

Be aware that warehouse clubs tend to encourage you to overbuy. A big family like mine can use up a 50-pound bag of rice in a reasonable amount of time. But a family of four? Maybe not. Also, don't get seduced by huge packages of "convenience" items. Dinosaur chicken nuggets in mega-size bags waste money even faster than dinosaur nuggets in small bags. If you've chosen to make them your "splurge of the week," fine. But impulse buys at warehouse stores make bigger dings in the budget than impulse buys at regular stores.

There's another factor to consider. (It applies to the big box stores like Walmart as well.) You'll be walking past a huge variety of items, including clothing and household items. While these items may not be groceries, they can still be very tempting—and potentially budget-wrecking. If you can't resist the siren's call of nonfood items, your budget might be better off if you avoid "everything" stores when you're grocery shopping.

Ethnic Grocery Stores: Hidden Treasures

Excellent deals can often be found at ethnic markets, even if your food tastes don't tend to the exotic. Spices tend to be a particularly good buy. Awhile back I needed turmeric, a seasoning that is used often in pickle-making and Ethiopian cooking. At the regular grocery store turmeric costs $5 for a 2-ounce jar. While on vacation I thought to stop at an Ethiopian market in a larger city. There I bought half a pound for $4, or one-fifth of what I'd have paid at the regular store. I won't have to buy it again for a long time, which also saves me time.

Another example: I love the flavor that sesame oil adds to stir-fries, but it's an expensive oil. My regular grocery store charges $4 for 8 ounces, or 50¢/ounce. The Korean market 40 minutes from my home charges $12 for a 56-ounce can, or 21¢/ounce. Needless to say, I rarely buy sesame oil at the supermarket.

At that same Korean grocery store, I can stock up on soy sauce, red pepper flakes, dried seaweed, and unusual types of noodles that are more expensive or unavailable at my regular grocery store. A few times I've stopped by the Vietnamese grocery store in our area. There I can get fresh lemongrass and some of the seasonings I use in Thai food. Indian groceries are also a wonderful place to shop for inexpensive spices, as well as fresh produce like cilantro, okra, and eggplant. You may find that rice is a bargain at ethnic markets, but don't assume it is. My warehouse club still beats the local Asian markets when it comes to rice prices.

Hispanic grocery stores are worth checking out, too. Again, the seasonings tend to be the best deals, but meat, flour, beans, and various other staples of Hispanic cookery can usually be found for reasonable prices.

Since I don't make frequent trips to ethnic markets, I tend to stock up mostly on nonperishable items, things that will last awhile. If your stores are more local, you can take advantage of their lower pricing on a regular basis.

> *Excellent deals can often be found at ethnic markets, even if your food tastes don't tend to the exotic.*

Dollar Stores

Don't forget to check out the dollar store for bargains. I've found small bottles of olive oil, boxes of cereal, frozen hash browns, and salad dressing for less than I can get them at the grocery store. I also routinely stock up on pasta at the dollar store. What they carry at any given time varies, and you can't always count on what you want being there, but it's worth visiting regularly and stocking up when you do find a good deal.

Grocery Outlet Stores

I don't get to the grocery outlet very often, but when I do, I try to look at everything they've got. Selection varies tremendously, and lots of what is available is highly processed food, which I don't usually buy. But every time I go, I find something that makes it worth the stop. Sometimes it's $1 cereal. At that price I grab a dozen boxes. Once I found big cans of dehydrated potato soup mix for $2. Those same cans were $7 at the warehouse club. Again, I grabbed a bunch when I saw them. Good thing—they only had them for a few weeks.

When you're deciding what to stock up on, remember that butter and cream cheese can be frozen. Recently I saw butter for less than $2 a pound and bought 10 pounds of it. Another store had cream cheese for 79¢ for an 8-ounce package, which is lower than I've seen it in a while. I bought six packages and put five into the freezer for later use. Milk also can be frozen. Just remember to pour half a cup out of the jug first, to allow for expansion.

storing u-pick apples

If you get a large quantity of apples from a U-pick orchard, the ideal storage location would be in an extra refrigerator. When I was a kid, my folks kept the apples in boxes on our cool back porch. Covered with blankets, they lasted for weeks. We have stored apples in our garage covered in blankets. The trick is to store only perfect apples, because it really is true that one bad apple can spoil the batch.

Farmer's Markets and U-Pick Farms

Since our family gardens, and we have our own apple and apricot trees, we don't do a lot of shopping at farmer's markets. But when summer fruit is in season and I'm ready to buy a bushel or two of peaches for canning, I usually check the farmer's market before I buy fruit at the grocery store. It's possible to find bargains, and often the selection of organically grown food is good. Our farmer's market also has a fairly good selection of health food. But prices can be high, so shop carefully. U-pick orchards are another good option to consider if the price is right. My family did that every year when I was a child, and I have many fond memories of those excursions, as well as the apples we ate for weeks afterwards.

What About Organic Food?

The organic food dilemma is a tough one. Who wants to feed their kids food laden with pesticides? But who can afford to pay double for organic apples? I understand that many people are convinced that organics are the only way to go. If that's your point of view, don't worry. I don't feel like there's no hope for your budget. Yes, you'll be spending more for your fresh food. But there are lots of other ways to save money.

For the record, I almost never buy organic food. And yet I think we do a good job of limiting our pesticide exposure. Let me explain

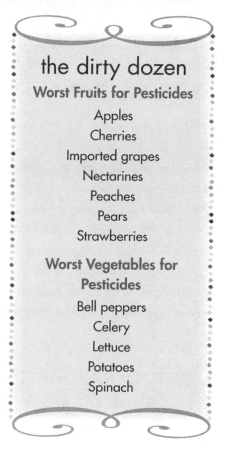

the dirty dozen

Worst Fruits for Pesticides

Apples
Cherries
Imported grapes
Nectarines
Peaches
Pears
Strawberries

Worst Vegetables for Pesticides

Bell peppers
Celery
Lettuce
Potatoes
Spinach

how. For starters, we have a garden. From June to October, our family gets homegrown fresh organic produce. I also freeze and can a lot of food for the winter. So we eat at least some organic food year-round.

We also wash fruit, and peel many of our fruits and vegetables. Studies have shown that washing and peeling potatoes reduces the pesticide load to undetectable levels, even when the plants have been heavily sprayed. Peeling fruit may be an especially good option for preschoolers and pregnant women, since infants and very young children are most at risk from pesticide exposure.

When washing fruits and vegetables, use cold running water and a very small amount of soap. Use a scrub brush on apples, carrots, potatoes, and other hard-surfaced produce. Make sure you rinse carefully. Don't bother buying soap products marketed specifically for washing produce. They're a waste of money.

Bananas and oranges are excellent fruit choices, especially since their thick skins keep the edible portion of the fruit mostly pesticide free. However, studies done on produce have found that some fruits and vegetables don't perform nearly as well. The list on page 47 highlights these "Dirty Dozen" fruits and vegetables.

From a budget point of view, you may find it reasonable to buy only organics for the produce on the "Dirty Dozen" list. Studies have concluded that buying organics of only these 12 items can reduce your pesticide exposure by 90%.

Chances are your family doesn't eat all 12 of these items on a regular basis. My family regularly eats five of them: apples, peppers, celery, spinach, and potatoes. Buying that amount of organic food wouldn't be nearly as expensive as buying organic everything.

Of course, you have to choose the best approach for your own family. I've found that educating myself about pesticide loads on fruits and vegetables actually makes me feel better in general about the produce choices I'm making for my family.

Comparing Meat, Poultry, and Seafood Prices

When you're standing in front of the meat display at the store, the sheer number of choices can feel overwhelming. Whole chicken is often affordably priced, but then you have to cut it up. Legs and thighs are another low-priced option. Boneless chicken breasts are convenient, but are they worth $2.29/pound when you can buy bone-in for $1 or less? Price isn't the only variable in this equation.

The table at right demonstrates the importance of servings per pound of meat by comparing cost per serving for a variety of proteins. As you can see, the number of servings per pound is extremely important in comparing the affordability of various options, and it's dependent on the amount of fat, skin, and bones in each. I've always wondered at what price boneless, skinless chicken breasts are a better deal than bone-in breasts. *Now I know: If boneless costs less than two times as much as bone-in chicken, that's the way to go.* The calculations in this table come from *www.cheapcooking.com*; this website contains an

meat cost per serving comparisons......

Type	Servings/pound	Sample price	Price/serving
Chicken			
Bone-in breasts	2.5	$1.29	$0.52
Bone-in thighs	2.5	$0.89	$0.36
Boneless breasts	4	$2.49	$0.62
Boneless thighs	3	$1.49	$0.50
Leg quarters	2	$0.79	$0.40
Whole	2.5	$0.99	$0.40
Beef			
Chuck roast	2	$2.49	$1.15
Cubed steak	4	$2.49	$0.62
Ground beef	4	$2.29	$0.57
New York steak	2	$7.99	$4.00
Round rump roast	3	$3.99	$1.33
T-bone steak	2	$5.99	$3.00
Top loin steak	3	$2.99	$1.00
Pork			
Bacon	6	$2.50	$0.42
Boneless top loin	3	$3.99	$1.33
Ham	5	$2.99	$0.60
Pork chops, blade	3	$2.29	$0.76
Pork roast	2	$1.49	$0.75
Sausage	4	$2.49	$0.63
Turkey			
Bone-in breasts	3	$1.99	$0.66
Ground	4	$1.49	$0.37
Legs	2.5	$1.49	$0.60
Whole	3	$0.99	$0.33
Seafood			
Imitation crab	3	$2.99	$1.00
Salmon, canned	5	$1.99	$0.40
Salmon, fresh	2	$6.99	$3.50
Salmon, frozen	2	$2.99	$1.50
Tilapia	3	$3.99	$1.33
Tuna, canned	5	$1.60	$0.32

purse killers

Watch out for all the little sneaky things that can pull money out of your pocket. Coffee at the drive-through on the way to work. Water bottles at the convenience store on a hot day. Chicken poppers from the grocery store deli. French fries or cinnamon rolls in the mall food court.

A little organization and forward thinking can save you a lot of money. Pack school lunches and set out the coffee pot the night before. Keep water bottles and crackers in your car for easy on-the-go snacks. Baggies of raisins and dry cereal in your purse will cheer cranky little shoppers, and make it easier to resist the siren's call of the mall's food court or the grocery store deli. You may still give in from time to time, but the more often you can walk past those expensive treats, the more money you'll save.

extremely helpful calculator into which you can type your own prices to figure the cost per serving of various types of meat, fish, and poultry.

Shopping Sales

There is definitely an art to shopping the sales at grocery stores. Many stores distribute weekly flyers that list the "loss leaders" along with other things that are on sale that week. The loss leaders are usually listed on the front and back of the flyer. Their name comes from the fact that the store will sometimes actually be losing money to sell the item at that price. They do this gambling on the chance that while you're at the store you will also buy other higher-priced items, which they hope will result in a net profit for the store.

Here's where your price book is golden. From the comfort of your own home, with price book and flyer in hand, you can determine which items are truly good deals and which are not. There are some stores from which I only buy the loss leaders, because their prices are simply too high otherwise.

What About Coupons?

I want to like coupons, really I do. I know lots of people who swear by them. Probably half a dozen times over the years I've decided to get serious about couponing. I've spent hours clipping them and organizing my coupon binder and scouring the sales for the best times to use those coupons.

But when I get to the store, coupons in my fist, I inevitably hit stumbling blocks. The store doesn't carry the brand that I want. Or they don't have the right size. Or I discover that the generic brand of the item is much cheaper.

Sure, I've saved some money at times. And each time I vow to try coupons again, I think that this time it will be a long-lasting change. But for me the hassle of fiddling with coupons always ends up not being worth the dollars saved.

One problem with coupons is that they tend to be for highly processed food and name brands, items I don't generally buy. However, if those types of foods are non-negotiable staples in your house, you may find that coupons are a good time investment for you. But too often coupons coax you to buy nonessentials.

I do still clip coupons now and then, especially when the coupon saves at least $1 on an item I buy often. For me, the most-useful coupons tend to be for toiletries and cleaning supplies. If you would like to give couponing a try, keep the following guidelines in mind:

One problem with coupons is that they tend to be for highly processed food and name brands.

☐ **Clip coupons only for needed items** that you buy regularly.

☐ **Always compare** the with-coupon cost to the cost of comparable generic brands.

☐ **Go through your coupon stash regularly** so you don't accidentally try to use a coupon that has expired.

There are some great couponing resources out there if you want to know more. Sites such as *www.CouponMom.com* and *www.coupons.com* are worth visiting if you'd like to better understand the ins and outs of coupon shopping.

Putting It All Together

Before I head out on a big shopping trip, I go through my grocery list and my cupboards and write down everything I need for the menus I have planned over the next couple of weeks. Then I divide up the list by store. Usually on a big trip, I'll plan to shop three or four stores. Depending on my needs, that list may include my favorite grocery store, another grocery store with good meat prices, the warehouse club, the dollar store, and the bread store or an ethnic market.

Before I leave, I also take a minute to look at that week's ads and write down the sale prices of things on my list. Since my favorite grocery store does no advertising, I won't know their sales until I get there. But they often beat the sale prices from other stores, so I'll shop there first and compare their prices with the ones I've written down.

Early in my shopping day, I also go to the stores where the selection varies the most. The dollar store is often a good place to buy pasta, but sometimes they're out of it. If I go there first, I can still get pasta at my favorite store if I need to. If my favorite store doesn't turn out to have good sales on meat that week, I'll take a few minutes to go to the meat store near the end of my trip.

My ideal plan is to shop with only one or two of my bigger kids, since they can actually help. But sometimes I need to bring younger kids, too. When that happens, I make sure to bring snacks and water, as well as a few toys to play with in the car. In the store kids get less bored if I give them small tasks to accomplish. When I'm in the produce aisle, I'll ask a child to fill a bag with oranges while I pick apples. Or in the cereal aisle, I'll send a child to get corn flakes while I select other cereals. This teaches them to shop, and it gets us out of the store faster.

You've Bought It: Now What Do You Do with It?

When I get home from one of my big-shop trips, I literally have mountains of food. I start by removing everything from the bags. Then I group items by type, and put away any fridge and freezer items that don't need further attention. The most time-consuming job by far is handling the meat and poultry.

finding a cheap freezer

If you end up deciding that you need a full-size freezer, don't immediately run to the appliance store and drop big bucks. You may be able to save hundreds by checking *www.craigslist.org*. Craigslist is a free classified ads website. On the main page, click on the state and city where you live, and you can find a multitude of items for sale. A recent check on Craigslist netted me at least a dozen leads on freezers for sale in my area. Several were less than five years old, which is great for energy efficiency, and were being sold for $300 or less.

Don't forget to check *www.freecycle.com* as well. Again, you'll need to follow the links to postings in your area. Everything listed on Freecycle is free. Yes, free. Appliances don't come through very often, but recently we found an older refrigerator that is currently providing extra cold space in our garage. I'm sure the energy efficiency isn't the best, but it's perfect at the end of the gardening season for holding extra cabbages and bushels of apples. Another place you can sometimes find a small fridge is outside college dorms at the end of the semester. College students throw all sorts of things away as they're packing to leave, and sometimes you'll see perfectly good dorm-size fridges next to dumpsters.

Yard sales are another great way to find an affordable freezer. We bought ours at a yard sale for $120, and it has been running beautifully for a decade. Keep in mind that as far as energy efficiency goes, an older freezer will cost more to run. For a 30-year-old freezer, that's about $75 a year, versus $35 for one manufactured in the last decade.

Beef and Pork Storage

When it comes to ground beef, I buy several family-size packages at a time. *Now, the last thing you want to do is toss eight pounds of beef into the freezer as is.* It's ridiculously hard to get a large block of meat thawed, even with the help of the trusty microwave. I usually cook ground beef as soon as I get it home, or I might form it into hamburgers, or make meatballs or meatloaf that go into the freezer (see page 72 for more on that).

Often I buy beef or pork roasts on sale and then cut them into slabs myself. The pork is used for pork chops, or I'll cut it into smaller pieces for stir-fry. Usually I cut the beef into cubes for stews or strips for stir-fry. The more cutting

Quart-size bags are a good size for a meal's worth of stir-fry meat.

I can do before the meat hits the freezer, the quicker my meals will come together at mealtime. I freeze pork chops in gallon-size zip-top plastic bags, enough for a single meal. Quart-size bags are a good size for a meal's worth of stir-fry meat.

Poultry Storage

I sometimes buy family-size chicken packs in which the chicken pieces have been individually frozen. These are convenient because they don't take any special handling once you get them home, but they're not the most economical option. If you want your grocery bill to hit its lowest possible level, it's better to watch for on-sale chicken and then stock up.

Often 10-pound packets of legs and thighs are very economical—yes, those big drippy plastic bags you can find at Walmart. They're not so pleasant to handle—but then again, raw meat usually isn't! But at 70¢/pound, you can quickly learn to get over any squeamishness. Some of the chicken I cook (see page 70 for more on that), then shred or chop and freeze it. I also like to freeze some pieces whole for a single meal—for my family that would be about a dozen pieces, but your family may only need six thighs or drumsticks to make a meal.

When bone-in chicken breasts are $1.25 or less/pound, I buy several packets, and freeze the breasts in twos or threes in quart- or gallon-size zip-top bags.

Cheese Storage

Once I've gotten the meat and poultry put away, I breathe a sigh of relief. Several other items also need my immediate attention, however. I often buy grated cheese in 5-pound packets. Even my large family will probably not use that much cheese before it goes bad in the refrigerator.

For me, the easiest way to handle this amount of cheese is to put it into the freezer as is. When I need cheese, I just thump the bag on the counter a few times before opening it. Usually enough cheese will release from the frozen clump for my meal. Then I just twist-tie the bag shut until I need it the next time.

Occasionally it's inconvenient to have all my cheese frozen, like when I want to serve some along with a baked potato bar or as a topping with a taco meal. If I think about it far enough ahead, I set out a bowl full of frozen cheese to thaw for an hour before the meal. But I don't always remember that in time. For that reason, you might consider repackaging a 5-pound package of cheese into three or four zip-top plastic bags, sticking several in the freezer for later use, and leaving one in the fridge for the current week's use. The down side of this is that it takes time and bags. However, you could reuse the same bags the next time you buy cheese.

Fruit and Vegetable Storage

A survey conducted by the University of Arizona showed that, on average, *Americans throw away 470 pounds of food a year because it has spoiled.* That includes tossing out the equivalent of half a pound of fresh produce per day. This is obviously a huge waste of money. You can prevent (or at least minimize) produce tossage in your house in two ways. First of all, eat the fastest-spoiling fruits and vegetables first. The sidebar on page 56 will help you remember which items to use early in the week and which ones will last a week or longer.

Second, baby your fruits and vegetables just a little. In general, fruits keep best if you remove them from the bag you brought them home in before you place them in the crisper drawer. Tomatoes and green peppers also do best when taken out of the bag. (Tomatoes do the very best if you leave them out on the counter until use. Cold actually has a negative effect on their flavor.)

Use a salad spinner to spin the extra water off your lettuce after you wash it. Too much water dramatically shortens the life of lettuce. If you don't want to pay full price for this gizmo, check in thrift stores. Or put your lettuce in a clean pillowcase and have your kid spin around in a circle outside. (I have found this second method to be impractical on a regular basis, but it does burn off pre-dinner energy in rowdy kids.)

A great way to add a few more days to the life of your leafy greens is to place a paper towel in the bag with them. The paper towel will soak up extra moisture and prevent rot. There's no need to buy those expensive produce

the lifespan of produce

In making this list I realized that, in general, the produce that spoils the fastest tends to be the most expensive, and the ones that last the longest are some of the best values for your dollar. The more you can slant your purchases towards the sturdier vegetables, the less you'll waste and the less you'll spend on produce in the first place.

When planning your meals, keep in mind which vegetables will need to be used first, and which will last in the fridge a week or more.

Lasts 1 to 2 weeks or more:
- apples
- beets
- cabbage
- carrots
- celery
- garlic
- onions
- potatoes
- winter squash

Eat within 1 week:
- bell peppers
- blueberries
- Brussels sprouts
- cauliflower
- grapefruit
- leeks
- lemons
- mint
- oranges
- oregano
- parsley
- peaches
- pears

- plums
- tomatoes
- watermelon

Eat within 4 days:
- apricots
- artichokes
- arugula
- asparagus
- avocados
- bananas
- basil
- broccoli
- cherries
- corn

- cucumbers
- dill
- eggplant
- grapes
- green beans
- lettuce
- mesclun
- mushrooms
- mustard greens
- pineapple
- spinach
- strawberries
- watercress
- zucchini and other summer squash

bags. Close the bag after you place the towel in it. The paper-towel treatment also works for produce such as zucchini, cucumbers, green beans, grapes, and mushrooms, but make sure to leave the bag partially open, though. This allows enough air circulation to prolong their life for a week or more. Mushrooms will get a little dried out stored this way, but they're no less useful for cooking even when they're a little dry.

Pantry Storage

I store garlic, potatoes, sweet potatoes, and onions in baskets in my pantry. Potatoes last longer if you take them out of the plastic sack. Store onions separately; the fumes will speed spoilage of other vegetables.

making fresh ginger last

I love to cook with fresh ginger—it's so much better than dried. But it doesn't last forever, and can get moldy in the fridge. Problem solved if you just keep your ginger in the freezer. I put mine in a plastic bag and, whenever I need some, I grate as much as I want with a regular cheese grater, then stick the rest back in the freezer. It will keep in the freezer for months.

To organize dried goods in my cupboards, I use plastic storage boxes the size of shoeboxes. The kind you can get in the dollar store works well. I use them to store things like dried beans, confectioners' sugar, brown sugar, and raisins.

In my pantry I have a couple of 18-gallon plastic bins with snap tops that slide underneath the lowest shelf. In these bins I store opened bags of things that I buy in bulk, such as 25-pound sacks of flour, sugar, and oats. This keeps them fresher longer and avoids any possible problems with bugs. If I didn't have a pantry, I would consider using under-bed storage for some of these items. In that case, I would buy large flat under-bed storage bins on wheels.

I also sometimes store bulky dried food items such as large bags of beans in plastic bins on garage shelves. *If you've stored things in unusual places, you might want to make a note of where you've put the items so you don't forget.* If you look around your home with an open mind, you may very well find storage in spaces that you hadn't thought of before.

Your Transformation into a Bargain Shopper

B ecoming an expert shopper takes time and patience. Begin with small changes and, once those become natural, add a few more strategies. Try not to get stuck in a rut when it comes to your shopping habits. If a new store opens, go check it out, price book in hand. Different times of the year may call for different shopping strategies. During soccer season, I have to fight the urge to buy convenience food, but the up side is that I find it easier to shop sales, since I'm out and about every day. Shopping multiple stores is easiest for me on days when my husband or a teenager can watch my younger kids. Your life may be different, but with a little creativity and a willingness to experiment, you will be able to come up with savings strategies that work for your own family.

action points:

- ☐ **Gather your receipts and begin** your price book with 20 items.
- ☐ **Add 10 items per week** until you have listed your top 100 purchases.
- ☐ **Check sales flyers** for "loss leader" items and stock up on best sales.
- ☐ **Visit a price club** or warehouse store to compare prices.
- ☐ **Visit an ethnic grocery store** to compare prices.
- ☐ **Visit a dollar store** or grocery outlet to check prices.
- ☐ **Work out a monthly shopping plan** that will allow you to shop on a regular basis at all the places where prices are the best.
- ☐ **Spend 15 minutes a day** working on your price book.
- ☐ **Investigate** which meats are most affordable in your area.
- ☐ **Organize your freezer** so that you're better able to stock up on sales.
- ☐ **If you need a freezer,** investigate purchasing a used one.
- ☐ **Clean out and organize your pantry** or food cupboards so that you have enough space to stock up when prices are best.

efficient cooking, good eating

What's Your Meal Plan?

Everyone has to deal with hunger pangs. That means we all have a meal-planning style, whether it involves endless list-making, or scouring the cupboards at 6 p.m., or swinging through the Golden Arches yet again. But some plans are kinder on the budget than others. As I describe various ways of coping with mealtime, see if you can identify your own style.

In Chapter 3 I talked a lot about cost comparison and careful shopping. *But there's another key component to every efficient shopping trip: meal planning.*

five fast meals: a rescue plan for crazy days

1

Jazzy Ramen Stir-fry
(page 131)

2

Spinach Frittata
(page 123)

3

Spaghetti Carbonara My Way
(page 164)

4

Sausage with Cabbage and Corn Sauté (page 148)

5

Curried Rice with Shrimp
(page 151)

Sometimes people hear the words *meal planning* and imagine an iron-clad menu that doesn't allow for an unusual day or times when you don't feel like cooking. But there are a number of different ways to approach putting a meal together, several of which allow for great flexibility. I'll walk you through some options so that you can pick a strategy (or strategies) that will work for your family.

Reactive Meal Planning

A reactive meal planner is someone who starts thinking about what's for dinner around 5 p.m. Sometimes the Reactor can figure out a meal made from ingredients she already has in the house, but more often than not an ingredient or two is missing, which means a 5:30 p.m. trip to the store. That's hardly ideal but if there's nothing in the house to eat, there's no way around it. Considering the number of cars in the supermarket parking lot between 5 and 6 p.m. each day, there are a lot of reactive meal planners in the world. And I've been that person plenty of times.

Reactive planning has the advantage of spontaneity. You can cook whatever you feel like cooking each evening. And when ideas fail you, you can use that as an excuse to go out to eat. Again.

The problem is, this is an expensive way to shop and eat. You end up shopping more often, which provides greater opportunity for budget-busting impulse buys. And extra shopping means extra time spent driving, cruising grocery aisles, walking to the back of the store to grab milk, and waiting in long checkout lines.

Another problem is that you're constantly trying to figure out what to cook. Yes, we all get into that trap from time to time when life gets busy. But for the

Reactor it's a habit. And I find that when I get behind and start doing last-minute meal planning, my creativity goes out the window.

High-Structure Meal Planning

A high-structure person plans a calendar full of pre-planned meals, right down to side dishes and desserts. There are many advantages to this type of meal planning. There are no daily decisions to be made about what to cook—you do all your thinking a week or more ahead of time. This allows you to shop ahead with exact knowledge of the items you will need each day. You're also less likely to discover that you're out of something and need to run to the store, which saves money.

When you plan this way, you can customize the menu to accommodate the activities for any given day. For example, on Saturday evening, when everyone is home to help, you can make a more labor-intensive meal. Soccer night may warrant a casserole out of the freezer. People who try this type of meal planning often find it to be wonderfully freeing.

The idea of planning to this degree scares a lot of people, however. They fear they'll lose all spontaneity, that they'll find themselves cooking things that they don't really feel like eating, or that when a day gets unexpectedly hectic, the meal schedule will feel like their master instead of their slave. The good news is that you can be a successful meal planner even if you don't happen to be a high-structure person.

Flexible Meal Planning

The planning method that I use is somewhere in between reactive and high-structure. I need the structure of a certain amount of planning, both to keep our budget at an affordable level and to simplify my life. But I also enjoy being able

my fridge list

I joke that my kids steal my brain cells. Some days are so hectic that I feel like I'm running on half a brain. One of the things that is a huge help in meal planning is my fridge list. I keep a piece of paper on the side of the refrigerator at all times. When I get low on an item, it goes on the list. The kids help by adding to this list as well, which means that by the time it is time to shop, I already have a jump start on the grocery list.

to decide from day to day what I'm going to cook, depending on what I'm in the mood for.

Here's how I handle that. I make a couple of major shopping trips a month. Before each trip, I plan a couple dozen meals for the next two weeks. Some of the meals may be listed twice. For example, our Sunday noon meal is typically hamburgers and home fries, so in a two-week span I serve that twice. Once I've gotten my meals figured out, I begin work on my grocery list. Looking down at my list of meals, I note which ingredients I have, and which I will need to buy, writing needed items on the grocery list. If I need several meals' worth of an ingredient, like chicken or cabbage, I'll put a hash mark on the grocery list for every use of the ingredient, so I know how much of each thing to buy at the store.

After I write down all needed dinner ingredients, I do the same for breakfast supplies such as eggs, flour, oatmeal, and orange juice. We rotate among five different breakfasts, so I don't really need to do special planning for that. I just need to keep the breakfast food in stock. I also try to keep cookie-baking supplies on hand most of the time, since homemade desserts help meals feel special.

Now here's where the flexibility comes in. I stick my lunch and dinner ideas list on the fridge, and each day when it's time to think about dinner, I simply pick something off the list to make. This lets me choose a meal that fits my level of busyness for the day and is something I'm in the mood to cook. Since I do a thorough shopping trip ahead of time, I know I have all the ingredients on hand.

The Two Times Five Meal Planner

I think that a flexible meal plan is a "best of both worlds" solution to meal planning, allowing both freedom and structure. For those of you who have never really gotten into the habit of meal planning, and find yourself going to the store every day or two, here's an easy way to begin meal planning. I call it the Two Times Five Meal Plan.

Here's what you do. Pick 10 meals that your family enjoys eating. Divide that list in half, making sure that both lists contain decent variety. You could make all sorts of different combinations, but here are some ways to vary the recipes on your list:

❶ One beef or seafood dish. This could be a dish where beef or seafood is the main component or a stir-fry in which the meat plays a smaller role.

❷ One chicken or pork dish.

❸ One double recipe of soup. The extra can be frozen or enjoyed for lunch.

❹ One meatless or almost-meatless dish. This could be a meal of beans and rice, a baked potato "bar," or a pasta dish that uses just a little bit of bacon as a flavoring.

❺ One meal such as a casserole that can be easily doubled and the second dish frozen. This will give you a meal for later in the week or to save for another week.

Once you have your two five-meal lists, read each recipe thoroughly for all the ingredients you'll need. Include the ingredients you commonly need for breakfast, school lunches, and snacks, and always keep those items in stock.

You might also enjoy including an experimental night, where you try out a brand-new recipe. Items for that meal should be listed, too. See the sample list on page 64 that shows space for each of these components.

The beauty of this type of planning is that it's completely flexible. You can cook what you want, when you want, with the knowledge that your pantry will always contain the ingredients for at least five meals.

Double-Batching

If the Two Times Five Meal Plan seems like too much to deal with, there is still hope. How about weekend double-batch cooking? If you cook double batches of your meals just two evenings a week, you will soon have a small reserve of meals on hand in the freezer to save you from the lure of takeout.

"two times five" meal planning— four simple steps

1 Pick 10 favorite meals and divide them into two lists of five meals each.

2 Make a complete shopping list for both lists. Include basic ingredients for easy breakfasts and lunches on the list.

3 Print the lists on sturdy paper and keep them in your wallet.

4 Each time before you shop, check your pantry, fridge, and freezer and buy the ingredients you need for one of the lists, alternating lists each time.

two times five meal plan

Meal:	Ingredients Required:
1 Beef or seafood	
2 Chicken or pork	
3 Meatless meal	
4 Soup (x2)	
5 Casserole (x2)	
Lunch food	
Breakfast food	
Snacks, drinks, baking supplies	
Experimental Night	

Ways to Save Money

Planning your meals ahead of time and shopping carefully will save you money. But there's another important piece that will help you keep your food costs low. It involves cooking with a frugal mindset. Don't worry—I'm not talking about hungry bellies and empty fridges here. I simply mean trying to get just a little more out of the food we buy.

Sometimes that may mean taking 30 seconds to scrape the last two servings out of the ketchup bottle. Other times it means using just a little less oil when frying chicken, so that the bottle of oil lasts a day or two longer. Or it can be shaking the crumbs out of a bread bag so it can be reused to wrap up that leftover pizza.

Beware of the Mega-Package

One thing I've noticed is that when I buy extremely large containers of things such as cheese and oil, I tend to use more at a time. Be aware if this is a tendency of yours, too. If it helps you be more moderate, you might consider portioning such items into smaller containers to make it less tempting to use so much. Another thing I do to make expensive oil, like sesame or olive oil, last longer is to mix it half and half with a less expensive oil. By doing this I get the flavor of the oil I want for half the price.

Making Meals Multiple Choice

One strategy for keeping meal costs down is, paradoxically, to offer more choice at each meal. Sure, you could just serve chicken and rice. But if you add a cooked vegetable and some sliced fruit, people will be eating a larger variety

five freezer meals: a rescue plan for crazy days

1
Spicy Chicken Enchiladas
(page 102)

2
Lighter Vegetable Lasagna
(page 168)

3
Grandma's Mushroom Chicken
(page 106)

4
Pork Chops with Apricot Sauce
(page 116)

5
Curried Chicken and Rice Casserole (page 105)

before-dinner snacking

I've found that the very best way to get kids to eat their veggies is to set out fresh raw veggies right before dinner. Kids tend to be very hungry at that point, and will often eat a good serving of veggies as they're waiting for the "real" food to show up.

of food, which is a healthier way to eat anyway. They'll also most likely be eating a little less of the most expensive food at the meal.

At each meal I usually make only enough meat, poultry, or fish for people to have a serving or a serving and a half. But I also include items that people can eat in unlimited amounts—depending on the meal, they might include rice, pasta, fruit, vegetables, and bread. I don't think it's necessary to serve huge amounts of meat. In fact, several meals a week at our house are vegetarian.

Some people might think this is deprivation. I disagree. Most Americans eat more meat than they need, and many of us are overweight. More meat isn't what most of us need.

If you have a question about appropriate serving sizes for meat, remember that one serving of meat or poultry is about the size of a deck of cards.

Filling Food

A while back I met a woman who told me that at her house there was always a pot of beans on the back burner of the stove. She was raising a bunch of hungry boys, and couldn't afford to buy as much meat as they would eat. But she figured that any time someone was really hungry, they could fill up on beans.

Also, almost any meal feels special when it's served with fresh bread. Often when I'm getting ready to serve a simple meal of soup or even leftovers, I will make a batch of biscuits or muffins. The bran muffin recipe on page 235 is a great one. You can make a big batch, bake what you need, and keep the remaining batter in the fridge for an easy addition to another meal. It serves the same purpose as that pot of beans on the back burner, but with the added pleasure that fresh bread brings to a meal.

Affordable Fruits and Vegetables

When it comes to fruit, I try to keep in mind what's most affordable. In the fall when we have lots of apples from our tree, and prices are reasonable in the store, kids can snack on apples whenever they want. In the spring when apples are expensive, I'll serve slices or half-apples instead of whole apples, and supplement them with bananas, since they're usually cheap. I'll also serve affordable vegetables, like carrot sticks, as snacks. Spinach is another vegetable that is fairly reasonably priced. I like to serve it instead of fresh salad greens.

Leftovers

I remember being shocked when someone told me she threw away leftover cooked chicken because it was too much of a hassle to put it away. I'm sure I looked at her like she'd sprouted a horn from her forehead, that's how odd that behavior seemed to me. I know I'm sounding like my German grandmother right now, but throwing away food is like throwing quarters into the trash. Many leftovers can be repurposed for other things. Bread heels can be saved to make Toasty Tuna Melt Casserole (page 119) or Stuffed French Toast Strata (page 254). Leftover scrambled eggs are great in fried rice. So is that last piece of leftover fried chicken.

Actually, almost any leftover vegetable or meat is a good addition to a soup or stir-fry. And plenty of leftovers taste delicious reheated for the next day's lunch. Remember, you've paid good money for that food. Why not use it?

I personally think that life is too short to drink bad coffee.

Jazzing Up Coffee at Home

I personally think that life is too short to drink bad coffee. Sometimes coffee-shop coffee can seem more appealing than coffee made at home because of all the flavor options they offer. But home coffee can be just as delicious as the $4/cup variety that calls to you on your way to work each day.

Here are some ideas for making coffee-shop coffee at home:

• **Get a coffee maker that can be set to brew at a specific time each day.** This will make it easier for you to make your morning cup yourself.

• **If you don't know which types of coffee you prefer, ask what is used in your favorite brew from the coffee shop.** They'll most likely be glad to tell you. Or try a few varieties from your grocery store. If you have the time to grind the beans yourself, you can buy a small coffee mill fairly affordably. But don't assume the best coffee is fresh ground and expensive. I've found that Costco, the warehouse store in our area, has excellent-tasting already-ground coffee that they sell under their Kirkland store brand.

• **Now comes the fun part. Sure, you can use expensive flavored creamer— it'll still be cheaper than coffee-shop coffee.** But try some more affordable ingredients as well. One-fourth of a teaspoon of vanilla, maple, or almond extract adds wonderful flavor to a plain cup of coffee. A sprinkle of cinnamon or nutmeg is another simple option. My sister swears by a slosh of sweetened condensed milk in her coffee.

Dealing with Picky Eaters

A friend once told me that when she was a little girl, she was so picky her mother dyed her mashed potatoes pink to coax her to eat them. Most moms don't resort to red dye #4 to get their kids to eat. But many moms at one time or another do wonder how to cajole their children to eat more than the (un)holy trinity of kid food: chicken nuggets, goldfish crackers, and fruit snacks. Highly processed foods like these tend to be expensive, and can make it hard for a mom to lower the grocery bill. But the good news is that even kids with a reputation for being picky can gently be encouraged to broaden their horizons.

My husband and I adopted two of our children at the ages of nine and 11. They were incredibly finicky when they first came home, and I wasn't sure if they would ever learn to enjoy the food at our house. Now, after a year, they happily eat most of what we offer. Sure, they still have a few idiosyncrasies, such as an aversion to cheese (a food very uncommon in Ethiopia), but seeing how their horizons have broadened in just a year has me even more convinced that most kids can be taught to enjoy a variety of food.

I've noticed that kids in big families tend to be less picky. I think this is related to sheer practicality. When you're feeding half a dozen kids, you'd go nuts trying to be a short-order cook for each and every child. Moms of big families tend to say, "Here's dinner. Take it or leave it."

With this approach kids learn to be more flexible. And here's something that moms of many know: Kids rarely starve themselves, despite their parents' fears. If they're given a reasonable variety of food, they'll eat enough to live. Nutrition isn't the only reason to encourage children to be good eaters. Picky kids become adults who worry about dinner invitations or trips outside of the U.S. because of the possibility of unfamiliar food. We do our kids a service by encouraging flexibility in eating.

But how do you do it?

The Just-Try-It Approach: Variety and persistence are the keys to raising healthy eaters. Don't give up if your kids seem to hate the first taste of new things. Some researchers have found that children need to try a food 10 times to get used to a new taste; others say the magic number is closer to 20. Except in the case of extreme (translate: gagging) aversion, in our family we encourage a couple of bites of everything presented at each meal, then allow the child to finish out the meal with other healthy items they enjoy more. I usually offer at least a couple of different foods at every meal, so that there are familiar options along with the new foods being offered.

The If-They-Make-It-They'll-Try-It Approach: A great way to encourage kids to try new food is to enlist their help in the kitchen. Even a four-year-old will enjoy thumbing through a colorful cookbook and helping you pick a new recipe to try. A second-grader can help make the grocery list. And a fifth-grader is old enough to cook a recipe on his own, with you nearby to answer questions. There is something about cooking for themselves that encourages kids to be brave when it comes to trying the actual dish.

The If-They-Grow-It-They'll-Try-It Approach: If you have a real veggie-hater, try gardening. Paging through a seed catalog or browsing a seed display at a local feed store is great fun for kids. Even a corner of a flowerbed is big enough to grow a few carrots or a tomato plant.

Keep Snacks Healthy: Another key to healthy eating is to keep between-meal snacks healthy. Kids who fill up with junk every couple of hours naturally are less interested in eating healthy food at mealtime. That doesn't mean you can't have goodies in the house. My teenage daughters keep us well supplied in homemade cookies. We have something sweet for dessert every day or two. But afternoon snacks are usually bananas or carrots.

Travel at the Dinner Table: Since we have children born in Ethiopia and Korea, I've made an effort to learn to cook items from each of these cuisines. Nearly every week our menu includes Korean and Ethiopian food. One nice thing about both these cuisines is that small servings of several things are offered at every meal. This variety increases the chance that kids will find something they enjoy. Consistently offering a wide variety of food will allow kids to grow up with a flexible palate.

Cooking Shortcuts

The final key to saving money on food is to find ways to make cooking at home doable for you. One great way is to involve your family on a regular basis. There are many steps to home cooking that are simple enough to be done by children. Two-year-olds can peel carrots. Five-year-olds can set the table. Eight-year-olds can slice cheese. Twelve-year-olds can chop onions. Involving your family will lighten your load, give you valuable time together, and teach your children skills they can use all their lives.

Prep cooking is another hugely helpful tool for speeding up cooking on busy days. Having meat and poultry cooked ahead of time is a great time-saver when making casseroles, stir-fries, and soups.

Pre-cooking Chicken

I often buy 10-pound packages of chicken leg quarters. As soon as I get home, I stick them in the slow cooker with 2 to 3 cups of chicken broth and cook them on Low 6 to 8 hours until the chicken is tender and falling off the bones. At that point, I let the meat cool for half an hour or so, then enlist my kids to help me pick the meat off the bones. Once the bones and skin have been removed, I freeze the cooked chicken in zip-top plastic bags or square plastic freezer containers. The containers I use hold about 2 cups of meat, which is enough for soup. For a stir-fry or a casserole, I use two containers.

making the most of your freezer space

Having a big freezer is a good money-saving strategy for a lot of families, including mine. But it's not a tightwad essential. With careful organization, it's possible to fit a lot of food into a small above- or below-the-fridge freezer.

Start by completely emptying the freezer you have now. Any food that has been in there a year or more should be used within the next day or so, or thrown away. Wipe out the freezer. Then think about ways to package food in space-saving ways. Gallon-size zip-top plastic bags stack nicely and can be used for everything from shredded zucchini, to taco meat, to the last dab of spaghetti sauce you're saving to use as pizza topping, to cooked beans, to leftover soup. Be sure to cool soup before putting it in a zip-top bag and don't lay anything on top of it until it's frozen.

If you often freeze casseroles, try to use similar-size casserole dishes for easy stacking. Pyrex dishes freeze without any problem, or you can use foil pans if you prefer. Using leftover containers that stack easily is another good tactic.

Many store-bought items are both boxed and bagged. By removing bagged pre-formed hamburger patties from their box, I save a few inches of space, and even more when the box is only partly full.

Chicken takes up much less space when it's already cooked, with the skin and bones removed, and stored in zip-top bags. You have the added convenience of having one step of that meal already done.

With a little careful planning, you may be amazed at just how much you can fit into a normal-size fridge freezer.

Pre-cooking Beef

I usually buy ground beef in family-size packs of 8 or 10 pounds. Soon after I arrive home from the store, I get out my two biggest skillets and set the hamburger to cooking. If I have time, I'll mince some garlic and onion and fry that in with the meat. But often I just add a bit of garlic and onion powder and cook it that way.

Once the beef is browned, I store it in 2-cup square plastic leftover containers. Again, this size allows me to use one or two containers for most meals. Storing the cooked meat in this size of container also makes it easier to thaw out before mealtime. I figure every time I use already-cooked meat in a meal, I am probably

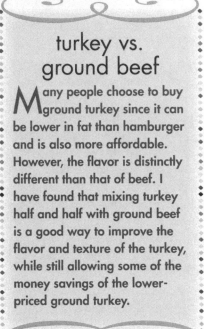

turkey vs. ground beef

Many people choose to buy ground turkey since it can be lower in fat than hamburger and is also more affordable. However, the flavor is distinctly different than that of beef. I have found that mixing turkey half and half with ground beef is a good way to improve the flavor and texture of the turkey, while still allowing some of the money savings of the lower-priced ground turkey.

shaving at least 10 minutes off the prep time for the meal.

I'll often leave some of the ground beef uncooked, however. This gets mixed with ground turkey to make my own meatloaf (see recipe on page 109). I freeze the meatloaf right in the pan in which I will be baking it—I like using a Bundt cake pan because the hole in the middle allows the meatloaf to cook more quickly and completely.

I also make my own meatballs by forming raw meat into 1-inch balls, then layering them with wax paper onto baking sheets. I freeze the meatballs raw, then transfer them to gallon-size zip-top plastic bags. This way I can take out just the number of meatballs I want, instead of having to defrost an entire bag at a time. Sometimes I also make my own hamburger patties, again freezing them on baking sheets separated by layers of wax paper, then transferring them to plastic bags.

Pre-prepping Veggies

I love everything about Panda Express. I love the luscious Chinese food, the wonderful smells, and the fact that you can be eating five minutes after you walk in the door. I also love looking at the trays and trays of beautiful, fresh, already-prepped vegetables displayed in the refrigerators behind the cash registers. In my dream kitchen, I would have a refrigerator like that and I would set it up just so I could look at the lovely vegetables.

Besides being a wonderful display item, prepped vegetables make cooking at the restaurant go so much more quickly. Obviously in a home, even one as full as mine, you don't need a gallon bin full of sliced onions. But if you want to minimize your time in the kitchen, you might just want to take a lesson from the Panda himself.

When you get out a couple of carrots to slice into a stir-fry, especially if you've enlisted your children to help you peel and slice, why not get out four more carrots and chop a few extra cups for a day or two from now when you will need carrots in a soup? When you're peeling garlic today, peel a couple more cloves for tomorrow. Stick the extras in a zip-top in the fridge. You'll thank yourself later.

One of the beauties of the Two Times Five Meal Plan is that you can easily look over your plans for the week and figure out just how many veggies you are going to need chopped during the week. On the weekend you just might have time to chop a few extra veggies to speed prep on a busier day in the middle of the week. You could even make this a Sunday-evening job for one of your children each week.

Serial Cooking

Now here's a beauty of an idea. Anytime you can make one cooking effort apply towards several meals, you're ahead of the game. We all benefit from this in the days after Thanksgiving when we have lots of leftovers. But there are many other ways you can double your benefit from the same amount of work.

For example, on Sunday you could cook a medium-size pork roast that would feed your family for a single meal. Or you could cook a truly enormous roast that would make Sunday dinner, plus pulled pork sandwiches for lunch on Monday, plus meat to add to a stir-fry on Tuesday. Don't even worry about not being able to eat it all in a few days. It's always an advantage to have already-cooked meat in the freezer.

Anytime you can make one cooking effort apply towards several meals, you're ahead of the game.

The same thing can be done with a pot of beans. A medium pot of beans could feed your family for one meal. Or you could toss twice as many beans into the pot, expending no extra energy (see the Bean Cooking Times chart on page 74). The first day you could have beans and rice. You can set aside several 2-cup servings of beans in zip-tops in the freezer for easy additions to soup on different days. You can add some beans to an enchilada casserole a day or two later. And you can have refried beans and chips later in the week for an easy lunch.

Once you've done serial cooking a few times, you'll get in the habit of thinking that way, and will likely come up with lots of ways to maximize the output from your time.

bean cooking times

Dried Beans (1 to 2 pounds)	Soaking Time	Regular Cooking Time	Pressure Cooking Time (15 pounds pressure)
Black (turtle)	overnight	1 hour	15 to 20 minutes
Black-eyed peas	overnight	1 hour	10 minutes
Chickpeas (garbanzo beans)	overnight	2 to 3 hours	15 to 20 minutes
Kidney	overnight	1½ to 2 hours	10 minutes
Lentil	none	40 to 50 minutes	not recommended
Lima	overnight	1 to 1½ hours	not recommended
Peas, split	none	45 to 60 minutes	not recommended
Pinto	overnight	1½ to 2 hours	10 minutes
Soybeans	overnight	3 to 4 hours	15 to 20 minutes
White (Great Northern, navy)	overnight	1 hour	4 to 5 minutes

*You can also cook beans in a slow cooker, on Low for 16 to 20 hours or on High for 7 to 9 hours; if cooking on High, check the beans a couple of times so you can add more liquid if needed.

This simple recipe is suitable for any type of bean. Beans will have the most flavor if they take up their seasoning while they cook. If you'll be using the cooked beans in another recipe, simply decrease the seasoning in that recipe to account for the seasoning you added to the beans during their initial cooking.

All-Purpose Cooked Beans

2 pounds dried beans, picked over
  and rinsed

12 cups water

2 to 4 tablespoons fat, such as bacon
  grease, margarine, or vegetable oil

1 tablespoon onion powder

2 teaspoons salt

1 teaspoon garlic powder

½ teaspoon black pepper

½ teaspoon ground red pepper

1. Combine all ingredients in a very large pot. Bring to a boil, uncovered, then reduce the heat to low or medium-low and simmer gently, partially covered, according to the recommended cooking time in the Bean Cooking Times chart (at left).

Cooking Efficiently

When putting together the recipes for this book, I tried to organize the tasks in each recipe to minimize time in the kitchen. Here are some of the time-saving strategies I've learned along the way:

• **Start your pasta or rice cooking at the beginning of prep time** so that it will be ready by the time the other food is ready.

• **Use precooked meat,** or cook the meat early in the meal prep while you're prepping other ingredients.

• **When stir-frying, partially thaw frozen food in the microwave** so as not to cool down the skillet in which you're cooking.

• **Always chop the vegetables that need the most cooking time first.** Cut up the quicker-cooking vegetables while the sturdier ones are cooking.

If you're unfamiliar with a recipe, it can sometimes be tricky to time it so that ingredients are ready when you need them to keep the recipe flowing along. To make these recipes work best for you, read through the entire recipe before you

save time and money with powdered milk

One quick trick I've discovered when making cream soups (see page 279) is to use powdered milk instead of cold milk straight out of the fridge. Powdered milk is usually cheaper than regular milk, and you don't notice the slight flavor difference when it's used in soup. And since you can use hot tap water instead of waiting for refrigerated milk to warm, this speeds the cooking time by 5 to 10 minutes.

Here's how I do it. When a soup calls for milk, I add an equivalent amount of water instead of the milk at the beginning of the cooking time. For example, if the recipe calls for 4 cups milk, I add 4 cups hot water. Right before serving, I measure enough powder to make the amount of milk called for by the recipe. I mix it briskly in a measuring cup with a little of the hot liquid from the soup, then dump it into the soup, stirring well. Adding the milk this late also means you decrease the likelihood of burning the soup to the bottom of the pot, something that can happen very quickly with a milk-based soup.

begin. If it seems like a lot is happening all at once, get some of the ingredient prep done before you begin cooking. Once you have made a recipe a time or two, you'll probably be comfortable enough with it to do it in the order that I've listed.

What's Next?

Now that we've talked about the basics of money-saving shopping, it's time for the fun part: the recipes. In the following chapters I'll be sharing my family's best-loved recipes, as well as many others that are both affordable and doable for busy families.

Keep in mind that the prep time listed at the beginning of each recipe also includes cook time. This way you can look at the recipe and know whether or not you have time to pull it together in the time you have left before dinnertime. For recipes such as the 30-minute stovetop dishes, you'll probably be actively cooking most of that time. Other recipes will include baking time, during which you can wander off and take a bubble bath (if you should be so lucky!).

The recipe chapters also include tips for saving money and time, as well as bits of mom wisdom you might find useful. They're there to make your life easier and your money stretch further.

As you cook with this book, you'll get a feel for various ways to make meals more affordable, which will make it easier to begin adapting other recipes on your own. Have fun, and don't be afraid to experiment!

action points:

☐ **Figure out your meal-planning style** and decide if you need to change your strategy to be more cost-effective at the store.

☐ **Choose a plan you'd like to try,** and make a meal plan based on it for the next week or two.

☐ **Go through your pantry** and figure out which staples you need to buy, as well as which items you need for the menus you've created.

☐ **When holding an ingredient in your hand,** ask yourself if it's possible to use a little less and get the same result. (The exception is seasonings. Seasonings keep food interesting, and tend to be only a small portion of the cost of a meal. So season away!)

☐ **Reorganize your freezer space** and decide if there might need to be a freezer in your future.

☐ **Get in the habit of prepping some of your meat** as soon as you get it home from the grocery store.

☐ **Freeze some meat, already cooked,** as a jumpstart to quick meals on busy days.

☐ **Next time you're cutting up vegetables,** prep some extra to speed meal prep on a busy day.

☐ **Enlist your family to keep you company** in the kitchen and to speed meal prep.

chapter 5

breakfast & lunch

Walk into the average home on a weekday morning and chances are you'll see sleepy-eyed people hunting for food and papers and shoes, while doing their best to get out the door on time. With all that going on, people need to be able to pull together breakfast quickly and easily.

Lunch presents other dilemmas. Packability is a virtue. Food that can be prepped the evening before is hugely helpful. And if you want your family to resist the lure of vending machines and fast-food restaurants, it also has to be appealing to both the eye and the taste buds.

Whether for breakfast or lunch, the recipes in this chapter will help you juggle all those demands, while keeping you within your food budget.

If you don't live in the South, you may not be familiar with grits. I first grabbed a carton of them out of curiosity, and discovered that they're just as quick and good as Cream of Wheat, but a lot more affordable. The trick is to stir them briskly, and then be creative with your toppings. Try fruit, jam, honey, brown sugar, vanilla, cinnamon, nutmeg, raisins, nuts, cheese, and, of course, butter. Experiment to see what your family enjoys the most or let everyone customize their own bowl. You can find grits in the breakfast foods aisle by the Cream of Wheat and oatmeal.

Breakfast Grits

serves 4   prep time: 15 minutes

2 cups milk
¼ cup honey, plus more for serving
½ teaspoon salt
¾ cup quick-cooking grits
Sliced fresh fruit

1. Combine milk, honey, and salt in a medium-size saucepan; add grits, stirring constantly. Bring to a boil over medium heat, stirring frequently.
2. Reduce heat to low; cook, stirring frequently, until thickened, about 5 to 7 minutes.
3. Serve warm, topped with fruit and additional honey to taste.

super-saver idea

To keep your breakfast costs low, aim to have hot cereal at least once or twice a week. Hot cereal tends to have more staying power than cold. It's the most affordable type of breakfast there is, especially if you steer clear of the prepackaged instant kind.

People all over the world eat versions of polenta every day, some for every meal. And no wonder—it's extremely affordable. To make smooth polenta, start by stirring the cornmeal into the liquid while it's still cold, and stir frequently as it cooks.

Maple Morning Polenta

serves 4 to 6   prep time: 20 minutes

3 cups cold water
1½ cups milk
2 cups cornmeal
½ teaspoon salt

½ cup pancake syrup, plus more for
  serving
2 tablespoons butter
½ cup raisins or dried cranberries

1. Combine water, milk, cornmeal, and salt in a medium-size saucepan, stirring briskly to combine. Cook over medium heat, stirring frequently, until mixture reaches a boil, about 10 minutes.

2. Reduce heat to low. Cook 3 to 5 minutes, stirring frequently, until mixture thickens.

3. Remove from heat. Stir in pancake syrup and butter; ladle into bowls. Top with additional syrup and sprinkle with raisins just before serving.

◆◆◆◆◆◆◆◆◆◆

This is a great warm breakfast on a winter morning—it tastes almost like dessert to me. If you don't want to use canned peaches, peel and slice 2 fresh peaches, and combine 1 cup orange juice with 1 cup milk for the liquid in the recipe.

Couscous with Peaches

serves 4   prep time: 15 minutes

One 16-ounce can sliced peaches,
  drained and liquid reserved
Milk, enough to total 2 cups of liquid
  when combined with peach juice
1 cup quick-cooking couscous

2 tablespoons butter
½ teaspoon ground nutmeg
2 tablespoons brown sugar, plus
  more for serving

1. In a small saucepan, heat reserved peach liquid and milk to simmering. Add couscous, butter, nutmeg, and brown sugar to pan; stir to combine.

2. Remove from heat; let sit until liquid is absorbed, about 5 to 10 minutes.

3. Top servings with sliced peaches and a dab of brown sugar.

· • · • • • · • • ·

If you're fortunate enough to have a rice cooker, you can make oatmeal even on days when you have only a few minutes to spend in the kitchen. A hot breakfast doesn't get any easier than this!

Rice-Cooker Oatmeal

serves 4   prep time: 20 minutes

4 cups cold water

2 cups quick-cooking oats

⅓ cup firmly packed brown sugar

2 tablespoons butter

1 teaspoon vanilla extract

1. Combine water and oats in rice cooker. Stir once and turn cooker on. Let cook until rice cooker switches over to "Warm," about 20 minutes.

2. Stir in brown sugar, butter, and vanilla. Serve immediately.

mom to mom

Oatmeal is an extremely affordable meal. Lots of people love it, including my husband. In the past I've not been a huge fan. That was before I learned a trick from friends of ours. They serve oatmeal topped with ice cream. Sounds terribly decadent, doesn't it? But when you think about it, ice cream is mostly cream and sugar, both of which are standard oatmeal toppings. If your kids don't love oatmeal, try a dollop of ice cream on top. They just might change their tune.

My mom kept us supplied in granola all during my growing up years. Granola has much more staying power and nutrition than your average cold cereal, and can be mixed up in minutes. Let your kids pick which "goodies" to use for added enjoyment.

Mary's Easy Granola

makes about 24 servings   prep time: 30 minutes

12 cups quick-cooking oats
½ cup all-purpose flour
1 tablespoon ground cinnamon
½ teaspoon ground nutmeg

4 cups "goodies" (nuts, raisins, sunflower seeds, trail mix, coconut, dried fruit)
1 cup vegetable oil
1 cup honey

1. Preheat oven to 325°F. Grease 3 large baking sheets with nonstick cooking spray.

2. In a very large bowl, combine oats, flour, cinnamon, nutmeg, and whatever "goodies" you are using. Mix well.

3. Combine oil and honey in a 2-cup glass measuring cup. Microwave on High 2 to 3 minutes until hot. Pour over dry ingredients and mix well.

4. Spread mixture over prepared baking sheets; bake until light to medium brown, 15 to 20 minutes. If you have a convection oven, bake all 3 pans at the same time. Otherwise, it's best to bake each pan individually on the center rack of oven.

5. Let granola cool. It will break up somewhat as you transfer it to a storage container, but try to leave some big chunks, as that makes it more interesting to eat. Store in an airtight container up to 4 weeks. (At our house, I'm lucky if it lasts 3 days!)

It wasn't until I started doing research for this book that I learned the secret of good French toast. First, don't use wimpy bread: Texas toast, French bread, or good sturdy homemade bread is best. Second, add a little flour to your egg mixture before dipping.

Restaurant-Style French Toast

serves 6   prep time: 20 minutes

⅓ cup all-purpose flour
¼ cup granulated sugar
¼ teaspoon salt
¼ teaspoon ground cinnamon
1 cup milk
4 large eggs

½ teaspoon vanilla extract
Vegetable oil or shortening
8 to 10 slices Texas toast or crusty French
   bread
Confectioners' sugar, sliced fruit, butter,
   and pancake syrup for serving (optional)

1. In a medium-size bowl, combine flour, sugar, salt, and cinnamon. Add milk, eggs, and vanilla; whisk briskly to remove any lumps of flour.

2. Grease a skillet or frying pan with a paper towel that has been dipped in oil or shortening. Heat skillet over medium-high heat until a drop of water sizzles when flicked onto skillet.

3. Dip both sides of bread slice into the batter briefly. Let some of the batter drip off, then place bread in skillet. Cook until golden brown on both sides, about 2 minutes on the first side and 1 minute on the second. If needed, add a little more oil to the skillet to cook all of the slices. Repeat procedure with remaining bread slices. Keep French toast warm in a low oven as you cook remaining slices.

4. Dust with confectioners' sugar and serve with butter, syrup, or fruit, if using.

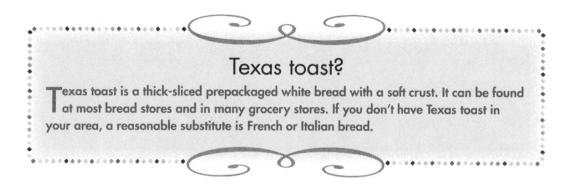

Texas toast?

Texas toast is a thick-sliced prepackaged white bread with a soft crust. It can be found at most bread stores and in many grocery stores. If you don't have Texas toast in your area, a reasonable substitute is French or Italian bread.

When you're serving pancakes, waffles, or French toast, don't forget to heat up your syrup in the microwave before setting it out. This helps keep your breakfast hot, and it adds a nice restaurant-style feel to your meal. You can put the syrup in a fancy little pitcher if you happen to have one. A small Pyrex measuring cup works well, too. You can find a recipe for homemade pancake syrup on page 272.

Short-cut Pancakes

makes 12 pancakes   prep time: 10 minutes

2½ cups Blue Ribbon Pancake Mix
  (page 277)
2 large eggs
2 cups tepid or warm (not hot) water

2 tablespoons butter, melted
½ teaspoon vanilla extract
Vegetable oil or shortening

1. Combine all ingredients except vegetable oil in a large bowl, whisking lightly until everything is mostly combined. (A few small lumps are OK.)

2. Lightly grease a skillet or frying pan with a paper towel that has been dipped in oil or shortening. Heat skillet over medium heat until a drop of water sizzles when flicked onto skillet.

3. Spoon about ½ cup batter onto skillet for each pancake. Batter will seem thick; use the back of a spoon to spread it out a little, if desired. Cook until top of pancake begins to look dry at edges. Flip and cook other side until golden brown. Keep pancakes warm in a low oven while you cook remaining batter.

For waffles: Prepare batter as directed above; cook in a hot, well-greased waffle iron for 3 to 4 minutes per waffle.

My family has been enjoying "Aunt Edie pancakes" ever since my aunt taught us how to make them. This was one of my favorite breakfasts as a child. It's actually just a simple recipe for crepes.

Aunt Edie Pancakes

serves 6 to 8   prep time: 25 minutes

4 cups milk

4 large eggs

2 tablespoons butter, melted

½ teaspoon vanilla extract

2 cups all-purpose flour

1 tablespoon granulated sugar

½ teaspoon salt

1 stick butter

2 cups confectioners' sugar

Sliced fruit (optional)

1. Combine first 7 ingredients in a large bowl to form a thin batter.

2. Spray a little nonstick cooking spray onto a large skillet. Place skillet over medium heat for a few minutes. Pour batter smoothly into hot skillet to make 6-inch round pancakes. Tilt the pan a little to spread the batter out as needed; these pancakes should be very thin. Cook until edges start to dry and curl up a little, 30 to 60 seconds. Flip and cook pancakes 20 to 30 seconds on other side. Remove pancakes from pan while bottom is still pale.

3. Immediately butter pancakes with the end of a stick of butter. Sprinkle each pancake with about 2 tablespoons confectioners' sugar, and roll up. Keep pancakes warm in a low oven until ready to serve. Before serving, top with fruit, if using, and sprinkle with an additional tablespoon confectioners' sugar.

quick tip

The batter for this recipe can be mixed ahead of time and kept in the refrigerator for up to a week for a super-easy breakfast any day of the week.

When John and I were newly married, we used to go to a certain diner every now and then for breakfast. They had the best potatoes in town. I liked their recipe so much that I came up with this similar version in my own kitchen. You can adapt this recipe to include any kind of vegetable you enjoy. We usually serve it with eggs and toast.

The crucial step to making good hash browns is washing the starch out of the potatoes. Set the grated potatoes in a colander and rinse well under cold running water until the water coming off the potatoes runs clear. Squeeze the potatoes firmly to remove excess water. Then they're ready to fry!

Hash Brown Combo

serves 4 to 6   prep time: 30 minutes

¼ cup vegetable oil

4 medium-size russet potatoes, peeled, shredded, rinsed, and squeezed dry

1 medium-size onion, minced

A handful of pepperoni slices, chopped

2 cloves garlic, minced

1 green or red bell pepper, seeded and chopped

1 teaspoon salt

½ teaspoon black pepper

2 ripe tomatoes, diced (I like Roma tomatoes for this)

1 tablespoon chopped fresh parsley

Shredded Cheddar cheese and sour cream for serving (optional)

1. Heat oil in a large cast-iron skillet over medium-high heat until hot. Add potatoes and onion; cook, without stirring, until mixture starts to brown, 3 to 4 minutes, then stir well. Cover and cook 2 to 3 more minutes.

2. Add pepperoni, garlic, bell pepper, salt, and black pepper. Turn heat down to medium-low. Cover and cook until potatoes are cooked through, 5 to 7 more minutes, watching to make sure they don't burn. If potatoes begin to stick before they're completely cooked, add ¼ cup water to skillet.

3. Stir in tomatoes and parsley, and remove from heat. Top with shredded cheese and serve with sour cream, if using.

These muffins can be baked, then refrigerated or frozen to eat later. Microwave
30 seconds (50 seconds if frozen) to reheat for a quick breakfast on a busy morning.

Eggy Breakfast Muffins

makes 12 muffins   prep time: 45 minutes

½ pound sliced bacon, minced
½ cup finely chopped onion
1 clove garlic, chopped
½ cup shredded raw vegetables
   (I usually use carrot and/or zucchini)
6 large eggs

½ cup milk
1 cup shredded Cheddar cheese
1 cup all-purpose flour
1 teaspoon baking powder
½ teaspoon salt
1 teaspoon minced fresh parsley

1. Preheat oven to 350°F. Grease and flour a 12-cup muffin tin; set aside.
2. Fry bacon over medium heat until crispy. Using a slotted spoon, remove bacon
to paper towels to drain. Reserve a tablespoon or so of grease in a small bowl,
then discard remaining grease in pan. Let pan cool, then wipe with paper towels
to remove any remaining bits of bacon. Return pan to medium heat. Add reserved
bacon grease, onion, garlic, and grated vegetables. Cook, stirring, until vegetables
soften, 3 to 5 minutes. Remove to a bowl to cool.
3. In a large bowl, beat together eggs, milk, and cheese. Add flour, baking powder, salt, parsley, bacon, and sautéed vegetables; stir together just until combined.
4. Fill each muffin cup three-quarters full. Bake until edges start to brown and tops
spring back when pressed, 20 to 25 minutes.

don't burn that bacon!

Use the oven! It cooks a little slower this way, but needs much less watching and
results in more evenly cooked meat. Simply spread your bacon (or sausage) on a
baking sheet and bake at 400°F. Turn the meat over halfway through the cooking time.
Bacon will cook in 15 to 20 minutes depending on how thick the slices are.

quick lunch ideas ....

The great thing about lunch is that it can be as simple as you want it to be. Some days we simply serve sliced cheese with crackers and fruit. Granted, that's when it's just the kids and me. When Dad's home, he requires more substantial fare. But lunch is the perfect meal for experimenting with simplicity.

If you pack lunches for school or work, it's important to streamline this process as much as possible. Many families do this by buying all sorts of individually wrapped convenience foods. But you pay big bucks for that convenience. The good news is that there are more affordable ways to have convenience.

The Sunday Lunchbox Party

One idea is the Sunday evening lunchbox party. Start by doing a bit of baking on Sunday afternoon: at least a batch of cookies or a pan of brownies. Make both if you really want your family to be happy with you. You might also make a batch of Honey-Granola Bars (page 232). You'll need zip-top bags in two sizes: sandwich-size and snack-size.

Other lunchbox party food to gather:

• Carrots, celery, broccoli, and other raw veggies your family enjoys
• Apples, oranges, grapes, raisins, and other fruit
• Olives or pickles
• Freshly popped popcorn, dried fruit, or big bags of pretzels or corn chips

Involve the family. Once you've gathered your supplies and your family, turn on some music and get to work. Divide your family into groups: one to slice veggies and fruit to put in snack-size zip-top bags (sliced oranges pack well since they don't discolor; apple slices can be tossed in a little lemon juice before being bagged up to keep from going brown); one to fill bags with chips, raisins, or popcorn; and another to wrap indiviual granola bars or brownies.

Figure out how many of each item you'll need. If four people each pack five lunches a week, you'll need 20 packages each of fruit, veggies, dessert, and snack items. You can vary the fullness of the bags by the appetite of the eater— dad gets 6 carrot sticks, and the 5-year-old gets 2.

Homemade is money saved. To save money, buy whole carrots instead of baby carrots and cut them into sticks yourself. Make your own cheese sticks by cutting up a log of Cheddar. Make your own single-servings of chips from a family-size bag to save even more money.

Freeze for freshness. Store cookies and other desserts in the freezer—they'll stay fresher that way. If you want, you can even make sandwiches ahead of time. Fillings that freeze well include peanut butter and jelly, lunchmeat, and cheese. Skip the mayo, though, because it changes consistency when frozen. Skip sandwiches entirely by packing whole-grain crackers alongside slices of cheese and lunch meat.

Try tortillas. Flour tortillas make excellent sandwich wraps. Peanut butter roll-ups are a lunchtime staple at our house. They're easy to eat and can be customized with the addition of raisins, chopped apples, or jam. Lunchmeat, cheese, and tuna work well in a flour tortilla, with no worries about smashed bread. Keep portion sizes in mind, though. One 10-inch tortilla has as many calories as 2 slices of bread. You may want to serve half-tortillas to your smaller children. Use plastic wrap to store your tortilla sandwiches, and they'll hold together better.

Keep it interesting. Children are more likely to eat their lunch when you serve small portions of a variety of different foods. Dips are also wonderful. Think of what your child would eat if he could dip it. Good dips include ketchup, peanut butter, yogurt, salsa, and ranch dressing. Keep an eye out for tiny dip containers—the dollar store is a good place to look.

Once you've gotten your bags filled for the week, designate boxes in the fridge and freezer in which to keep lunch food. An hour of preparation on a Sunday evening will make it possible to pack lunches in just a minute or two on a busy school or work morning. Approaching it in an organized way will mean you'll be eating better, too.

For other lunchtime ideas, be sure to check out the salads on pages 211–219. Many of those recipes make excellent lunches, and can be stored in the fridge for several days, which adds to their convenience.

This is a jazzed-up version of scrambled eggs. We've been cooking it for years, and my family really enjoys it. It's a good way to use up stale taco chips. If you don't have taco chips, substitute torn flour or corn tortillas.

Mexican Migas

serves 6   prep time: 25 minutes

6 large eggs
¼ cup water
2 tablespoons butter
4 cloves garlic, minced
½ cup chopped onion
1 to 2 jalapeños, seeded and minced
   (optional)
½ cup chopped green bell pepper

1 to 2 medium-size ripe tomatoes,
   chopped
1 teaspoon ground cumin
2 cups broken taco chips
1 tablespoon minced fresh cilantro
Salt and black pepper to taste
Salsa or picante sauce (optional)
Flour tortillas or toast (optional)

1. Whisk together eggs and water in a medium-size bowl.
2. Melt butter in a large heavy skillet over medium heat. Add garlic, onion, and jalapeños (if using); cook until onion softens, 3 to 5 minutes, stirring every couple of minutes. Add bell pepper, tomatoes, and cumin; cook for several minutes more until liquid steams off and mixture starts to look dry.
3. Add beaten egg mixture to pan; cook until eggs begin to set but are still shiny with a little bit of liquid. Stir in taco chips and cilantro. Continue to cook until eggs look done. Season with salt and black pepper.
4. Serve migas with salsa or picanté sauce and warm flour tortillas or toast, if using.

Variation: Feel free to get creative with this recipe. Good additions include any kind of chopped meat, herbs, cooked vegetables, or cheese.

These rollups are sure to be a hit in your child's lunchbox. They can be eaten either warm or cold. Wrap extras in twos and threes and freeze them for quick lunchbox food another day. Using frozen bread dough speeds the prep considerably, but if you'd like an even more affordable option, this can be made using the pizza dough recipe on page 226.

Easy Pizza Rolls

makes about 24 small rolls   prep time: 30 minutes

1 loaf frozen bread dough, thawed
4 ounces cream cheese, softened
One 6-ounce can tomato paste
2 teaspoons dried oregano

1 teaspoon garlic powder
1 teaspoon onion powder
1½ cups shredded mozzarella cheese
1 cup chopped pepperoni

1. Preheat oven to 375°F. Coat a large baking sheet with nonstick cooking spray.
2. Roll out bread dough into a rectangle, making it as thin as you can (the thinner the dough, the better these will be). Spread softened cream cheese evenly over dough. Spread tomato paste evenly over cream cheese. Sprinkle evenly with oregano, garlic powder, and onion powder. Top evenly with mozzarella and pepperoni.
3. Roll up jelly-roll style, starting at long end. Cut log into 1-inch-thick rounds, like you do when you're making cinnamon rolls. Place rolls, cut sides down, onto prepared baking sheet, leaving a little space for them to expand. Bake until golden brown, about 20 minutes.

super-saver idea

Instead of endlessly buying little cans of cooking spray, try making your own. All you have to do is purchase a spray bottle at the dollar store, fill it with your own olive oil, and spray away. The mist isn't quite as fine as it is from a can of cooking spray, but you'll end up using less oil than you will pouring it from a bottle.

This simple recipe is our go-to lunch two or three times a week when our tomato plants are producing. Even a child can manage the prep, and you can be eating your meal within 10 minutes.

I call for hamburger buns because they're easy and I usually have a package in the freezer. But this recipe is even better with good homemade rolls or sturdy French bread. Sometimes we also add pepperoni to the melt. Experiment and see what your family likes best.

Summertime Tomato Melts

serves 4 to 6   prep time: 10 minutes

super-saver idea

If you're a gardener wondering what to do with green tomatoes still on the vine in the fall, pick them before the frost. If you wrap them individually in newspaper and store them in a cool place, they'll ripen and be ready to eat in a few weeks. We regularly have fresh tomatoes in December using this trick.

4 hamburger buns
2 cloves garlic, peeled
3 tablespoons olive oil
2 ripe tomatoes, sliced
Sliced cheese of your choice

1. Preheat broiler.

2. Split open hamburger buns and place on a baking sheet, cut sides up.

3. Mash garlic and combine with olive oil. Using a spoon or a basting brush, drizzle oil mixture evenly over each hamburger bun, spreading it around to coat. Place baking sheet 4 to 6 inches away from the source of heat, and broil buns 2 to 3 minutes until they are golden brown. Remove from oven.

4. Place 1 slice of tomato and 1 slice of cheese on top of each bun-half. Return to oven and broil until cheese melts, 3 to 4 more minutes. Remove from oven and serve warm.

This recipe can be used as a party snack or a great addition to a school lunch. Freeze extras to enjoy another day.

Cream Cheese Pinwheels

makes 24 bite-size pinwheels   prep time: 20 minutes, plus 2 hours chilling time

One 3-ounce package cream cheese,
    softened
1 tablespoon store-bought or homemade
    (page 276) dry ranch dressing mix
¼ cup minced celery
1 green onion, very thinly sliced
¼ cup sliced pitted olives (optional)
Three 10-inch flour tortillas
4 slices deli ham, turkey, or roast beef

1. In a small bowl, beat softened cream cheese and ranch dressing mix together until smooth. Add celery, green onion, and olives (if using). Mix well.

2. Divide mixture evenly among tortillas, spreading to coat. Top each tortilla with 2 slices of meat; roll up tortillas tightly and wrap in plastic. Refrigerate tortillas at least 2 hours or overnight to set. Slice into 1-inch-thick rounds.

things I love!

my cheese slicer

A good cheese slicer makes a block of cheese last much longer than cutting it with a regular knife. After years of breaking wimpy wire cheese cutters, I've finally found one that lasts. My Pampered Chef cheese knife has a "plane" that allows you to shave extremely thin slices, and a regular knife for times when you want thicker pieces. It comes with a lifetime guarantee, so I expect that it will be the last cheese slicer that I need to buy.

This recipe is a delicious improvement on your standard grilled cheese sandwich. If you have already-cooked chicken set aside in the freezer, this goes together really quickly. It's also a great use for leftover turkey after Thanksgiving. If you happen to have extra cranberry sauce, that makes an excellent addition as well.

Chicken and Apple Sandwiches with Melted Cheese

serves 4   prep time: 30 minutes

3 tablespoons butter, at room temperature
8 slices white or whole-wheat bread
2 cups cooked chicken, cut into small pieces

4 ounces cream cheese, cut into thin slices
1 Granny Smith apple, peeled, cored, and thinly sliced

1. Preheat oven to 350°F. Grease a large baking sheet with nonstick cooking spray.
2. Spread butter on 1 side of each slice of bread. Arrange 4 bread slices onto prepared baking sheet, butter sides down. Divide chicken evenly among the 4 bread slices on pan and top each evenly with cheese and apple slices. Top with remaining bread slices, butter sides up.
3. Bake for 10 minutes, then flip sandwiches and bake until crispy and golden, about 10 more minutes. Cut sandwiches in half and serve immediately.

With its golden braided top and sesame-seed topping, this bread looks like it's much more difficult to make than it actually is. I often make this the day before we leave on a trip. It's easy to eat in the car and is more interesting than sandwiches. Plus the recipe is very versatile. I sometimes use sliced ham and Cheddar cheese instead of the sausage and cream cheese called for in the recipe. Or you can substitute ground beef that you've seasoned with 1 teaspoon each onion powder, garlic powder, and paprika.

Sausage Sandwich Braid

serves 6 to 8   prep time: 45 minutes

1 pound bulk pork sausage

½ cup chopped onion

1 rib celery, chopped

¼ cup chopped green bell pepper

1 clove garlic, minced

4 ounces cream cheese, cubed

2 green onions, chopped

2 tablespoons minced fresh parsley

2 loaves frozen bread dough, thawed

1 large egg, lightly beaten

Sesame seeds and/or poppy seeds for
 topping

1. Preheat oven to 350°F.

2. Cook sausage, onion, celery, bell pepper, and garlic in a medium-size skillet over medium heat until pork is no longer pink and vegetables are tender; use a large spoon to break pork into small pieces as it cooks.

3. Drain grease from meat in pan; stir in cream cheese, green onions, and parsley. Cook, stirring frequently, over low heat until cheese melts; set aside.

4. Knead both thawed loaves of dough into 1 lump. Roll bread dough out onto a 10 x 12-inch baking sheet. Spread sausage mixture down middle of rectangle, leaving 3 inches of dough uncovered on both long sides and 1 inch uncovered at the short ends. On each long side, cut ¾-inch-wide strips 3 inches into the center of the dough, right up to where the filling starts. Starting at one end, fold alternating strips at an angle, forming a braid over the filling. Crimp ends of dough to close braid. Brush dough with beaten egg. Sprinkle with sesame seeds.

5. Bake until golden brown, 20 to 25 minutes. Let cool slightly, then cut into 1½-inch-thick slices.

These chimichangas are crunchy and wonderful. Since they're oven-baked, not fried, they're lower in calories than your standard chimi.

You can make these in large quantities, freeze in individual zip-top bags, and zap in the microwave 2 minutes to reheat.

Crunchy Baked Chimichangas

serves 4 to 6   prep time: 40 minutes

1½ cups chopped cooked chicken

½ cup picante sauce or your favorite salsa, plus more for serving

1 cup shredded Cheddar cheese, plus more for serving

2 green onions, chopped, plus more for serving

1 teaspoon ground cumin

1 teaspoon garlic powder

1 teaspoon onion powder

1 teaspoon salt

½ teaspoon black pepper

½ teaspoon dried oregano

Six 8-inch flour tortillas

2 tablespoons butter, melted

Salsa for serving

1. Preheat oven to 400°F.

2. Combine chicken, picante sauce, cheese, green onions, cumin, garlic powder, onion powder, salt, pepper, and oregano in a medium-size bowl. Divide mixture evenly among center of tortillas. Fold opposite sides of tortillas over filling, then roll up from the bottom and place, seam sides down, onto a baking sheet. Brush with melted butter.

3. Bake until golden brown, about 25 minutes. Garnish with additional cheese and green onions; serve salsa on the side.

Variation: This recipe is very flexible. Try substituting browned ground beef for the chicken and adding a little taco seasoning. Or make a filling with cooked chicken, chopped steamed broccoli, and ½ cup ranch dressing.

This recipe is super quick and makes a great addition to a lunchbox along with sesame crackers, taco chips, or toasted bread cut into quarters.

Middle Eastern Hummus

serves 6   prep time: 5 minutes

One 15-ounce can chickpeas, rinsed
  and drained
1 tablespoon sesame oil
2 to 3 tablespoons olive oil
¼ cup fresh lemon juice

3 cloves garlic, peeled
1 teaspoon ground cumin
½ teaspoon salt
¼ teaspoon black pepper

1. Combine all ingredients in a food processor or blender; process until smooth. If mixture is too thick, add a little water to dilute to preferred consistency. Serve at room temperature. Store in an airtight container in the fridge up to 1 week.

• ◆ • ◆ ◆ ◆ • ◆ • •

A friend of mine keeps single-serving containers of refried beans handy in her freezer so that her teenage boys can zap an easy snack anytime.

Refried Beans

serves 6   prep time: 6 hours, mostly cooking time, plus soaking overnight

One 1-pound package dried pinto beans
4 cups water
¼ cup bacon grease (optional)
1 tablespoon garlic powder

2 tablespoons powdered chicken bouillon
2 tablespoons chili powder
2 tablespoons butter
Taco chips, tortillas, or rice

1. Place beans and water in a large pot. Soak overnight.
2. Drain beans with a colander and rinse thoroughly. Add 2 cups fresh water to pot; stir in bacon grease, if using, and next 3 ingredients. Bring to a boil. Cover and reduce heat to low. Simmer 5 to 6 hours, stirring occasionally. Beans are done when they are very soft.
3. Add butter to beans and mash well. Serve with taco chips, tortillas, or rice.

casseroles & oven meals

asseroles are frugal-family staples: They make the most of moderate portions of meat, can often be made ahead and frozen for later use, and, in many cases, offer simple one-dish dining options.

Casseroles warm easily and also make good leftovers. Don't be intimidated if a recipe makes more than your family can use in one meal. Having great leftovers in the fridge makes it much easier to resist the siren's call of fast food. At our house we have a leftover meal at least once a week. I go through the fridge and pull out the week's leftovers, and the kids get to pick what they want to eat. My kids love choosing their favorites, and I love not having to cook.

This elegant version of lasagna is lower in fat and more affordable than standard lasagna. You can use fresh spinach instead of frozen, if you prefer.

Chicken Lasagna Florentine

makes one 9 x 13-inch casserole; serves 6 to 8   prep time: 1 hour 15 minutes

12 lasagna noodles, cooked according to
   package directions and drained
1 tablespoon olive oil
3 cups chopped chicken
One 10-ounce package frozen chopped
   spinach, thawed and squeezed to
   remove excess water
2 large eggs
½ cup shredded mozzarella cheese
1 teaspoon dried basil
1 teaspoon dried oregano
½ teaspoon ground nutmeg

White Sauce:
¼ cup (½ stick) butter
2 teaspoons garlic powder
1 teaspoon dried parsley
¼ cup all-purpose flour
1 chicken bouillon cube, dissolved in
   1 cup hot water
2 cups milk
¼ cup grated Parmesan cheese

Topping:
½ cup shredded mozzarella cheese

1. Preheat oven to 350°F. Coat a 9 x 13-inch casserole dish with nonstick cooking spray.

2. Heat olive oil in a medium-size heavy skillet over medium-high heat until hot. Add chicken; cook until lightly browned and no longer pink. In a large bowl, combine cooked chicken with spinach, eggs, ½ cup mozzarella, basil, oregano, and nutmeg.

3. To make white sauce, melt butter in a medium-size saucepan over low heat. Add garlic powder, parsley, and flour; stir until well combined. Gradually add chicken bouillon and milk, stirring frequently. Stir in Parmesan; continue to stir until thick and creamy. Remove from heat.

4. To assemble lasagna, layer half of lasagna noodles in the prepared baking dish. Top with half of the chicken-spinach mixture and half of the white sauce. Repeat with remaining noodles, chicken mixture, and white sauce. Sprinkle evenly with ½ cup mozzarella. Bake until bubbly and mozzarella begins to brown just a bit, about 25 minutes.

You can tailor the vegetables in this pot pie to suit your own family's likes and dislikes. Frozen mixed vegetables are the easiest. Other vegetables that we enjoy are broccoli, pearl onions, potatoes, sweet potatoes, and cabbage. Pick what's in season and most affordable. Almost any vegetable will work. Just make sure that the vegetables are mostly cooked before you put them into the casserole dish.

Chicken Pot Pie with Cheesy Biscuit Topping

makes one 9 x 13-inch casserole; serves 6 to 8   prep time: 1 hour 15 minutes

Filling:

One 1-pound bag frozen mixed vegetables

¼ cup (½ stick) butter, divided

1 cup chopped onion

4 cups cubed chicken

¼ cup all-purpose flour

1 teaspoon salt

1 teaspoon black pepper

1 teaspoon dried thyme

1 teaspoon dried basil plus 1 tablespoon minced fresh basil (optional)

2 cups chicken broth

1 cup sour cream

Cheesy Biscuit Topping:

2 cups all-purpose flour

2 teaspoons baking powder

1 teaspoon baking soda

1 teaspoon salt

1 teaspoon dried thyme

1 teaspoon dried basil

½ teaspoon black pepper

½ cup vegetable shortening, cut into bits

1 cup shredded Cheddar cheese

2 large eggs, beaten

1½ cups milk

1. Microwave vegetables on High 2 minutes to begin to thaw.

2. In a large heavy skillet, melt 2 tablespoons butter over medium-high heat. Add onion; cook until soft and slightly brown, stirring occasionally. Add slightly frozen vegetables and cook until heated through, 5 to 7 minutes. Transfer to a bowl, and set aside.

3. Melt remaining 2 tablespoons butter in same skillet over medium heat. Add chicken and cook through, stirring a few times. Reduce heat to medium-low. Add flour, salt, pepper, thyme, and 1 teaspoon dried basil, stirring to coat chicken. Quickly add broth and cook until mixture begins to thicken. Add sour cream and mix until combined. Return vegetables to the skillet and stir. Reduce heat to low and let cook slowly for a few more minutes while you prepare the biscuit topping.

4. Preheat oven to 400°F. Coat a 9 x 13-inch casserole dish with nonstick cooking spray.

5. To prepare topping, in a large bowl, combine flour, baking powder, baking soda, salt, thyme, 1 tablespoon fresh basil (if using), and pepper. Add shortening and blend with your fingertips or a pastry blender until mixture resembles coarse meal. Add cheese; toss to combine. Add beaten eggs and enough of the milk to form a very soft, wet dough.

6. Pour filling into prepared casserole dish. Spoon biscuit mixture in clumps evenly over top of casserole until filling is covered. If your casserole dish seems very full, you may want to put a baking sheet under it in the oven to catch any drips. Bake until biscuit dough is puffed and filling is bubbling, 25 to 35 minutes.

* * * * * * * * * *

This recipe takes only a few minutes to put together, and will make you feel industrious and well organized every time you smell it cooking. You can serve it with either rice or pasta; personally, I think it's best over egg noodles cooked al dente.

Slow-Cooker Chicken Cacciatore

serves 4 to 6   prep time: 15 minutes to prep, then 3 to 4 hours on High or 7 to 9 hours on Low

1 large onion, thinly sliced

3 to 4 pounds bone-in chicken thighs

Two 6-ounce cans tomato paste

Two 4-ounce cans sliced mushrooms

1 green bell pepper, seeded and finely chopped

2 to 4 cloves garlic, minced

2 teaspoons dried oregano

1 tablespoon sweet paprika

1 teaspoon dried basil

½ teaspoon celery powder

2 tablespoons brown sugar

1 teaspoon salt, or more to taste

½ cup dry white wine or chicken broth

3 tablespoons olive oil

1 teaspoon crushed red pepper (optional)

1. Layer onion over bottom of a 4- to 6-quart slow cooker. Add chicken pieces to cooker. Combine next 12 ingredients and red pepper, if using; pour over chicken in cooker. Cover and cook on Low 7 to 9 hours or on High 3 to 4 hours.

2. Serve over pasta or rice.

Chewy flour tortillas, chunky salsa-spiced chicken, and crispy browned cheese—no wonder this casserole is a huge favorite at our house. It's so easy to make that you might as well pop two of them out and put one in the freezer. If you're fortunate enough to have a few servings left over, it warms up beautifully in the microwave.

Spicy Chicken Enchiladas

makes two 9 x 13-inch casseroles; each serves 8   prep time: 1 hour

2 tablespoons vegetable oil

4 pounds boneless, skinless chicken breasts
  or thighs, cut into 1-inch cubes

4 cloves garlic, chopped

1 medium or large onion, minced

3 to 4 cups frozen corn or two 15-ounce
  cans whole-kernel corn, drained

One 28-ounce can tomato puree or
  three 8-ounce cans tomato sauce and
  1 cup water

1 cup spicy salsa, plus more for serving

½ cup store-bought or homemade
  taco seasoning mix (page 274)

Twenty 8-inch flour tortillas

4 cups shredded Cheddar cheese

Sour cream for serving

1. Preheat oven to 375°F.

2. Heat oil in a very large skillet over medium-high heat until hot. Add half of the cubed chicken, waiting to stir until chicken begins to brown on one side. Stir chicken once, and let other side brown. Remove cooked chicken from pan, and set aside in a bowl. Repeat with remaining half of chicken, and add to bowl.

3. In the same skillet, cook garlic, onion, and corn, stirring a few times until onion is tender, 5 to 7 minutes. Add cooked chicken to pan, and stir well.

4. Pour ½ cup tomato puree into each of two 9 x 13-inch casserole dishes and spread to coat the bottom of each dish.

5. Add remaining puree to chicken in pan. Add salsa and taco seasoning; bring to a simmer over medium heat. Let it simmer 5 minutes or so.

6. While chicken simmers, put a double layer of tortillas in the bottom of each casserole dish. Tear tortillas as needed to make them fully cover the bottom of each dish. Once chicken mixture has simmered for a few minutes, layer one quarter of the mixture into each casserole dish. Sprinkle 1 cup cheese over chicken in each dish, then add another layer of tortillas. Divide remaining chicken mixture evenly between casserole dishes, and top chicken evenly with remaining cheese.

7. Bake casserole 30 minutes or until bubbly and cheese on top is nicely browned. Let sit 10 minutes before serving. Serve with sour cream and additional salsa.

8. Cover remaining casserole tightly with aluminum foil, label, and freeze up to 6 months. To cook frozen casserole, thaw overnight in the refrigerator and bake until casserole is bubbly, 30 to 35 minutes. You may also cook it frozen, in which case it will need to bake 50 to 55 minutes.

tomato substitutions

I use a lot of tomato puree, since that is how I can my garden tomatoes. One 28-ounce can of store-bought tomato puree is roughly equivalent to a quart of home-canned tomatoes (4 cups). You can also substitute three 8-ounce cans of tomato sauce and 1 cup of water for a quart of canned tomato puree. Check prices and see what is most affordable at your store.

This recipe can be doubled and the extra casserole frozen (see step 8 in Spicy Chicken Enchiladas, page 103, for directions). Instead of the traditional red spicy sauce, this recipe has a white sauce with a cheese and broccoli filling. If you like your food mild, skip the Anaheim pepper.

Chicken-Broccoli Enchiladas

makes one 9 x 13-inch casserole; serves 6 to 8   prep time: 45 minutes

super-saver idea

Many casserole recipes use canned condensed cream soup as their binding agent. You may notice that the recipes in this chapter don't. Making your own white sauce with various flavorings is easy and cuts the cost in the average recipe by $1 to $2. That may not sound like a lot, but multiply that by a couple of casseroles a week for a year, and you'll see how small amounts of money saved here and there can add up to hundreds in savings each year.

2 cups broccoli cut into bite-size pieces
2 tablespoons vegetable oil
3 boneless, skinless chicken breasts or 6 thighs, cut into bite-size pieces
1 clove garlic, minced
1 Anaheim pepper (optional), seeded if you want less heat and minced
¼ cup all-purpose flour
2 cups milk
1 teaspoon ground cumin
1 teaspoon salt
½ teaspoon black pepper
Twelve 6-inch corn tortillas, divided
2 cups shredded Cheddar cheese
Sour cream, tortilla chips, and salsa for serving

1. Preheat oven to 375°F. Grease a 9 x 13-inch casserole dish.
2. Bring a medium-size pot of salted water to a boil. Add broccoli; cook until crisp-tender, 4 to 5 minutes. Drain.
3. Heat oil in a large skillet over medium-high heat until hot. Add chicken, garlic, and Anaheim pepper, if using; cook, stirring occasionally, until chicken is cooked through.

4. Reduce heat to medium-low. Sprinkle flour over chicken; toss to coat evenly. Add milk, cumin, salt, and black pepper; mix well. Cook over medium heat until mixture is well heated and starts to thicken, 7 to 10 minutes. Stir in drained broccoli, and cook for a few more minutes.

5. Layer 6 tortillas in bottom of prepared casserole dish, tearing them as needed to fully cover the bottom. Top with half of the chicken mixture, and sprinkle with half of the cheese. Repeat layers with the remaining tortillas, chicken, and cheese. Bake until bubbly and cheese starts browning a bit, 25 to 30 minutes. Serve with sour cream, tortilla chips, and salsa.

◆ ◆ ◆ ◆ ◆ ◆ ◆ ◆ ◆ ◆

This savory casserole is a great way to get another meal from a little bit of leftover chicken or turkey.

Curried Chicken and Rice Casserole

makes one 8-inch square casserole; serves 6   prep time: 50 minutes

2 tablespoons butter

2 ribs celery, chopped

1 medium-size onion, minced

2 carrots, chopped

1 apple (a tart apple such as Granny Smith is best, but any type will work), peeled, cored, and chopped

2 cups uncooked brown rice

2 cups diced cooked chicken

5 cups chicken broth

1 cup milk or plain yogurt

1 tablespoon curry powder

1 teaspoon black pepper

Salt to taste

Additional curry powder (optional)

1. Preheat oven to 350°F.

2. Melt butter in a large skillet over medium-high heat. Add celery, onion, carrots, and apple; cook, stirring for a few minutes. Add next 7 ingredients; stir until well combined.

3. Pour mixture into an 8-inch square casserole dish. Sprinkle with additional curry powder, if using. Bake 45 minutes or until bubbly and rice is tender.

Several times when my children have spent time with my sweet mother-in-law, she has served them this easy chicken dish. They all love it, even the mushroom-haters. In fact, one of my boys praises it so highly that, along with his other gifts, she now gives him a pan of this every year for his birthday. If you like, you can double the sauce to have extra to serve over rice or pasta alongside the chicken.

Grandma's Mushroom Chicken

makes one 9 x 13-inch casserole; serves 6   prep time: 1 hour 15 minutes

Almost without exception, the cheapest way to buy bone-in chicken pieces is to buy whole chickens on sale and cut them up yourself. Bought that way, you can get chicken for as cheap as 69¢/pound. The trick to removing the drumsticks, wings, and thighs is to cut at the joint between the bones, which you can feel out with your fingers before cutting. After you've cut up one or two chickens, it'll take you all of 5 minutes to reduce a whole chicken to 10 serving pieces. You can save the backbones in the freezer to make your own chicken broth.

1 medium-size fryer, cut into 10 serving pieces, or 2 to 3 pounds bone-in chicken thighs
¼ cup (½ stick) butter
1 medium-size onion, minced
¼ cup all-purpose flour
2 cups chicken broth
1 teaspoon curry powder
2 cups sliced fresh mushrooms or 2 small cans, drained
1 cup shredded sharp Cheddar cheese

1. Preheat oven to 350°F. Grease a 9 x 13-inch casserole dish.
2. Remove skin from chicken pieces. Place chicken in prepared dish so that all pieces fit in a single layer.
3. Melt butter in a medium-size skillet over medium heat. Add onion, and cook until it begins to soften, stirring occasionally. Sprinkle with flour; stir. Add broth and curry powder; simmer until mixture begins to thicken. Add mushrooms and cheese, stirring until cheese blends in. Pour sauce evenly over chicken. Bake until chicken is cooked through, about 1 hour.

This casserole makes a very hearty vegetarian dish. But if you have die-hard meat-lovers who balk at the thought of meatless meals, try simmering half a pound of turkey sausage or Italian sausage in with the sauce. An even quicker way to add meat to an otherwise vegetarian red sauce is to add a cup of chopped pepperoni.

Baked Ziti Casserole

makes one 9 x 13-inch casserole; serves 8 to 10   prep time: 1 hour

1 pound uncooked ziti pasta

1 tablespoon butter

1 large onion, chopped

1 clove garlic, chopped

4 cups tomato puree or one 28-ounce can

⅓ cup Spaghetti Seasoning Mix (page 274)

1 cup sour cream

1½ cups shredded mozzarella cheese

2 tablespoons grated Parmesan cheese

1. Preheat oven to 350°F. Coat a 9 x 13-inch casserole dish with nonstick cooking spray.

2. Bring a large pot of lightly salted water to a boil. Add pasta, and cook until al dente, about 8 minutes; drain.

3. Melt butter in a large skillet over medium heat. Add onion and garlic; cook, stirring frequently, until browned. Add tomato puree and spaghetti seasoning; simmer 15 minutes. Remove from heat, and stir in sour cream.

4. Spread pasta over bottom of prepared casserole dish. Pour sauce over pasta. Sprinkle with mozzarella and Parmesan. Bake until cheeses melt, 20 to 30 minutes.

This recipe can be prepared in one pan if you use a large cast-iron skillet. Cook your meat and vegetables in the skillet, add the remaining ingredients, then pop the whole thing into the oven to finish cooking.

Spanish Rice Bake

serves 4   prep time: 45 minutes

½ pound lean ground beef

½ cup finely chopped onion

1 clove garlic, chopped

½ cup chopped green bell pepper

One 14-ounce can tomato puree (2 cups)

3 cups water

1½ cups uncooked long-grain white rice

1 tablespoon chili powder

1 teaspoon salt

1 teaspoon brown sugar

½ teaspoon ground cumin

½ teaspoon Worcestershire sauce

½ teaspoon black pepper

½ cup shredded Cheddar cheese

2 tablespoons chopped fresh cilantro

1. Preheat oven to 375°F.

2. Preheat a large heavy skillet, preferably cast iron, over medium-high heat until hot. Add ground beef and cook until all the pink is gone, breaking it up into small pieces with the side of a spoon. Reduce heat to medium-low, and drain off the excess fat from meat. Stir in onion, garlic, and bell pepper; cook, stirring occasionally, until onion begins to soften, 3 to 4 minutes. Add remaining ingredients up to pepper; cook over medium-high heat until simmering.

3. If you're not using a cast-iron skillet, carefully pour contents of skillet into a 2-quart ovenproof casserole dish. Bake 20 to 25 minutes, stirring once, until rice is tender.

4. Remove from oven and sprinkle with cheese and cilantro before serving.

Variations: This dish can be a great vegetarian side dish simply by omitting the ground beef. If you would like to prepare it with brown rice, be sure to add 20 more minutes to the bake time.

Meatloaf uses up a lot of meat in one meal, so I only serve it once a month or so. But it's delicious and very quick to put together. I like to serve meatloaf with baked potatoes, since they take the same amount of oven time. If you get a lot of ground beef on a good sale, consider making a meatloaf or two for the freezer.

Hearty Meatloaf

serves 6   prep time: 1 hour 15 minutes

Meatloaf:
1 pound lean ground beef
1 pound ground turkey
1 medium-size onion, minced
1 clove garlic, chopped
2 medium-size or large eggs
½ cup quick-cooking oats
¼ cup ketchup
2 tablespoons Worcestershire sauce
2 teaspoons salt

1 tablespoon paprika
1 teaspoon dried parsley or
   1 tablespoon chopped fresh
1 teaspoon black pepper

Glaze:
¼ cup firmly packed brown sugar
¼ cup ketchup
1 teaspoon Dijon mustard
1 teaspoon dry mustard

1. Preheat oven to 400°F.
2. Combine meatloaf ingredients in a large bowl. Mix well, using a large spoon. Press mixture into an 8-inch square casserole dish.
3. Combine glaze ingredients in a medium-size bowl until well mixed, and drizzle evenly over top of meatloaf in pan. Bake for 1 hour.

Variation: Another excellent glaze for this meatloaf is the Teriyaki Sauce on page 271.

quick tip

Instead of making this in a casserole dish, bake the meatloaf in a 10-inch Bundt pan. Because of the hole in the middle, it'll cook faster and more evenly.

This wonderful one-dish meal is comfort food at its finest. If it seems too time consuming to make your own mashed potatoes, you can use instant instead. But home-cooked taste better and cost less. Don't forget to enlist your little ones to help with peeling potatoes. Even a three-year-old is big enough to operate a potato peeler!

Shepherd's Pie

makes one 8-inch square casserole; serves 4   prep time: 1 hour

One of the best things you can stash in your freezer is precooked ground beef in 1- or 1½-pound packages. I usually cook my hamburger as soon as I get home from shopping, then stick it into the freezer in zip-top plastic bags. Having already-cooked ground beef will easily shave 10 minutes off your mealtime prep, a big bonus on those nights when your hungry family is stalking the kitchen.

5 medium-size russet potatoes, peeled and quartered

1½ pounds ground beef

Salt to taste

1 teaspoon black pepper

2 medium-size carrots, thinly sliced

1 medium-size onion, chopped

2 tablespoons butter

2 tablespoons all-purpose flour

1 cup beef broth

2 teaspoons Worcestershire sauce

1 cup frozen or fresh peas

1 cup frozen or fresh corn kernels

2 tablespoons sour cream

1 large or medium-size egg

¼ cup milk

1 teaspoon salt

½ teaspoon black pepper

1 teaspoon sweet paprika

1. Place potatoes in a large saucepan; cover generously with salted water. Bring to a boil and continue to boil until potatoes are fork-tender, about 15 minutes. Drain off water.

2. While potatoes boil, preheat a large skillet over medium-high heat until hot. Add ground beef, and cook until all the pink is gone, breaking it up into small pieces with the side of a spoon. Season with salt and pepper. Add carrots and onion; cook for 5 more minutes, stirring frequently.

3. Melt butter in a small skillet over medium heat. Whisk in flour until smooth. Whisk in broth and Worcestershire; cook, stirring, until mixture thickens. Add gravy to the skillet with the meat and vegetables. Stir in peas and corn; cook until heated through, about 5 minutes.

4. In a small bowl, combine sour cream, egg, milk, salt, and pepper; whisk until well combined. Add sour cream mixture to potatoes; mash until well blended and potatoes are almost smooth.

5. Preheat broiler to high. Grease an 8-inch square casserole dish.

6. Pour meat mixture into prepared dish. Spoon potato mixture evenly over meat mixture. Sprinkle with paprika. Broil 6 to 8 inches away from heat until potatoes are evenly browned.

My mom made this recipe often when I was a child. She prepared hers with the crust on the bottom, but I prefer to make mine by simply dropping the crust across the top of the pie.

Chili Corn Pone Pie

serves 4 to 6   prep time: 1 hour 15 minutes

There's nothing wrong with buying a can of beans to prepare this recipe. But to make the recipe the most afford-able, consider cooking up a big batch of beans (see page 75) and freeze them in 1- or 2-cup portions. This recipe takes 2 cups of cooked beans.

Filling:

1 pound ground beef

1 small onion, chopped

One 15-ounce can kidney or small red beans, drained

½ cup frozen or canned (drained) corn kernels

1½ cups tomato sauce (about 12 ounces)

1 tablespoon chili powder

1 teaspoon ground cumin

1 teaspoon salt

Crust:

¾ cup cornmeal

¾ cup all-purpose flour

½ teaspoon salt

1½ teaspoons baking powder

½ teaspoon baking soda

1 large egg, beaten

¾ cup milk

2 tablespoons vegetable oil

Topping:

½ cup shredded Cheddar cheese

1. Preheat oven to 350°F.

2. Preheat a large heavy skillet over medium-high heat until hot. Add ground beef, and cook until no longer pink, breaking it into small pieces with the side of a spoon. Remove beef from skillet; add onion to skillet. Cook onion until it begins to soften, 3 to 5 minutes. Add remaining filling ingredients; stir well to combine. Simmer until heated through, 5 to 10 minutes.

3. In a medium-size bowl, combine cornmeal, flour, salt, baking powder, and baking soda. Add beaten egg, milk, and oil to flour mixture; mix well to form a soft dough.

4. Spread meat mixture over the bottom of a 9-inch pie pan. Drop tablespoonfuls of the corn bread mixture all over the top of the pie, distributing it as evenly as possible. Sprinkle cheese across the top. Bake 45 minutes, or until cheese is flecked with brown and filling starts to bubble out the sides.

super-saver idea

In many recipes that call for ground beef, I often substitute half of the beef with ground turkey without it affecting the flavor at all. This reduces the fat and also usually the cost. In stores near me, ground turkey costs $1.39/pound versus nearly $2/pound for regular hamburger. Using 100% turkey will taste a bit different from ground beef. So if your family is used to beef, I would suggest you add turkey gradually and see what proportion your family enjoys.

This recipe is basically a pot roast except the meat is cubed, which makes it quicker to cook and easier to serve to children. If you prefer, instead of roasting it in the oven, cook this meal in a 4- to 6-quart slow cooker on Low for 5 to 7 hours.

Roast Beef and Vegetable Bake

makes one 9 x 13-inch casserole; serves 6   prep time: 1 hour 15 minutes

Sometimes it can be tempting to buy beef already cut into cubes. But that isn't usually the most affordable way to go. For recipes like this one, I usually buy a large roast and cut as much from it as I need for the dish. That allows me to cut the meat exactly how I want it, and it also lets me choose a less-expensive cut of beef.

1 tablespoon olive or vegetable oil

1½ pounds beef chuck roast, cut into 1-inch cubes

1 green bell pepper, seeded and chopped

1 onion, chopped

1 carrot, sliced

2 ribs celery, chopped

2 cups very finely slivered green or Napa cabbage

2 teaspoons sweet paprika

1 teaspoon salt

1 teaspoon black pepper

¼ teaspoon crushed red pepper

Pinch of ground cinnamon

Pinch of ground cloves

2 cups beef broth

½ cup red wine (optional)

4 medium-size russet potatoes, peeled and thinly sliced

1 large sweet potato, peeled and thinly sliced

1. Preheat oven to 400°F. Coat a 9 x 13-inch casserole dish with nonstick cooking spray.

2. Heat oil in a large skillet over medium heat until hot. Add beef, and cook until evenly brown on all sides. Transfer to a plate, leaving any juice in the pan.

3. In same skillet, add bell pepper, onion, carrot, celery, and cabbage; cook, stirring occasionally, until vegetables soften, 5 to 7 minutes. Return beef to skillet. Add paprika, salt, black pepper, red pepper, cinnamon, and cloves. Stir in broth and wine, if using. Simmer for a few minutes. Remove skillet from heat.

4. Layer bottom of prepared dish with potato and sweet potato slices. Pour beef and vegetable mixture over potatoes in dish. Bake, covered with aluminum foil, until potatoes and beef cubes are tender, about 45 minutes.

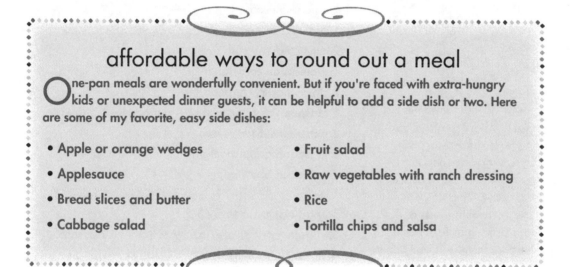

affordable ways to round out a meal

One-pan meals are wonderfully convenient. But if you're faced with extra-hungry kids or unexpected dinner guests, it can be helpful to add a side dish or two. Here are some of my favorite, easy side dishes:

- Apple or orange wedges
- Applesauce
- Bread slices and butter
- Cabbage salad

- Fruit salad
- Raw vegetables with ranch dressing
- Rice
- Tortilla chips and salsa

This crowd-pleasing recipe is extremely easy to prepare and bakes in 1 hour flat. I often serve it when company comes, since, as it cooks, I'm free to set the table and do other dinner preparations.

Pork Chops with Apricot Sauce

serves 6   prep time: 1 hour 30 minutes

I've found that sometimes I can buy pork roasts on sale for a better price than pork chops. When that happens, I buy several roasts and slice them about ¾ inch thick to make my own boneless pork chops as soon as I get home. I then stack them with wax paper separating the chops and freeze until I need them.

2 to 3 pounds boneless pork chops

1 onion, minced

1 cup apricot jam

2 cups chicken broth

1 tablespoon cornstarch

2 cloves garlic, chopped

1 teaspoon dry mustard

2 teaspoons dried thyme

1 teaspoon ground ginger

1 teaspoon black pepper

1. Preheat oven to 375°F.

2. Place pork chops in a 9 x 13-inch casserole dish. In a medium-size bowl, whisk together remaining ingredients; pour over top of pork chops. Cover pan with aluminum foil; bake until chops are cooked through, about 1 hour.

3. Remove from oven. To serve, ladle the sauce from pan over chops after plating.

My kids named this Easter casserole because it combines ham with cheesy potatoes, two of their favorite Easter foods. It's a great way to make the most of leftover ham. A good accompaniment for this dish is Southern-Style Fresh Cabbage Salad (page 218).

Easter Casserole

serves 6   prep time: 1 hour 15 minutes

¼ cup (½ stick) butter
1 small onion, very finely chopped
¼ cup all-purpose flour
2 cups milk
1 teaspoon salt
½ teaspoon black pepper
1 cup sour cream

6 cups peeled and diced russet potatoes
   (5 medium-size potatoes)
2 cups peeled and diced sweet potato
   (1 large sweet potato)
2 cups cubed fully cooked ham
1 cup shredded Cheddar cheese, divided
¼ cup chopped green onions

1. Preheat oven to 375°F. Coat a 9 x 13-inch casserole dish with nonstick cooking spray.

2. Melt butter in a large heavy skillet over medium heat. Add onion; cook until onion begins to soften, stirring occasionally. Whisk in flour until onion is evenly coated. Add milk, salt, and pepper, stirring occasionally until mixture simmers and begins to thicken. Add sour cream; stir to combine.

3. In a large bowl, combine potatoes, ham, ½ cup cheese, and green onions. Spread potato mixture into prepared dish. Pour white sauce over potato mixture. Sprinkle with remaining ½ cup cheese. Bake until bubbly and potatoes are fork tender, 50 to 60 minutes. Let stand 5 minutes before serving.

Variation: I prefer to use green onions, but if your family enjoys green bell peppers, they would make a nice substitution for the green onions.

This recipe is excellent with Spanish Rice Bake (page 108). You can also use these beans in Chili Corn Pone Pie (page 112) instead of buying canned beans.

Boston Baked Beans

serves 6   prep time: 15 minutes, plus soaking overnight; 4 hours cooking

2 cups dried navy beans, picked over
   and rinsed
½ pound sliced bacon, chopped
1 medium-size onion, finely diced
½ cup ketchup
¼ cup firmly packed brown sugar

2 tablespoons molasses (a darker molasses
   will give a stronger flavor)
1 tablespoon Worcestershire sauce
½ teaspoon salt
½ teaspoon black pepper
½ teaspoon dry mustard

1. Soak beans overnight in cold water to cover.

2. Transfer beans and soaking water to a large saucepan; bring to a simmer over low heat. Continue to simmer until beans begin to soften, about 1 hour. Drain and reserve liquid.

3. Preheat oven to 325°F.

4. In a large skillet over medium heat, cook bacon and onion until both begin to brown, about 10 minutes.

5. Combine drained beans, browned bacon and onion, and remaining ingredients in an ovenproof pan (I use the same cast-iron skillet that I used to cook the onion and bacon), and stir to combine. Pour in enough of the reserved bean cooking water to cover beans, probably about 3 cups. Cover pan with aluminum foil or a lid. Bake, stirring every hour or so, until beans are tender, 2 to 3 hours. Remove lid about halfway through cooking, and add more liquid if necessary to prevent beans from becoming dry.

One of the recipes my family enjoys is tuna on toast—basically a tuna cheese sauce served over hot buttered toast. This casserole version has the flavor of the original, but with more eye-appeal, as well as being easier to serve and eat.

Tuna makes an affordable meal and has the additional advantage of already being cooked, which can really speed along meal preparation. This recipe would also work with canned salmon.

Toasty Tuna Melt Casserole

makes one 9 x 13-inch casserole; serves 6   prep time: 40 minutes

10 to 12 ounces dry bread cubes
   (use crouton recipe on page 284 or
   buy stuffing mix—the kind with the
   seasonings in a separate packet)
Three 6-ounce cans any kind of tuna,
   packed in water and undrained
½ cup very finely minced onion

¼ cup (½ stick) butter, melted
½ teaspoon black pepper
½ teaspoon curry powder
3½ cups milk
2 medium-size or large eggs
1 cup grated or shredded cheese
   of your choice

1. Preheat oven to 400°F.

2. Grease a 9 x 13-inch casserole dish. Pour bread cubes into dish. If you're using bagged stuffing, discard seasoning packet or save for another use.

3. In a large bowl, whisk together tuna, onion, melted butter, pepper, curry powder, milk, and eggs. Pour tuna mixture over top of bread cubes in dish. Using clean hands or a flat spatula, press bread cubes into the liquid, so that most of the bread becomes dampened. Sprinkle with cheese.

4. Bake until casserole starts to puff up, cheese has melted, and bread cubes have some browned, crunchy-looking edges, 20 to 30 minutes.

This casserole can also be prepared with 1 pound of any white-fleshed fish cut into bite-size chunks in place of the shrimp. Tilapia and catfish are fairly affordable options.

Herbed Seafood Casserole

makes one 8-inch square casserole; serves 4   prep time: 40 minutes

1 large egg
½ cup milk
1 cup plain yogurt or sour cream
¼ cup chopped fresh parsley or
  1 tablespoon dried
1 teaspoon dried basil
1 teaspoon dried oregano
4 cloves garlic, minced

½ pound angel hair pasta, cooked
  according to package directions
  and drained
1 cup mild salsa
1 pound medium-size shrimp, peeled and
  deveined
1 cup shredded mozzarella cheese

1. Preheat oven to 350°F. Coat an 8-inch square casserole dish with nonstick cooking spray.
2. In a medium-size bowl, whisk together egg, milk, yogurt, parsley, basil, oregano, and garlic.
3. Spread cooked pasta over bottom of prepared dish. Cover evenly with salsa and shrimp. Pour egg mixture over top. Sprinkle with cheese.
4. Bake until cheese melts and begins to brown, about 30 minutes. Remove from oven and let stand 5 minutes before serving.

Quiche is an elegant and affordable meal. Serve it alongside a green or fruit salad. I don't often buy half-and-half; I've found that evaporated milk makes a great substitute and has a long shelf life, which means fewer trips to the store!

Spinach-Cheddar Quiche

serves 6   prep time: 1 hour

4 large eggs, lightly beaten
1¼ cups half-and-half or
   evaporated milk
½ cup mayonnaise
2 tablespoons all-purpose flour
1 teaspoon Dijon mustard
1 teaspoon salt
1 teaspoon black pepper

½ teaspoon ground nutmeg
1 medium-size onion, chopped
One 10-ounce package frozen chopped
   spinach, thawed and squeezed dry
1 cup shredded Cheddar cheese
One 9-inch deep-dish unbaked pie crust
   (or use my recipe on page 245 to make
   your own)

1. Preheat oven to 350°F.

2. Whisk together eggs, half-and-half, mayonnaise, flour, mustard, salt, pepper, and nutmeg. Add onion, spinach, and cheese; mix thoroughly.

3. Pour mixture into prepared pie crust; bake until the filling is set and the top is golden brown, about 45 minutes.

Eggs are one of the best bargains in the frugal fridge. There aren't too many other sources of protein that only cost a buck for an entire family, and can be cooked into a yummy meal in 20 minutes or less. On days when I'm not feeling imaginative, I'll sometimes serve scrambled eggs and toast for dinner. A frittata is a more elegant solution, but just as quick. This recipe and the one that follows are just ideas to get you started. Feel free to adapt these recipes to suit the tastes of your family.

Broccoli-Pasta Frittata

serves 6   prep time: 30 minutes

4 ounces uncooked spaghetti

2 cups broccoli cut into bite-size pieces

2 tablespoons butter

1 cup thinly sliced onion

1 clove garlic, minced

8 large eggs

½ cup milk

1 tablespoon chopped fresh basil
   or 1 teaspoon dried

½ teaspoon salt

1 cup shredded Monterey Jack cheese

1. Bring a medium-size pot of salted water to a boil. Break spaghetti in half and place in boiling water. Stir once. After 4 minutes, add broccoli to spaghetti in pot. Cook 4 more minutes. Drain and set aside.

2. Preheat oven to 425°F. Generously grease a 2-quart casserole dish (or, if you have a cast-iron skillet, bake this dish right in the skillet).

3. Melt the butter in a skillet over medium heat. Add onion and garlic; cook, stirring, until tender.

4. In a large bowl, beat eggs, milk, basil, and salt until combined. If using a cast-iron skillet, pour in egg mixture then broccoli and spaghetti. If using a casserole dish, pour egg mixture, sautéed onion and garlic, broccoli, and spaghetti into prepared dish. Sprinkle with cheese. Bake until eggs are set, 15 to 20 minutes. Let stand 5 minutes before serving.

Spinach Frittata

serves 4 to 6   prep time: 20 to 30 minutes

8 large eggs
½ teaspoon black pepper
1 to 2 tablespoons olive oil
1 small onion, chopped
1 to 2 cloves garlic, minced or pressed

4 cups fresh spinach, washed well,
    heavy stems removed, and torn
    into medium-size pieces
½ cup cottage cheese

1. Beat eggs and pepper in a large bowl.
2. Heat oil over medium heat in a large broiler-proof skillet. Add onion and garlic; cook until soft, 4 to 5 minutes, stirring occasionally.
3. While onion and garlic sauté, preheat broiler.
4. Add spinach to skillet; cook, stirring occasionally, until spinach is limp. Stir in cottage cheese. Pour egg mixture into skillet. As eggs begin to set, run a metal spatula around the edge of the skillet, lifting the mixture up so that uncooked egg mixture flows underneath. Continue cooking and lifting until most of egg mixture is set.
5. Place pan under broiler 4 to 6 inches from heat. Broil for a few minutes, watching closely, until top of frittata sets. Cut into wedges and serve immediately.

mom to mom

Frittatas are a great way to get your kids to eat vegetables without really knowing it—just chop that broccoli or spinach up fine and by the time they realize it's good for them, it'll just be a tasty memory.

chapter 7

stir-fries & skillet meals

S tir-fry and skillet dishes are a mainstay at our house for a variety of reasons. They're quick. They present vegetables in an appetizing way. There are flavor combinations to suit every taste. And they make the most of moderate amounts of meat, which is a huge key to saving money at the grocery store.

Think of the recipes in this chapter as a springboard for your own creative experimentation. Learn what flavors your family enjoys, then customize the recipes to your own liking.

We have two Korean sons who came to us via adoption. A Korean friend of mine showed me how to make this traditional dish for my son's first birthday. In Korea, meat is only one portion of the meal, along with several other side dishes, plus rice. One simple side is a bowl of lettuce leaves in which to wrap the beef. Another green option is the Southern-Style Fresh Cabbage Salad on page 218.

Korean Barbecued Beef (Kalbi)

serves 6   prep time: 30 minutes, plus marinating overnight

2 pounds round steak

⅓ cup soy sauce

1 cup firmly packed brown sugar

2 tablespoons sesame oil

¼ cup lemon-lime soda

3 cloves garlic, minced

2 green onions, chopped

1 teaspoon black pepper

1 teaspoon sesame seeds

1. Thinly slice beef against the grain. Mix remaining ingredients together in a glass baking dish. Add steak; cover and marinate overnight.

2. Preheat grill. Remove beef from marinade, and grill to desired degree, turning slices over at least once while cooking.

super-saver idea

When you're in the mood for steak, don't automatically reach for the strip steak or ribeye, which can be crazy expensive. Cuts like flank steak, skirt steak, hanger or flat-iron steak, round steak, and London broil are generally a lot less expensive. Give them a nice long turn in a boldly flavored marinade, and you'll be rewarded with tons of flavor. Just be careful not to overcook them and make sure to cut them against the grain. Stock up when you see them on sale.

I adapted this recipe from one in an old cookbook called *African Cooking* (Time-Life Foods of the World series, 1970). You can skip the hot chili pepper and only use sweet peppers if your family isn't big on spicy food. The turmeric adds authentic flavor to the dish, but if you don't have any on hand, you can leave it out. Serve this with rice or over egg noodles.

Spicy Ethiopian Beef in Green Pepper Sauce (Zilzil Alecha)

serves 4 to 6   prep time: 45 minutes

3 green bell peppers, 2 coarsely chopped
　　and 1 cut into strips
1 tablespoon seeded and finely chopped
　　jalapeño pepper
2 cloves garlic, finely chopped
1 tablespoon peeled and finely chopped
　　fresh ginger

1 teaspoon turmeric
1 teaspoon salt
1 teaspoon black pepper
2 large white or yellow onions, peeled
¼ cup olive or vegetable oil, divided
1½ pounds round steak, thinly sliced
　　against the grain

1. Combine 2 chopped green peppers, hot pepper, garlic, ginger, turmeric, salt, and black pepper in a food processor. Blend at high speed, scraping down sides as needed, until smooth. Scoop into a bowl; set aside.

2. Finely chop onions, either in food processor or by hand. Place onions in a heavy 10- to 12-inch skillet and cook over medium-low heat until soft and dry, 5 to 6 minutes, stirring often and watching constantly. When onions begin to brown, add 2 tablespoons oil and cook 2 to 3 more minutes, stirring occasionally. Transfer onions to a bowl.

3. Heat remaining 2 tablespoons oil in same skillet until hot. Add beef strips, a handful at a time, and cook, turning pieces regularly and removing them to a platter as they brown. Once all beef is cooked, return onions to skillet and increase heat to medium-high. Add green pepper strips, stirring constantly; cook 2 to 3 minutes until strips are soft. Stir in green pepper puree and bring to a boil.

4. Return beef and any accumulated juices to green pepper sauce in skillet. Reduce heat to low, cover partially, and simmer 6 to 8 minutes.

This recipe is great for warding off a craving for restaurant-style stir-fry. To make broccoli stems more tender, be sure to peel them before stir-frying.

Mongolian Beef and Broccoli

serves 4   prep: 40 minutes, plus marinating time

Marinade:

¼ cup lemon-lime soda

2 tablespoons water

1 tablespoon cornstarch

1 tablespoon soy sauce

Sauce:

¼ cup soy sauce

1 tablespoon sesame oil

1 tablespoon sugar

1 tablespoon oyster sauce

1 teaspoon Worcestershire sauce

1 teaspoon black pepper

Stir-fry:

1 pound beef flank steak, thinly sliced against the grain

1 bunch broccoli, cut into bite-size pieces

1 tablespoon cooking oil (sesame is best)

3 cloves garlic, minced

1 tablespoon peeled and grated fresh ginger or 1 teaspoon ground

2 leeks, thinly sliced

2 green onions, thinly sliced

1. Mix together marinade ingredients in a glass baking dish; add beef, and marinate at least 30 minutes (or overnight to maximize the tenderizing effect of the marinade).

2. Mix together sauce ingredients; set aside.

3. Bring 1 to 2 inches of water to a boil in a medium-size pot. Add broccoli and cook until crisp-tender, 3 to 5 minutes, stirring occasionally. Drain and set aside.

4. To stir-fry, heat oil in a wok over high heat until hot. With a slotted spoon, remove beef from marinade, reserving marinade to add in later. Add beef to wok and stir-fry for a couple of minutes until meat begins to brown. Add garlic, ginger, broccoli, and leeks; stir-fry 3 to 5 minutes. Add sauce to wok along with meat marinade, stirring well to combine and coat beef and vegetables. Cook until hot and bubbly. Stir in green onions right before serving. Serve hot over rice.

A Korean friend shared this recipe with me. She told me that this is often served in the summertime in Korea when gardens are overrun with zucchini. Serve it over rice. My kids enjoy this sprinkled with crunchy chow mein noodles.

Summer Hamburger Zucchini Stir-fry

serves 4   prep time: 30 minutes

1 medium-size zucchini

1 teaspoon salt

1 tablespoon oil (sesame oil is best but olive oil is fine, too)

½ cup diced onion

1 pound ground beef

2 cloves garlic, minced

1 tablespoon soy sauce

Salt and pepper to taste

Chow mein noodles (optional)

You can buy frozen vegetables already chopped, ready for stir-fry, but you'll save money by chopping fresh vegetables yourself, and the job goes much faster with a decent knife. You don't need a big fancy set. One good-quality paring knife will take you a long way. Go to a kitchen supply store and ask for recommendations. If you choose a straight knife with a nonserrated blade, you'll be able to sharpen it yourself with a sharpening stone, which will greatly enhance the usability of the knife.

1. Peel zucchini and slice it in half lengthwise. If there are visible seeds, run a spoon down the center of each half to scrape them out. Cut zucchini into bite-size cubes and toss in a bowl with salt. Let sit for 10 to 15 minutes. This will draw out some of the water.

2. Heat oil in a large heavy skillet over medium-high heat until hot. Add onion and cook until it begins to soften, 3 to 4 minutes. Add ground beef and garlic, breaking up beef with the side of a large spoon. When beef is brown, drain off any excess oil or fat.

3. Drain any water that has collected in the bowl with zucchini. Add zucchini and soy sauce to beef. Cook over medium heat for 5 minutes or so, stirring occasionally. Season with salt and pepper (but remember, zucchini will have taken up some salt as it released water in the bowl before cooking, so taste before salting). Sprinkle with chow mein noodles, if using.

This Mexican-flavored dish, with its soft, chewy tortillas and meat, reminds me of enchiladas, but is much quicker to make. Once you've prepared this a time or two, you'll be able to put it together in 15 minutes flat. I serve it with taco chips for a little crunch, along with salsa and sour cream to make it easy for everyone to customize the heat of the dish to their own liking.

Mexican Tortilla Skillet

serves 4 to 6   prep time: 25 minutes

1 pound ground beef

1 clove garlic, minced

1 packet store-bought or homemade
   taco seasoning mix (page 274)

6 burrito-size flour tortillas

2 cups pureed canned or fresh tomatoes

½ cup salsa

½ cup shredded Cheddar cheese

1 green bell pepper, seeded and
   chopped (optional)

1. Heat a large skillet over high heat until hot. Add ground beef, garlic, and taco seasoning. Cook until beef is browned, breaking it into small pieces with the side of a spoon and mixing everything together.

2. While beef is browning, slice tortillas into 1-inch squares. A pizza cutter or scissors works well for this.

3. Add tomatoes, salsa, and cut-up tortillas to skillet and cook for 5 minutes over medium heat. If it seems dry, you can add a little water. Once this is heated through, sprinkle cheese over top and cover for a few minutes. Once cheese is melted, it is ready to serve. Sprinkle with chopped green pepper (if using) for a little color, crunch, and a healthy dose of vitamin C.

Don't ask me why, but very often the price of the tortillas sold in the Hispanic foods section of a supermarket is lower than that of the tortillas sold in the refrigerator case of the very same supermarket. Check it out at your store.

This dish can be made with chard, spinach, or romaine lettuce—whatever is most afford-able. Kids love it because they can make their own rolls. I'm always amazed at the large amount of "greenery" that my kids consume when I serve this dish.

Thai Wraps

serves 6 or more   prep time: 25 minutes

1 pound romaine lettuce, Swiss chard, or fresh spinach, separated into individual leaves

2 carrots, peeled

1 onion, peeled

3 cloves garlic, peeled

1 rib celery

½ cup minced fresh vegetable of your choice (tomato, cucumber, or celery)

1 tablespoon olive oil (if using ground turkey)

2 pounds lean ground beef (or 1 pound ground turkey and 1 pound lean ground beef)

¼ cup fish sauce or soy sauce

1 or 2 cups leftover cooked rice (optional)

Salt and black pepper to taste

1. Wash lettuce, chard, or spinach, spinning or shaking off as much water as possible. Set aside in a colander or bowl lined with a paper towel. Cut any heavy stems from spinach.

2. Shred carrots. Chop onion and garlic, slice celery, and mince any other veg-etable that you desire. You can also add leftover scrambled eggs to this recipe.

3. Heat a large skillet over medium-high heat, then add beef and cook until browned, breaking it up into small pieces with the side of a large spoon. If you're using ground turkey, add oil before adding turkey. Or, you can add a little water to skillet as you cook to prevent sticking and cook at a little bit lower temperature.

4. Once meat is cooked through, remove it from pan using a slotted spoon. Add chopped, sliced, and minced veggies to skillet and cook in remaining oil over medium heat until soft, 5 to 7 minutes, stirring a few times.

5. Return meat to pan and mix with vegetables. Add fish sauce. Add rice, if using. Add salt and pepper. Cook over medium heat for a few more minutes, stirring, until ingredients are well mixed and heated through. Serve by wrapping leaves of lettuce, chard, or spinach around several tablespoons of the meat mixture.

This recipe goes together in a snap but you can save yourself even more time if you cut up extra onions, carrots, and broccoli when prepping another meal and keep them on hand in the fridge. This is also a great way to use up leftover ham.

Jazzy Ramen Stir-fry

serves 4 to 6   prep time: 25 minutes

2 tablespoons sesame or olive oil
1 onion, cut in half, then into long
   thin slivers
1 carrot, thinly sliced on the diagonal
2 cups slivered cabbage
1 clove garlic, minced
3 packages oriental-flavor or chicken-
   flavor ramen noodles
1 cup bite-size broccoli florets

1 cup water
2 tablespoons soy sauce
2 tablespoons sugar
2 tablespoons cornstarch
½ teaspoon peeled and grated fresh
   ginger (optional)
2 cups cubed ham
Sprinkle of sesame seeds (optional)

1. Bring a medium pot of salted water to a boil.

2. Meanwhile, add oil to a wok or large heavy skillet; let oil get very hot over high heat. Add onion and carrots; cook without stirring 1 to 2 minutes to allow vegetables to brown on 1 side first, then stir-fry 1 to 2 more minutes. Stir in cabbage and garlic; stir-fry 3 to 4 more minutes. Reduce heat to medium.

3. Add ramen noodles and broccoli to pot of boiling water; boil 2 to 3 minutes. (Be sure not to cook longer than 3 minutes or the noodles will get too soft!) Drain and rinse briefly.

4. Meanwhile, in a measuring cup or small bowl, combine water, soy sauce, sugar, cornstarch, ginger (if using), and 1 packet of ramen seasoning mix. Mix until well combined. Pour over cooked vegetables in the wok. Add ham and sesame seeds (if using). Simmer for a few minutes until liquid in wok is bubbly and thickens. Add cooked broccoli and ramen noodles to wok; stir to coat completely with sauce before serving.

I ate this dish in Ethiopia, served over rice. The Ethiopian version is much spicier than this one, but both have good flavor, and make a satisfying meal.

Ethiopian Sloppy Joes

serves 6   prep time: 40 to 50 minutes

1½ pounds ground beef

4 cloves garlic, minced

3 large onions, finely minced or pureed in food processor

¼ cup store-bought or homemade (page 275) Easy Berbere, or 1 tablespoon chili powder and ½ teaspoon ground cumin for a milder flavor

5 medium-size russet potatoes, peeled and cut into small cubes

2 ripe tomatoes, chopped very fine or pureed in food processor, or one 8-ounce can tomato sauce

2 cups water

6 hamburger buns

1. Heat a very large skillet or heavy-bottomed stockpot over high heat, then add beef and garlic; cook until beef is browned, breaking into small pieces with the side of a spoon. Spoon off as much fat as possible, then push beef and garlic to edges of pan, making an empty space in the center. (Some fat will still probably be in the meat and come to the center of pan; that's fine.)

2. Add onions to the center of pan and cook over medium heat, stirring a couple of times, until some of liquid evaporates, 2 to 4 minutes. Add berbere and stir to combine everything. Add potatoes, tomatoes, and water; stir well. Cook, covered, over medium heat until potatoes are tender, about 30 minutes, stirring frequently. Reduce heat and add a bit more water if mixture starts to stick to bottom of pan. There should be a moderate amount of sauce.

3. Serve warm ladled over hamburger buns.

This colorful dish is loaded with vitamins and flavor. You can substitute regular potatoes if you don't have sweet potatoes, but sweet potatoes really add to the overall taste.

Beef with Sweet Potatoes and Spinach

serves 4 to 6   prep time: 30 minutes

1 pound lean ground beef

4 cloves garlic, minced

2 medium-size sweet potatoes

1 teaspoon sesame seeds

1 pound fresh spinach

1 cup water

¼ cup soy sauce

2 tablespoons cornstarch

1. Heat a large skillet over medium-high heat. Add beef and garlic; cook until beef is browned, breaking into small pieces with the side of a large spoon.

2. While meat cooks, peel and cube sweet potatoes.

3. When beef is half cooked, drain off any accumulated fat. Add sweet potatoes and sesame seeds; continue to cook.

4. Meanwhile, rinse spinach well, remove any heavy stems, and coarsely chop.

5. When beef is well browned and sweet potato cubes are starting to soften, about 10 minutes, combine water, soy sauce, and cornstarch until cornstarch dissolves. Pour over contents in skillet. Simmer until sweet potato cubes are soft but not mushy, another 10 to 12 minutes.

6. Just before serving, add spinach and 2 to 3 more minutes until spinach is wilted, stirring once. Serve over hot rice.

I was overjoyed when a Panda Express restaurant was built near my home. There were two main reasons for my delight: Their names were chow mein and orange chicken. This version of orange chicken has helped me resist the siren's call of the panda more than a few times.

Orange Chicken, Panda-Style

super-saver idea

If you have access to ethnic grocery stores in your area, make sure to scope out what they carry and their prices. In many cases, you'll find their prices beat those at the supermarket hands down. In an Asian market, you'll want to stock up on products like soy sauce, hoisin sauce, oyster sauce, fish sauce, rice vinegar, and sesame oil; you'll very likely be able to buy at least twice the amount for what it costs you to buy a small bottle in the supermarket.

serves 6   prep time: 40 minutes

2 pounds boneless, skinless chicken breasts
   or thighs, cut into bite-size cubes
1 large egg
1½ teaspoons salt
½ teaspoon black pepper
1 tablespoon vegetable oil plus additional for frying
½ cup plus 1 tablespoon cornstarch, divided
¼ cup all-purpose flour

Orange Chicken Sauce:
¼ cup sugar
¼ cup white vinegar
2 tablespoons soy sauce
2 tablespoons water
Grated zest from 1 orange

Stir-fry:
1 tablespoon peeled and minced or
   grated fresh ginger
1 teaspoon minced garlic
Dash of red pepper flakes
¼ cup chopped green onions
¼ cup water
1 tablespoon sesame oil

1. Place cubed chicken in a large bowl. Add egg, salt, black pepper, and 1 tablespoon oil. Mix well. Stir together ½ cup cornstarch and flour in a large shallow bowl. Add chicken pieces, a handful or two at a time, and stir to coat evenly. Tap off any excess.

2. Pour about 1 inch oil in a wok or deep, heavy skillet and heat to 375°F. If you don't have a thermometer, heat oil until it starts to ripple. Add chicken pieces, a small handful at time, and fry until golden and crisp, 3 to 4 minutes. Remove chicken from oil with a slotted spoon and drain on paper towels. Set aside. When cooking the next batch, you will probably need to reduce heat to keep chicken from cooking too fast and possibly add a bit more oil.

3. Once all chicken is cooked, reserve a couple of tablespoons of oil from pan in a separate bowl. Clean wok. Combine sauce ingredients in a large measuring cup and whisk until sugar dissolves.

4. Heat wok for 15 seconds over high heat. Add reserved oil back into pan. Add ginger, garlic, red pepper, and green onions; stir-fry 2 to 3 minutes. Add sauce and bring to a boil. Add cooked chicken, stirring until well mixed. Combine remaining 1 tablespoon cornstarch with ¼ cup water until smooth; add to skillet wth orange sauce and chicken. Heat until sauce is thickened; stir in sesame oil. Serve with rice.

super-saver idea

Sesame oil adds a wonderful Asian flair to many stir-fry recipes, but it's expensive. To make my sesame oil last longer, I use half sesame oil and half ordinary vegetable oil. This imparts the richness of sesame oil to the recipe without breaking the bank. You can employ the same technique to stretch extra-virgin olive oil. I keep small bottles of all three of these oils in the cupboard right next to my stovetop, making it very simple to use two different oils in a recipe. You might also consider adding regular oil to a half-full bottle of sesame or olive oil to get the same 50-50 mix, saving you money and the hassle of grabbing two oils each time you're stir-frying. If you don't use your sesame oil that frequently, be sure to keep it in the fridge, otherwise it will go rancid pretty quickly.

Being able to prepare authentic-tasting foreign-cuisine food at home makes it easier to resist restaurant food. You can find Thai fish sauce in many large supermarkets and in Asian markets. A whiff of it might concern you—the smell is potent. But it adds a wonderful authenticity to Thai food. I like to add a splash to stir-fries and soups as well. It lasts a year or more in the fridge.

Thai Chicken Curry

serves 6   prep time: 30 minutes

2 cups canned or Homemade
   Coconut Milk (recipe follows)
2 pounds boneless, skinless chicken
   (thighs work well)
3 tablespoons store-bought or homemade
   Thai Red Curry Paste (recipe follows)

3 tablespoons fish sauce or soy sauce
2 tablespoons sugar
1 tablespoon butter or olive oil
1 jalapeño pepper (optional), seeded and
   cut into long, micro-thin slivers

1. Place a heavy skillet or wok over medium heat. Add coconut milk and bring to a simmer. Cut chicken into bite-size pieces while you wait. Once coconut milk begins to simmer, add curry paste, fish sauce, and sugar, and whisk until well mixed. When mixture begins to boil, add chicken and cook through, stirring every few minutes. This will take 10 or more minutes, depending on the size of your skillet. You can put a lid on your skillet to speed cooking.
2. Near the end of cooking, add butter and jalapeño, if using. Stir to incorporate melted butter. Serve with rice.

Homemade Coconut Milk

makes 2 cups   prep time: 15 minutes

2 cups boiling water
1 cup sweetened shredded coconut

1. Combine boiling water and coconut in a heatproof bowl. Let stand 10 minutes.
2. Whiz liquids together in a blender or food processor for 30 seconds. (Watch out for hot water splashes.)

3. Strain mixture through cheesecloth or a wire strainer, discarding coconut. Or, skip straining step and just add coconut along with coconut milk. This makes for less waste and adds flavor to the recipe.

• • • • • • • • • •

This delightful paste adds a complex kick that works with a variety of foods. Though it has some heat, it's not blazing hot. It can be kept in the fridge in an airtight container for a month. If you have some left over after making Thai Chicken Curry, try adding a tablespoon to a pot of soup, or in the wok with your favorite stir-fry vegetables.

Thai Red Curry Paste

makes about ½ cup   prep time: 15 minutes

1 lime, zest peeled away with vegetable
   peeler and discarded
1 teaspoon peeled and grated fresh ginger
4 cloves garlic, peeled
1 teaspoon ground coriander
1 teaspoon ground cumin

1 teaspoon salt
1 green bell pepper, seeded and cut
   into a few pieces
8 fresh red chili peppers, seeded
2 tablespoons olive oil

1. Whiz all ingredients together in a food processor until smooth.

Substitutions: The paste will be most flavorful made with fresh ingredients. But if you don't want to run to the store, here are some substitutions. Instead of fresh ginger, try ½ teaspoon ground ginger. If you don't have limes, try 2 tablespoons bottled lime or lemon juice. You can substitute 2 tablespoons chili powder for the fresh red chili peppers. But remember, the more substitutions you use, the less authentic your flavors will be. And, whatever you do, use fresh garlic. There's nothing quite like it.

A couple of years ago we attended an "Africa" night at a local university, where a variety of wonderful African foods were served for dinner. The thing I liked best was a delicious peanut chicken dish that sent me scampering to the internet for a recipe as soon as I got home. The recipe I found was from *The Congo Cookbook* (*www.congo cookbook.com*). I changed the recipe quite a bit in an attempt to replicate the food we'd had at the university that evening. My family loves this adaptation of the original, served over rice. The original recipe calls for homemade peanut butter. If you'd like to use fresh ground peanut butter, you can grind your own at the grocery store, or whirl some roasted peanuts in your food processor if you happen to have them. Usually I make this recipe with regular peanut butter and think it turns out fine, though it's a little sweeter than it would be with natural peanut butter.

West African Peanut Chicken

serves 4 to 6   prep time: 30 to 40 minutes

¼ cup peanut oil (or any cooking oil)

2 pounds boneless, skinless chicken breasts or thighs, cut into bite-size pieces

3 medium-size onions, minced or pureed in food processor

2 cloves garlic, minced

3 cups pureed tomatoes (or 2 cups tomato sauce and 1 cup water)

1 cup water

½ cup peanut butter

1 teaspoon cayenne pepper or red pepper flakes (optional)

½ teaspoon black pepper

1 tablespoon salt

1 green bell pepper, seeded and diced

2 ripe tomatoes, diced

1. Heat oil over high heat for 3 to 4 minutes in a deep pot or large heavy skillet. Add chicken pieces, half at a time, and fry on both sides until nicely browned. Once all chicken pieces are cooked, set aside in a covered bowl to keep warm.
2. Add onions and garlic in same pot; cook until onions are soft and begin to brown, stirring occasionally. Add pureed tomatoes and 1 cup water; reduce heat to medium, bring to a simmer, and let simmer for a few minutes.
3. Return chicken to pot. Stir in peanut butter. Mixture will look clumpy for a minute, but will mix in nicely once it heats up. Add cayenne pepper, black pepper, and salt. Simmer over low heat 10 to 15 minutes.
4. Stir in diced green pepper and tomatoes; simmer for 3 to 4 more minutes.

This recipe is somewhat more time-consuming than others I've included. You may find it a better use of your time to double up on the recipe for an extra meal down the line. Go ahead and fry all the chicken, using two skillets to speed the process. Freeze half of the chicken. When you're ready to cook, reheat (still frozen) on a baking sheet in the oven for 10 to 15 minutes, just as you would store-bought chicken strips.

Parmesan Chicken Strips

serves 4 to 6   prep time: 45 minutes

2 pounds boneless, skinless chicken
  breasts
1 cup all-purpose flour
2 teaspoons salt
½ teaspoon black pepper
1 teaspoon sweet paprika
2 large eggs

1 tablespoon water
1 sleeve saltine crackers, smashed in
  a zip-top plastic bag or whirled in
  the blender
¾ cup grated Parmesan cheese
½ cup olive oil for frying
2 tablespoons butter

1. Slice each chicken breast diagonally into 4 or 5 strips.
2. Get out 3 bowls. In bowl #1, combine flour, salt, pepper, and paprika. In bowl #2, whisk together eggs and water. In bowl #3, combine cracker crumbs and cheese.
3. Working with a handful of chicken strips at a time, dredge chicken in flour mixture, coating evenly and tapping off any excess. Dip chicken in egg, coating evenly, then transfer to the bowl of cracker crumbs. Press the crumbs firmly against the strips so they adhere. Set strips on a plate and repeat with remaining chicken.
4. In a large heavy skillet, heat oil and butter together over medium heat until butter melts and mixture is hot. Reduce heat to medium-low. Working in batches, cook chicken until no longer pink in the center, 3 to 4 minutes per side; don't let strips touch each other while cooking. Remove from pan and keep warm while you finish cooking remaining chicken.

This is another recipe that gives your kids assembly options. I'll often cook onions and peppers separately, and set them out in separate bowls, so the children can choose which vegetables they want on their fajitas.

Easy Chicken Fajitas

serves 4   prep time: 20 minutes

2 tablespoons vegetable or olive oil, divided

3 boneless, skinless chicken breast halves, cut across into strips

1 recipe Fajita Seasoning (recipe follows), divided

½ cup water

2 large onions, slivered

3 bell peppers (one each of green, yellow, and red is prettiest, but not essential), slivered

2 cloves garlic, minced

12 fajita-size flour tortillas, wrapped in a cloth and warmed in the microwave 1 to 2 minutes

Salsa and sour cream for serving (optional)

1. Heat 1 tablespoon oil in a large skillet over medium-high heat until hot. Add chicken strips and cook, stirring a couple of times, until almost cooked through, 5 to 6 minutes. Add half of fajita seasoning and water, mix well, and let chicken finish cooking. Transfer chicken to a bowl; cover to keep warm.

2. Heat remaining 1 tablespoon oil in skillet until hot. Add onions and peppers; cook, without stirring, until tender and some caramelized brown bits begin to show up in pan, 3 to 4 minutes. Stir; add garlic and remaining fajita seasoning. Let cook about 2 more minutes. Stir vegetables into seasoned chicken. (Or serve the vegetables separately.)

3. Serve the fajita mixture on warm tortillas with salsa and sour cream on the side, if using.

If you're feeling ambitious, make multiple batches of this and store in foil packets for up to 1 year to use whenever the urge for fajitas hits you.

Fajita Seasoning

makes 5 to 6 tablespoons   prep time: 5 minutes

1 tablespoon cornstarch

2 to 3 tablespoons chili powder
(vary according to how spicy you like it)

1 teaspoon salt

1 teaspoon powdered chicken bouillon

1 teaspoon sweet paprika

1 teaspoon garlic powder

½ teaspoon onion powder

½ teaspoon ground cumin

½ teaspoon black pepper

1. Combine all ingredients in a small bowl. Set aside and use just as you would the seasoning packet that comes in those taco kits at the store.

cutting up chicken

Chicken is easiest to cut into small pieces or strips if it's half frozen. There are several ways to get the perfect cutting consistency:

• If you're the organized type, you can put the package of frozen chicken in the fridge in the morning so that it will be partially thawed by dinner (set it on one of the top shelves in the fridge, where it's slightly warmer).

• If you're disorganized like me, stick the frozen chicken in the microwave for a couple of minutes before cutting it up. This works best if you cook on High for a minute, turn meat, then cook for another minute, repeating for a total of 3 to 4 minutes. Quit when you can pry the meat apart, but it's still partially frozen.

• If your chicken is fresh, put it in the freezer for a couple of hours before cutting it.

• If you're disorganized *and* your chicken is fresh, you'll just have to cut it that way!

Frying individual batches of chicken in this wonderful recipe takes a bit of time, but using frozen Asian vegetables is a good time-saver.

Sesame Chicken and Vegetable Stir-fry

serves 4   prep time: 40 to 60 minutes

things I love!

my rice cooker

Many of the recipes in this chapter are accompanied by rice. In my opinion a rice cooker belongs in the kitchen of every busy family. Before I got mine, I'd joke that dinner wasn't done until the rice pot boiled over. I was constantly forgetting about it. And forget cleaning it. Now that I have my rice cooker, I just add rice and water, turn it on, and walk away. The rice cooks perfectly, then switches to Warm until I need it. I've discovered several other things cook beautifully in the rice cooker as well, including oatmeal and polenta. Get a rice cooker; you won't regret it.

2 tablespoons sesame seeds

3 boneless, skinless chicken breast halves

Marinade:

2 tablespoons light soy sauce

2 tablespoons all-purpose flour

2 tablespoons cornstarch

2 tablespoons water

1 teaspoon sesame oil

¼ teaspoon baking powder

¼ teaspoon baking soda

Sauce:

1 cup chicken broth

½ cup water

2 tablespoons white vinegar

2 tablespoons soy sauce

2 tablespoons sesame oil

1 cup sugar

¼ cup cornstarch

1 teaspoon Asian chili paste, or more if desired

1 clove garlic, minced

Stir-fry:

One 16-ounce bag frozen mixed Asian stir-fry vegetables

2 tablespoons plus 1 cup vegetable oil

1. Toast sesame seeds in a dry skillet over medium heat for just a few minutes, constantly shaking skillet, until seeds turn medium brown. Set aside.

2. Cut chicken into 1-inch cubes. Mix marinade ingredients together in a large bowl; add chicken, stir to coat evenly, and let marinate for 10 minutes.

3. Combine sauce ingredients in a small pot. Bring to a boil, stirring continuously until sugar and cornstarch have dissolved. Turn heat down to low and keep warm.

4. Thaw frozen vegetables in microwave on High 2 to 3 minutes. Heat 2 table-spoons oil in a wok or large heavy skillet set over medium-high heat until hot. Increase heat to high, and stir-fry vegetables until crisp-tender, 3 to 5 minutes. Remove to a bowl and cover to keep warm.

5. To the same pan, add remaining 1 cup oil and heat to about 350°F. Add marinated chicken pieces a few at a time so that they do not touch each other. Fry, turning until all sides of chicken are golden brown. Remove from hot oil using a slotted spoon and drain on paper towels. Repeat with remaining chicken. Reduce heat after the first batch is done cooking to keep chicken from cooking too fast. You also may need to add a little more oil, as some oil is used in cooking.

6. Just before you're finished deep-frying, reheat sauce until simmering. Transfer drained chicken to a platter. Add vegetables, and pour hot sauce over chicken and vegetables. Stir to coat. Sprinkle with toasted sesame seeds. Serve with rice.

I have to warn you up front that this recipe, though delicious, can be rather alarming to make. When it comes time to blacken the spices, you'll literally have smoke wafting out of your skillet. Remember to turn on your stove's exhaust fan. And yes, chocolate does seem like an odd thing to add to a main dish, but it results in a deep, satisfying flavor.

Chicken Mole

serves 4 to 6   prep time: 30 minutes

2 pounds boneless, skinless chicken breasts or thighs, cut into bite-size pieces

Coarsely ground black pepper to taste

¼ cup olive oil, divided, or more as needed

3 tablespoons mild chili powder

1½ teaspoons ground cumin

1½ teaspoons ground cinnamon

1 teaspoon cayenne pepper (optional)

2 ounces unsweetened chocolate

Three 14.5-ounce cans stewed tomatoes (I puree mine before adding it; my kids like it better that way.)

1 clove garlic, minced

2 green bell peppers, seeded and chopped

1. Sprinkle chicken with black pepper. Heat 2 tablespoons oil over high heat in a deep 4-quart pot. Add chicken and cook until just cooked through, stirring a few times. Set chicken aside in a covered bowl to stay warm.

2. Reduce heat to medium-high and add remaining oil to pot. Add chili powder, cumin, cinnamon, and cayenne, if using. Mix well, adding a little more oil if needed until spice mix is wet with oil. Heat spices until they're blackened and smoking, 4 to 6 minutes.

3. Reduce heat to low and add chocolate. Stir into spice mixture with a heatproof rubber spatula.

4. When chocolate is fully melted, add tomatoes and garlic. Bring to a boil and simmer over medium heat for 10 minutes, stirring occasionally.

5. Stir cooked chicken and green peppers into sauce and simmer 5 more minutes. Serve over hot rice.

The pork mixture is also excellent served over rice or noodles.

Sautéed Pork Sandwiches with Mustard Sauce

serves 4   prep time: 30 minutes

2 pounds pork loin, trimmed of fat

2 tablespoons butter, divided

2 tablespoons olive oil, divided

1 large yellow onion, cut into long thin shreds

2 cups sliced mushrooms

1 cup beef broth

1 tablespoon Dijon mustard

1 tablespoon soy sauce

1 tablespoon cornstarch

4 hoagie rolls, toasted

1. Cut pork loin across the grain into ¼-inch-thick slices; cut slices into 2- to 3-inch-long strips.

2. Heat 1 tablespoon butter and 1 tablespoon oil in a large heavy skillet over medium-high heat until hot and butter melts. Add onion and cook, without stirring, 2 to 3 minutes. Don't stir until you start to see some browned bits. Add mushrooms and cook 2 to 3 more minutes, stirring once or twice. Remove onion and mushrooms to a separate bowl.

3. In the same skillet, heat remaining 1 tablespoon butter and 1 tablespoon oil over medium heat until hot and butter melts. Add half of pork and cook 3 to 5 minutes, or until it's the way you like it. Transfer to a bowl and cook remaining pork in the same way. Set aside pork and keep warm.

4. In the same skillet, quickly whisk together broth, mustard, soy sauce, and cornstarch while broth is still cold. Heat mixture over medium heat until bubbly and starting to thicken. Return pork, onion, and mushrooms to broth mixture in skillet. Mix well and heat through. Serve spooned over toasted hoagie rolls.

My interest in ethnic cooking began at our wedding when we were given a wok as a present. It came with a cookbook, from which I chose this very unauthentic recipe for sweet-and-sour hot dogs. The recipe became a family favorite. My only suggestion is that you use good-quality hot dogs. My favorite is Falls Brand Beef. In most cases I'm very happy to buy generic, but not when it comes to hot dogs.

Sweet-and-Sour Hot Dog Stir-fry

serves 6   prep time: 25 minutes

One 16-ounce package hot dogs
1 tablespoon olive or sesame oil
One 12- to 16-ounce can pineapple
    (chunks or tidbits)
One 6- to 8-ounce can mandarin oranges
3 tablespoons cornstarch

1 teaspoon peeled and grated fresh ginger
    or ½ teaspoon ground ginger
¼ cup white vinegar
¼ cup firmly packed brown sugar
1 green bell pepper, seeded and chopped

1. Cut hot dogs into ¼-inch-thick "coins." Heat 1 tablespoon oil in a wok or large heavy skillet over medium heat until hot. Add hot dogs and stir-fry until they are a little brown.

2. Meanwhile, open both cans of fruit. Pour liquid from cans into a medium-size bowl. Add cornstarch, ginger, vinegar, and brown sugar to juice; whisk together until cornstarch and sugar dissolve. Pour sauce over hot dogs in skillet. Simmer over medium heat until sauce begins to thicken.

3. Add pineapple and green pepper and stir gently. Cook until pineapple is warmed through, 2 to 3 minutes. Remove skillet from heat and distribute mandarin oranges across top of mixture. Serve over hot rice.

Variations: If a stir-fry with hot dogs doesn't appeal to you, try making this exactly the same way except with cubed chicken. You can also add some thinly sliced onions, if you like.

This Tex-Mex recipe is extremely simple. The lemon-lime soda works to tenderize the pork.

Melt-in-Your-Mouth Pork Carnitas

serves 4 to 6   prep time: 3 hours, mostly cook time

One 3-pound pork butt
1 can lemon-lime soda
2 cups water
2 teaspoons salt

Twelve 8-inch flour tortillas, warmed
Salsa and sour cream or guacamole
   for serving

1. Trim pork of excess fat; cut into 2- to 3-inch cubes. Combine pork cubes in a large heavy pot with soda, water, and salt. Bring to a simmer over high heat, then reduce heat to low and continue to simmer, uncovered, for 2 hours. Do not stir.
2. After 2 hours, turn heat up to medium and cook, covered, until all liquid has evaporated and pork fat has rendered, about 45 minutes. Stir a few times, just often enough to keep pork from sticking hard to bottom of pan. If it starts to stick, add a little more water as you complete cooking time. When done, pork will be brown on both sides, and just a little liquid fat will remain in pot. Pork will be so tender that it will fall apart at a touch.
3. Serve pork in warm tortillas with salsa and sour cream or guacamole.

Italian sausages are often an excellent value, especially when they're on sale. As with anything, make sure to compare prices between brand names and sausages that are packaged by the store's butcher.

Sausage with Cabbage and Corn Sauté

serves 4 to 6   prep time: 25 minutes

Try slicing the sausages into ¼-inch "coins" before cooking them. After they're cooked, stir them into the sautéed cabbage and onion with the corn. If you do this, you can get away with using only 1 pound of sausage instead of 1½ pounds, since cutting the meat into smaller pieces makes it go further.

8 sweet Italian sausages (about 1½ pounds)
1 tablespoon olive oil
Half of a small head green cabbage, cored and thinly sliced (about 6 cups)
1 large onion, cut in half and thinly sliced into half-moons
¼ cup balsamic vinegar
1 cup corn kernels (cut from 2 fresh ears or thawed frozen)
½ teaspoon kosher salt
½ teaspoon black pepper

1. Heat a large skillet over medium-high heat. Prick sausages with a fork and cook, turning occasionally, until browned all over and cooked through, 10 to 12 minutes. Transfer to a plate and cover with aluminum foil to keep warm.
2. Heat oil in a skillet over medium heat. Add cabbage and onion; cook, stirring occasionally, 5 minutes. Add vinegar and cook, stirring occasionally, until cabbage is just tender, 3 to 4 more minutes.
3. Stir in corn, salt, and pepper. Cook 2 to 3 more minutes. Serve with sausage.

I came up with this recipe one day when I had a bunch of root vegetables to use but didn't know what to make. I wasn't sure what everyone would think of it, but the kids loved it enough that they now request it.

Pork tenderloin isn't something I buy regularly, but when it's on a good sale it can be fairly affordable. An alternative cut is pork roast.

Barbecued Root Veggies and Pork

serves 4 to 6   prep time: 40 minutes

1½ pounds pork tenderloin

4 russet potatoes, peeled

1 sweet potato, peeled

2 carrots, peeled

1 small winter squash of your choice, peeled and seeded

2 tablespoons olive oil

¼ cup Worcestershire sauce

¼ teaspoon black pepper

Salt to taste

1. Cut pork and vegetables into 1½-inch cubes. Toss everything together in a large bowl with oil, Worcestershire, pepper, and salt. Spread in a single layer over a large oiled baking sheet.

2. Set sheet on gas grill, and cook with lid down over low heat. Grill, stirring every 3 to 5 minutes, until meat is cooked through and vegetables are tender and getting brown, 15 to 20 minutes.

Variations: This is a very flexible recipe. If you aren't in the mood to barbecue, you can roast everything in a 450°F oven, which will take 12 to 18 minutes. And if your family likes other root vegetables better than the ones listed, feel free to pick ones that your family enjoys. I've also tried this with peeled and cubed pumpkin, beets, and kohlrabi, as well as Brussels sprouts that have been cut in half and boiled for 3 minutes.

Usually when I make rice for another meal I make extra with this recipe in mind. Fried rice turns out best if you make it with cooled rice. Along with the ingredients listed here, you can add almost any finely chopped vegetable or cooked meat. I sometimes even toss in the last dab of scrambled eggs left over from breakfast.

Fried Rice

serves 4 to 6   prep time: 15 minutes

I have several children who don't especially like onions. I've found that in many dishes I can puree the onions in a food processor, then stir-fry them in a dry skillet for a few minutes to evaporate any extra liquid before adding them. It makes the onions less obvious and more palatable to little children who might otherwise pick them out, while still adding flavor to the dish.

4 cups cooled cooked rice
2 tablespoons sesame oil
2 tablespoons vegetable oil
1 carrot, shredded
¼ cup finely chopped onion or scallions
2 cloves garlic, chopped
½ cup finely chopped ham or pepperoni
¼ cup soy sauce

1. If rice has been refrigerated, microwave 3 minutes or so to cut down on total cook time.
2. Heat oils in a wok or large heavy skillet over medium heat until hot. Add carrot and onion; cook, stirring frequently, until onion is soft and starting to get browned bits. Add garlic and ham, stirring well. Immediately add rice, stirring well to coat with oil. At this point, you can also add any other vegetables, cooked egg, or leftover cooked meat that you'd like to use. Cook over medium-high heat, without stirring, about 3 to 4 minutes so that some of rice gets browned bits.
3. Drizzle soy sauce evenly over rice in pan; stir well. Cook for a few more minutes. Serve this with additional soy sauce on the side.

This Indian-style meal goes together very quickly and feels like a nice treat. Add more curry powder if you like it spicy.

Curried Rice with Shrimp

serves 4   prep time: 25 minutes

2 tablespoons olive oil

1 large onion, finely chopped

2 carrots, thinly sliced

2 russet potatoes, peeled and cut into 1-inch cubes

2½ cups chicken broth

2 cloves garlic, minced

2 teaspoons curry powder

1 cup uncooked long-grain white rice

½ teaspoon black pepper

1 pound medium-size shrimp, peeled and deveined

¼ cup chopped fresh basil or 2 teaspoons dried

1. Heat oil in a large skillet over medium heat until hot. Add onion, carrots, and potatoes; cook, stirring occasionally, until they start to soften, 6 to 8 minutes. If vegetables begin to stick, add a little slosh of chicken broth to skillet.

2. Add garlic and curry powder; cook, stirring until fragrant, about 2 minutes. Add rice, broth, and pepper. Bring to a boil. Reduce heat to medium-low, cover, and simmer for 15 minutes.

3. Add shrimp; stir, cover, and cook, stirring occasionally, until shrimp are opaque and rice is tender, another 5 to 7 minutes. Sprinkle with basil and serve.

things I love!

my cast-iron skillet

Over and over in the recipes in this book I use the phrase "in a heavy skillet." Nonstick skillets have their place, but if I could have only one pan in my entire kitchen, I would choose a big cast-iron skillet. They're amazingly versatile and cook evenly. Once you get one seasoned (smear it with Crisco, then bake for an hour at 350°F), they're almost as easy to clean as nonstick. And they last forever—literally—whereas every nonstick pan I have ever owned eventually left me wondering how much Teflon my kids were ingesting along with their fried rice.

Here's a nice vegetarian dish that is affordable and easy to make. You can make it with either yellow or green split peas.

Spicy Split Peas

serves 4   prep time: 1 hour

1 cup dry split green peas, rinsed, drained, and picked over

3 cups vegetable broth (water and bouillon is fine)

1 onion

2 cloves garlic, finely minced or mashed through a garlic press

3 tablespoons butter

½ teaspoon ground turmeric (optional)

1 jalapeño pepper, seeded and cut into very thin threads

Salt to taste

1. Bring peas to a boil in broth in a medium-size saucepan. Reduce heat to low and simmer 50 to 60 minutes.

2. While peas are cooking, peel onion; cut into several pieces, and process into a puree in a food processor. Transfer puree to a dry medium-size skillet and cook over medium heat, stirring frequently, 3 to 4 minutes, just until some of onion juice cooks away. Reduce heat to medium-low. Add garlic, butter, turmeric (if using), hot pepper, and salt. Cook, stirring occasionally, until onion softens.

3. Pour onion mixture into pot with split peas as they continue to cook. Check peas every now and then to make sure there is enough liquid to keep them from sticking. Add a little more water, if necessary, near the end of cooking time. When peas are soft but not mushy, remove pot from heat. You can serve as a stew, or spoon it over rice.

chapter 8

perfect
pasta

When I'm rushed for time and I have hungry kids milling around, my first thought is almost always pasta. It's quick. It's affordable. The kids love it. I love it. And it can be customized in dozens of delicious ways.

I like to keep at least two or three different types of pasta in my kitchen: Spaghetti and egg noodles are regulars. Bow-tie and spiral pasta are frequent residents of my cupboard as well. The recipes in this chapter only touch on the tremendous variety of pasta that is out there. Try something new this week!

I added cubed chicken to a Moroccan side dish to turn it into a main dish. I liked that it called for using mint tea bags as flavoring instead of mint leaves, since I usually keep tea around but I don't often have mint.

Chicken-Mint Couscous with Raisins and Apricots

serves 4   prep time: 30 minutes

2½ cups water

8 peppermint tea bags

½ cup chopped dried apricots

1 cup uncooked couscous

1 pound boneless, skinless chicken
   breasts or thighs

2 tablespoons olive oil

½ cup raisins

2 tablespoons butter

2 teaspoons salt

¼ teaspoon ground cinnamon

2 tablespoons chopped fresh mint
   (optional)

1. Bring water to a boil in a medium-size saucepan. Remove from heat. Add tea bags and apricots; steep 10 minutes.

2. Remove tea bags from water. Add couscous to pan (no need to remove the apricots). Stir to combine and let stand 20 minutes, covered (no extra heat is needed).

3. While couscous is soaking up tea, cut chicken into bite-size pieces. Heat olive oil in a large skillet over medium-high heat until hot. Add chicken and cook until no longer pink in the center, stirring a few times.

4. When couscous has been sitting for 20 minutes, add it to skillet along with raisins, butter, salt, cinnamon, and chopped mint, if using. Stir well to combine. Serve immediately.

You can use almost any shape of pasta in this recipe, but my family is very partial to bow-ties. I usually buy them at the dollar store, which is where I can get them the cheapest.

Mexican Bow-tie Pasta with Chicken

serves 6   prep time: 25 minutes

1 pound uncooked bow-tie pasta
1½ pounds boneless, skinless chicken thighs
    or breasts
2 tablespoons butter
2 cloves garlic, crushed
¼ cup all-purpose flour
½ cup milk
1 cup chicken broth
1 cup salsa
One 8-ounce package cream cheese, cut
    into ½-inch cubes

1. Cook pasta in boiling salted water according to package directions. Drain and set aside.
2. Meanwhile, cut chicken into bite-size pieces. Melt butter in a large skillet over medium heat. Add chicken; cook, stirring, 4 to 5 minutes. Add garlic and continue to cook until chicken is just cooked through. Stir in flour; slowly pour in milk and broth, stirring constantly. Add salsa and cream cheese and stir until sauce is hot and bubbling and cream cheese is melted and smooth.
3. Add drained pasta to skillet; stir until pasta is coated with sauce and everything is well combined. Serve immediately.

quick tip

Chicken Cacciatore (page 156), Mexican Bow-tie Pasta with Chicken, and Cheesy Chicken Penne (page 157) will come together even faster if you use already-cooked chicken. When I get home from a big shopping trip, I usually cook up a bunch of chicken pieces in the slow cooker. This gives me some nice broth to use in recipes—I can never have too much chicken broth! And it also gives me a whole lot of cooked chicken to freeze in zip-top bags, so that I can pull them out on evenings when I need dinner to happen very quickly. If you use already-cooked chicken, skip the browning step.

This tomato-rich pasta dish is one I made many times as a newlywed. It's easy to put together and can be served over rice if you don't have egg noodles.

Chicken Cacciatore

serves 6   prep time: 40 minutes

¼ cup (½ stick) butter

1 pound boneless, skinless chicken breasts
   or thighs, cut into bite-size pieces

1 onion, minced

1 green or red bell pepper, seeded and
   chopped

2 ribs celery, thinly sliced

1 clove garlic, minced

One 28-ounce can crushed tomatoes or
   3 cups pureed fresh or canned tomatoes

1 cup sliced mushrooms

⅓ cup loosely packed fresh parsley
   leaves, chopped, or 1 tablespoon dried

2 tablespoons sweet paprika

1 teaspoon dried basil

1 teaspoon dried oregano

¼ teaspoon salt

¼ teaspoon black pepper

12 to 16 ounces uncooked egg noodles

secret

1

to restaurant-style pasta

For the best-tasting pasta, always salt the water before adding pasta. It should have enough salt to taste like the ocean. This will make the most of the flavor of any sauces you add, and will mean that you'll need less salt in the sauce.

1. Melt butter over low heat in a large skillet; add chicken and cook, stirring a few times, until lightly browned. Remove chicken from skillet to a plate.

2. Add onion, bell pepper, celery, and garlic to skillet and cook, stirring, until vegetables are tender. Return chicken to skillet and add remaining ingredients, except egg noodles. Cover and simmer 20 minutes.

3. Meanwhile, cook egg noodles in boiling salted water according to package directions. Drain and add to skillet. Toss until noodles are coated with sauce and everything is well combined. Serve.

My family really enjoys this dish, especially when I prepare it with sliced olives.

Cheesy Chicken Penne

serves 4 to 6   prep time: 1 hour

12 ounces uncooked penne pasta

2 tablespoons butter

1 large onion, cut in half and thinly sliced into half-moons

1 pound boneless, skinless chicken breasts or thighs, cut into bite-size pieces, or about 2 cups chopped cooked chicken

2 cups pureed canned or fresh tomatoes

2 small or medium-size ripe tomatoes, diced

¼ cup chopped fresh cilantro

One 6-ounce can tomato paste

Salt and black pepper to taste

½ pound thinly sliced salami, summer sausage, or pepperoni

1 cup shredded Monterey Jack cheese

1 cup sliced pitted olives (optional)

Small handful of fresh parsley leaves, chopped

1. Preheat oven to 375°F. Grease a 9 x 13-inch casserole dish.

2. Cook pasta in boiling salted water according to package directions.

3. While pasta cooks, melt butter in a large skillet over medium heat; cook onion, stirring, until softened. Add chicken; cook until no longer pink, 5 to 7 minutes, stirring a few times. Add tomato puree, diced tomatoes, cilantro, and tomato paste; season with salt and pepper. Mix thoroughly.

4. Drain cooked pasta and add to skillet; stir until coated with sauce. Pour mixture into prepared dish. Top with salami, cheese, and, if using, olives.

5. Bake until cheese is melted and casserole is bubbly, about 20 minutes. Sprinkle with parsley and serve.

secret

2

to restaurant-style pasta

Butter and olive oil. You suspected it, didn't you? Restaurant pasta is loaded with it. Most home cooks will not want to use the amount of fat that restaurant food contains. After all, restaurant food is supposed to be an occasional treat, not a way of life. But using a little real butter or olive oil in sauces and when sautéing vegetables will greatly enhance the mouth-feel of the food.

This pasta dish reminds me a bit of pot roast and vegetables, the kind you cook in a slow cooker for hours, except this version takes less than an hour. To make this even more rib-sticking, try adding a couple of diced potatoes.

Hearty Beef and Noodles

serves 6   prep time: 45 minutes

¼ cup olive oil, divided

2 large onions, cut in half and thinly sliced into half-moons

1 cup all-purpose flour

1 tablespoon dried thyme

1 teaspoon salt

1 teaspoon black pepper

1½ pounds lean beef round, cut into 1-inch cubes

3 cups beef broth

3 tablespoons balsamic vinegar

3 medium-size or large carrots, thinly sliced

8 to 10 ounces frozen peas (about 1 cup)

10 to 12 ounces uncooked bow-tie pasta

¼ cup chopped fresh parsley

Salt to taste

1. Heat 2 tablespoons olive oil in a large skillet over medium-high heat. Add onions and cook, stirring occasionally, until some onions start to get a little browned, about 10 minutes. Remove onions to a bowl.

2. In a bag, combine flour, thyme, salt, and pepper. Add beef cubes and toss well to coat with flour. Remove cubes from bag, shaking off any excess flour.

3. In same skillet, heat remaining 2 tablespoons olive oil over medium heat until hot; add beef, and brown on all sides. When brown bits start to stick to bottom of skillet, add broth, vinegar, carrots, peas, and onions. Simmer, covered, 30 minutes, stirring occasionally.

4. Meanwhile, cook noodles in boiling salted water according to package directions. Drain, rinse briefly, and set aside, covering to keep warm.

5. When beef is cooked through and carrots are tender, stir in parsley and season with salt. Serve beef mixture over warm noodles.

My aunt gave me her recipe for beef stroganoff when John and I first got married. I used that recipe for years before adapting it to be made without cream of mushroom soup. Once you've made this recipe a few times, you'll probably be able to get the whole thing on the table in 30 minutes. It's a quick, easy, delicious meal.

If you want to save a few calories and even more money, you can leave out the cream cheese. It's yummy but not essential.

Quick Beef Stroganoff

serves 6   prep time: 30 minutes

1 pound uncooked egg noodles
1 pound lean ground beef
1 cup sliced mushrooms (optional)
2 tablespoons butter
2 cloves garlic, minced
2 tablespoons all-purpose flour

2 cups milk
¼ cup ketchup
4 ounces cream cheese
½ cup sour cream
Salt and black pepper to taste

1. Cook egg noodles in boiling salted water according to package directions. Drain and keep warm.
2. Meanwhile, in a large skillet over medium heat, brown ground beef until no pink shows; using a slotted spoon, remove beef to paper towels to drain. Drain most of the fat from pan, leaving just a tablespoon or so to cook mushrooms.
3. If you're using mushrooms, add them to skillet and cook 1 to 2 minutes. Remove them to the bowl with beef.
4. Again, in the same skillet, melt butter over medium-high heat. Add garlic and cook, stirring, 1 minute. Add flour. Whisk well to break up any clumps. Slowly add milk, whisking, and heat until bubbly and sauce starts to thicken. Add ketchup, cream cheese, and sour cream. Whisk until smooth and heated through.
5. Return beef and mushrooms to skillet. Add drained pasta and stir until well combined. Season with salt and pepper, then serve.

This is Korean picnic food. It's good when hot, but the flavors are more fully developed at room temperature. Add almost any thinly sliced cooked vegetable you like.

The cellophane noodles can be found in Asian markets or in the Asian food section of many grocery stores. Grayish white in color, they're made from sweet potatoes and look like vermicelli noodles. If you can't find them, use vermicelli cooked *al dente*.

Korean Glass Noodles (Chap Ch'ae)

serves 4   prep time: 25 minutes

When I was a kid, I remember hating two things: stringy cooked tomatoes and big chunks of cooked onion. Several of my kids are like that as well. I've found that some vegetables are better received if I simply puree them before serving. That way, the kids get all the nutrition but in a covert kind of way. They (hopefully) will eventually become accustomed to the flavors without having to deal with troublesome texture issues.

8 ounces uncooked Tangmyon cellophane noodles or vermicelli
½ pound lean ground beef
2 to 4 cloves garlic, or to taste
1 carrot, cut into matchsticks
1 bunch green onions (5 to 6), cut into 1-inch lengths
4 to 5 mushrooms, sliced, then cut into matchsticks
1 cup coarsely chopped fresh spinach
¼ cup soy sauce
2 tablespoons sesame or olive oil
1 tablespoon sugar
2 teaspoons sesame seeds

1. Cook noodles in plenty of boiling salted water until soft, 8 to 10 minutes. Drain, then rinse under cold running water.
2. Meanwhile, heat a medium-size skillet over medium heat until hot. Add beef and garlic; cook until beef is no longer pink, breaking into small pieces. Add carrot and green onions; cook 3 to 4 minutes, stirring a few times. Add mushrooms and spinach; cook 2 to 3 minutes, stirring a few times.
3. In a small bowl, combine soy sauce, sesame oil, sugar, and sesame seeds. Add to skillet and toss. Add noodles; toss well before serving.

This recipe goes together quickly once you have the vegetables chopped. And instead of ground beef, you can use a ½ pound of frozen meatballs.

Hamburger Lo Mein

serves 6   prep time: 40 minutes

1 recipe homemade Teriyaki Sauce
   (page 271)
12 to 16 ounces uncooked thin egg
   noodles or fettuccine
½ pound ground beef
2 cloves garlic, minced

1 onion, very thinly slivered
2 carrots, very thinly slivered
3 bell peppers (a variety of colors looks
   prettiest), seeded and thinly slivered
2 to 3 ripe tomatoes, cut into wedges

1. Prepare teriyaki sauce while noodles cook in boiling salted water according to package directions. Drain and keep warm.

2. Heat a large heavy skillet over medium-high heat until hot. Add beef and garlic; cook until beef is no longer pink, breaking into small pieces. Drain fat from pan and transfer beef to a bowl.

3. Heat skillet over high heat. (There's no need to wash it; you'll want a little oil glossing the pan.) Add onion and carrots to pan; let cook a couple of minutes (resist the urge to stir for at least 2 to 3 minutes!). Let onion and carrots soften and start to caramelize to a nice, deep brown color on 1 side, as this develops a sweetness in the vegetables. Once vegetables have gotten some of these sweet brown bits, stir and let cook 1 to 2 minutes longer. If vegetables start to stick, add a slosh of oil or water to pan. Add peppers, and stir-fry 2 to 3 minutes. Stir in teriyaki sauce.

4. Right before serving, add reserved beef and tomato wedges, and toss with hot pasta.

super-saver idea

Lean ground beef is the healthiest, of course, and has the least waste. But I usually just buy whatever grade is cheapest and drain off excess fat after cooking. If you would like to get rid of even more fat, try boiling the beef. This takes away some of the flavor of beef, but you can add flavor back in with seasonings.

When I was growing up, lasagna was one of my favorite foods. This recipe is similar to my mom's, with a few of my own tweaks. It does take a little time to make, but it freezes beautifully, so I always make at least two, which is a much better time investment. Just cover the second casserole with foil and freeze it for a busy day.

Three-Cheese Lasagna

serves 6   prep time: 1 hour 15 minutes

super-saver idea

In my grocery store, 1 pound of cottage cheese costs at least a dollar less than a pound of ricotta, and makes almost no flavor difference in lasagna. I almost always use it instead of ricotta.

Meat Sauce:

1 pound ground turkey

1 pound bulk hot Italian sausage

1 medium-size onion, minced

4 cloves garlic, minced

Two 14-ounce cans crushed tomatoes or 4 cups
    pureed fresh or canned tomatoes

Two 6-ounce cans tomato paste

1 tablespoon sugar

⅓ cup Spaghetti Seasoning Mix (page 274)

Pasta:

12 uncooked lasagna noodles

Cottage Cheese Filling:

One 16-ounce carton cottage cheese

1 large egg

¼ cup chopped fresh parsley or 1 tablespoon dried

Cheese Topping:

4 cups mozzarella cheese, shredded

1 cup grated Parmesan cheese

1. Heat a large, deep heavy skillet or large pot over high heat until hot. Add turkey and sausage; cook until well browned and no pink remains, using a spoon to break it into small pieces.

2. Push meat out to sides of the pan to make a well in the center. Place onion and garlic in the well and cook until softened, stirring occasionally. Add tomatoes, tomato paste, sugar, and spaghetti seasoning; stir together with onion, garlic, and meat. Reduce heat to medium and simmer 20 minutes.

3. Preheat oven to 375°F. Grease a 9 x 13-inch casserole dish.

4. Cook pasta in boiling salted water according to package directions. Drain and set aside.

5. Meanwhile, in a medium-size bowl, combine cottage cheese, egg, and parsley. In another bowl, combine mozzarella and Parmesan.

6. Arrange 6 noodles across the bottom of prepared casserole dish. Spread half of cottage cheese mixture over noodles, then half of meat sauce, then half of cheese topping. Repeat layers.

7. Bake until cheese is bubbly and starting to brown, about 30 minutes. Remove from oven and let cool 10 minutes before cutting to let cheese firm up a bit.

Variation: You could skip the turkey and use all sausage if you like, but turkey is lower in fat and lower in cost, and works very well in this recipe.

secret

3

to restaurant-style pasta

Don't overcook your pasta! Always aim to cook your pasta al dente, which means the very core of the pasta should still have a tiny bit of firmness to it. In most cases you can achieve this by following package directions and cooking pasta for the shortest recommended time, but I always pull out a noodle and taste it before I drain. Be sure to set your timer so you don't forget.

This lightning-fast recipe always gets rave reviews at my house, probably because everything tastes better with bacon.

Spaghetti Carbonara My Way

serves 6   prep time: 20 minutes

1 pound uncooked spaghetti
½ pound sliced bacon, cut into
   ½-inch pieces
1 medium-size onion, very finely minced
2 cloves garlic, minced

2 tablespoons finely chopped fresh basil
   or sage
2 large eggs, well beaten
½ cup grated Parmesan cheese
Salt and black pepper to taste

1. Cook spaghetti in boiling salted water according to package directions.

2. Meanwhile, cook bacon in a large heavy skillet over medium heat until nicely crispy. Remove bacon from skillet using a slotted spoon to a small bowl. (Do NOT dump out bacon drippings, because that's where this recipe gets its flavor.)

3. Cook onion, garlic, and basil in bacon drippings, stirring, over medium heat until onion is softened.

4. Drain the hot pasta and return to pot. Immediately pour onion, garlic, and bacon drippings over hot pasta and toss well. Pour beaten eggs over pasta and stir them quickly into pasta so that they coat pasta as evenly as possible. It is important that pasta still be steaming hot for this step, since it is the heat from the pasta that will cook the eggs. Add cheese and reserved bacon; stir again. Season with salt and pepper to taste. Serve immediately.

Sometimes I bread and fry fish, and sometimes I bake it. But last summer, when I had a lot of zucchini and tomatoes, as well as a bunch of small chunks of catfish, I came up with this recipe, which makes the most of all three.

Bacon, Catfish, and Zucchini Pasta

serves 6   prep time: 40 minutes

1 pound uncooked bow-tie pasta

1 teaspoon olive oil

½ pound sliced bacon, cut into ½-inch pieces

1 pound catfish fillets, cut into bite-size pieces

1 clove garlic, minced

2 cups cubed (1-inch) zucchini

2 cups cubed (1-inch) ripe tomatoes

1 teaspoon salt

½ teaspoon black pepper

Grated Parmesan cheese (optional)

1. Cook pasta in boiling salted water according to package directions. Drain and toss with olive oil. Set aside and keep warm.

2. Meanwhile, cook bacon over medium heat in a large heavy skillet until nicely browned. Remove bacon to drain on a paper towel.

3. Add catfish and garlic to bacon drippings in skillet and cook stirring a few times, until catfish is fully cooked, about 5 minutes. Remove catfish to a bowl and set aside.

4. Add zucchini and tomatoes to skillet and cook until they begin to soften, about 5 minutes. Return bacon to skillet and stir well. Add drained pasta, stirring to combine. Return fish to skillet and stir gently (try not to break the fish into smaller pieces). Add salt and pepper, and serve topped with a little cheese, if using.

Variation: I chose catfish for this recipe because I can usually buy catfish nuggets for less than $2/pound. However, you can substitute a different fish if you like. Firmer-textured fish will probably work best. A very soft fish like tilapia will quickly break up when stirred together with the pasta—not a problem taste-wise, just not as attractive as the chunky look you get with catfish.

Because it's made with shrimp, this recipe is a little more expensive than others. But if you make it only every now and then, it won't break the bank and it feels like a real treat. If you use already-cooked shrimp, it's possible to pull together the whole meal in the time it takes to boil the pasta.

Shrimp Fettuccine

serves 4 to 6   prep time: 20 minutes

secret

4

to restaurant-style pasta

Before draining your pasta, grab a measuring cup and scoop out a cup or so of the pasta water, setting it aside. Then, when making your pasta sauce, if it turns out a little thick or is too dry, you can add some pasta water to give the sauce a rich moistness.

12 ounces uncooked fettuccine
4 tablespoons (½ stick) butter, divided
1 onion, finely chopped
3 cloves garlic, minced
1 pound medium-size shrimp, peeled and deveined
1 tablespoon fresh lime juice
2 teaspoons chopped fresh basil
½ cup white wine or chicken broth
1 teaspoon salt
1 teaspoon chopped fresh parsley
Grated Parmesan cheese (optional)

1. Cook fettuccine in boiling salted water according to package directions. Drain, toss with 1 tablespoon butter, and keep warm.

2. Meanwhile, heat remaining 3 tablespoons butter in a large skillet over medium heat until butter melts. Add onion and garlic; cook, stirring, until onion softens, 3 to 4 minutes. Toss shrimp with lime juice. Add basil, wine, salt, and shrimp to skillet. Simmer over medium heat until warmed through, about 10 minutes. Sprinkle with parsley.

3. Serve over warm pasta with grated cheese on the side for anyone who wants it.

I came up with this recipe to make better use of a huge sage plant in our backyard. If you can't find sage for a good price, try using basil, an herb that is often cheaper at the grocery store.

Sage and Spinach Penne

serves 4   prep time: 20 minutes

1 pound uncooked penne pasta
1 cup packed fresh sage leaves
2 cups fresh spinach, heavy stems discarded
2 cloves garlic, peeled
2 teaspoons salt
Black pepper to taste
1 tablespoon fresh lemon juice
½ cup extra-virgin olive oil
½ cup grated Parmesan cheese

1. Cook pasta in boiling salted water according to package directions. Drain, reserving a little cooking water in case you need it later for the sauce, and keep warm.

2. Meanwhile, pulse together sage, spinach, garlic, salt, and pepper in a food processor. Pulse until finely chopped. Add lemon juice.

3. With the food processor running, drizzle olive oil into the feed tube a little at a time until mixture becomes smooth and creamy. Then add cheese and pulse to combine.

4. Toss sauce with warm pasta, adding a little reserved cooking water if needed to help sauce spread better.

quick tip

If you have a good-size sage or basil plant in your yard, you might consider harvesting some of the leaves in good weather and freezing them for winter use. Last summer I pureed big bunches of washed sage leaves in my food processor with a little olive oil. I froze the puree in ice cube trays. Then I popped the frozen herb chunks out of the tray and kept them in zip-top plastic bags in the freezer. This makes it a snap to add sage to a soup or a pasta recipe, even in the wintertime.

This lower-fat version of lasagna is also lower in cost. If a 9 x 13-inch casserole is too big for your family, try making it in two 8-inch square pans, freezing the extra one for another day. Reduce the cooking time by 5 minutes for the smaller casserole size.

Lighter Vegetable Lasagna

serves 6 to 8   prep time: 50 minutes

vegetarian meals

Vegetarian meals tend to be healthy and affordable. If you're trying to acclimate your family to a partially vegetarian diet, gradual is the way to go. This veggie lasagna is a nice place to start. If you think your family will balk at the idea of vegetables only, you could add a cup or two of cooked chicken to the middle layer. Or, if you like, you could make it half vegetarian and half with chicken.

1 pound uncooked lasagna noodles

2 cups shredded mozzarella cheese

1 cup grated Parmesan cheese

¼ cup extra-virgin olive oil

1 medium-size onion, cut in half and thinly sliced into half-moons

4 cloves garlic, minced

8 cups fresh spinach, washed well, heavy stems discarded, and torn into bite-size pieces

1 red bell pepper, seeded and diced

1 green bell pepper, seeded and diced

8 ounces mushrooms, sliced

½ cup chopped fresh cilantro

1 tablespoon dried basil

1 teaspoon salt

½ teaspoon black pepper

1. Preheat oven to 375°F. Grease a 9 x 13-inch casserole dish.

2. Cook lasagna noodles in boiling salted water according to package directions.

3. Meanwhile, mix cheeses together in a medium-size bowl and set aside.

4. In a large skillet, heat 2 tablespoons olive oil over medium heat until hot. Add onion and cook, stirring, until softened. Add garlic and cook 1 minute. Add remaining 2 tablespoons olive oil, spinach, bell peppers, mushrooms, cilantro, basil, salt, and black pepper and cook just until spinach wilts, 3 to 5 minutes. Remove from heat.

5. Arrange half of lasagna noodles in prepared casserole dish. Cover noodles with half of spinach mixture. Sprinkle half of cheese mixture over spinach. Repeat layers with remaining lasagna, spinach, and cheese. Bake until cheese is melted on top and edges are starting to get a little brown, 25 to 30 minutes. Let cool 10 minutes before cutting.

• • • • • • • • •

This is a wonderfully quick vegetarian meal.

Spinach and Ricotta Pasta

serves 4 to 6   prep time: 20 minutes

1 pound uncooked bow-tie pasta

2 tablespoons olive oil

4 green onions, chopped

One 10-ounce package frozen spinach,
    thawed and squeezed dry, or 4 cups
    chopped fresh spinach

1 teaspoon salt

½ teaspoon black pepper

¼ teaspoon ground nutmeg

1 cup ricotta cheese

1. Cook pasta in boiling salted water according to package directions. Drain and keep warm.

2. Meanwhile, do your chopping, then, in a large skillet, heat olive oil over medium heat. Add green onions and cook, stirring, until wilted, about 3 minutes. Add spinach, salt, pepper, and nutmeg and cook until heated through, about 3 minutes, stirring a few times.

3. Stir cheese into mixture and heat through. Add warm pasta and toss until coated with sauce and everything is well combined.

super-saver idea

You can use ricotta or cottage cheese in this dish. If you'd like the texture of ricotta but prefer the lower cost of cottage cheese, whiz cottage cheese in the food processor for a few seconds to make it smoother.

Here's a wonderful way to use up extra produce in the summertime when it's plentiful and you want to get in and out of the kitchen quickly. If you like, you can add some sautéed cubed zucchini along with the tomatoes. The vegetables in this recipe should be just lightly cooked.

Fresh Summer Spaghettini

serves 6   prep time: 20 minutes

mom to mom

When I'm serving a vegetarian main dish, I try to also include a salad and some kind of bread or dessert. Occasionally I'll also offer cheese and crackers, or I'll set out leftover breakfast pancakes along with a jar of peanut butter. This gives options to my hungry teenagers, and makes it less likely that they'll be hungry in an hour.

12 ounces uncooked spaghettini or angel hair pasta

3 tablespoons olive oil

4 green onions, coarsely chopped

2 cups cherry tomatoes, cut in half

3 cloves garlic, crushed

8 to 10 fresh basil leaves

Salt and black pepper to taste

4 ounces mozzarella cheese, cut into ½-inch cubes

½ cup grated Parmesan cheese

1. Cook pasta in boiling salted water according to package directions. Drain, reserving cooking water; keep warm.

2. Meanwhile, heat olive oil in a medium-size skillet over medium heat until hot. Add green onions, tomatoes, and garlic and cook until heated through, 2 to 4 minutes. Add basil and season with salt and pepper. Add ½ cup reserved cooking water to veggies. Add both cheeses, stir to combine, and remove from heat. Serve immediately over warm pasta.

A few years ago when John and I couldn't go out for Valentine's Day, our older daughters cooked us a lovely dinner, which they served at a little table in our bedroom, complete with candles, music, and menus. This is one of the dishes they served us that evening. You can also make this recipe with shrimp if you like.

Shell Mac with Broccoli and Mushrooms

serves 4   prep time: 25 minutes

12 ounces uncooked shell pasta
2 cups chopped broccoli
¼ cup (½ stick) butter
1 cup sliced mushrooms
¼ cup all-purpose flour
½ teaspoon garlic powder
1 teaspoon onion powder
2 cups milk
½ cup grated Parmesan cheese
1 teaspoon dried parsley

1. Cook pasta in boiling salted water according to package directions. Five minutes before the end of cooking time, add broccoli to pasta pot and continue to cook until pasta is al dente. Drain, reserving 1 cup cooking water; keep warm.

2. Melt butter in a medium-size skillet over medium heat. Stir in mushrooms and cook a couple of minutes. Add flour, garlic powder, and onion powder, then slowly stir in milk. Add cheese and parsley; stir to combine. Add pasta and broccoli and stir to coat with sauce. If sauce is too thick, add a little reserved cooking water to thin it a bit.

mom to mom

Since several of my kids are not enthusiastic mushroom-eaters, I often serve the mushrooms on the side for this dish. You could do the same thing with the broccoli. However, if you want your children to become better veggie-eaters, consider asking your child to skip only one vegetable. I often use this tactic when we get "combo" pizzas. Each kid is allowed to pick off one most-hated item, but then must eat the rest. The more variety kids are encouraged to eat, the wider their tastes will eventually become.

I like the way the slivers of vegetables mimic the shape of the pasta in this recipe. You want pretty "ribbons," not mush, so be sure not to overcook the vegetables.

Zucchini-Carrot Fettuccine

serves 6   prep time: 20 minutes

12 ounces uncooked fettucine

1 onion, peeled

1 carrot

1 medium-size zucchini

¼ cup (½ stick) butter

1 teaspoon garlic powder

¼ teaspoon red pepper flakes, or more to taste

¼ cup chopped fresh parsley or 1 tablespoon dried

1 cup chicken broth

1 cup milk

1 tablespoon cornstarch

Salt and black pepper to taste

½ cup crumbled feta cheese

1. Cook pasta in boiling salted water according to package directions. Drain, reserving a little cooking water, and keep warm.

2. Meanwhile, cut onion into thin slices, then cut slices into long, thin slivers. Peel carrot and zucchini, discarding peels. Continue to "peel" the flesh of carrot and zucchini into long, thin shreds using the vegetable peeler, and keeping vegetables in separate piles.

3. Melt butter in a large heavy skillet over medium-high heat. Add onion and cook, without stirring, until it starts to brown a bit, 2 to 3 minutes. Stir, then cook 2 to 3 more minutes. Add carrot shreds to skillet, stirring well to distribute carrot among the onion. Cook 3 to 4 minutes, stirring once or twice. Add zucchini shreds, garlic powder, red pepper flakes, and parsley, stirring well to combine. Add broth and let simmer over medium heat until carrot shreds are crisp-tender, about 5 minutes.

4. In a small measuring cup, combine milk and cornstarch. Pour mixture into skillet, mixing well, and let cook for a few more minutes, until liquid thickens around vegetables. If sauce gets too thick, add a little reserved pasta cooking water to thin it to your preferred consistency. Pour sauce and vegetables over warm pasta. Season with salt and pepper. Serve immediately, sprinkling a little cheese over each serving.

Did you know that you can make homemade macaroni and cheese almost as fast as boxed? And that it tastes twice as good? Give this cheesy-good recipe a try, and I'm guessing you'll become a convert.

I like making this with sharp Cheddar, but because it's more expensive, I usually use medium-sharp Cheddar, along with the cream cheese and Parmesan. Once you've made this recipe a few times, you'll probably find that you can have the sauce done by the time the pasta is cooked.

Better-than-Boxed Macaroni and Cheese

serves 6   prep time: 25 minutes

12 to 16 ounces uncooked elbow macaroni

¼ cup (½ stick) butter

¼ cup all-purpose flour

3 cups milk

1 teaspoon dry mustard, like Colman's

1 teaspoon garlic powder

2 teaspoons salt

½ teaspoon black pepper

2 cups shredded Cheddar cheese (Monterey Jack or Colby is fine, too)

4 ounces cream cheese (optional)

½ cup grated Parmesan cheese, plus more for serving

Sweet paprika (optional)

1. Cook macaroni in boiling salted water according to package directions. Drain and keep warm.

2. Meanwhile, in a large saucepan, melt butter over medium heat. Add flour and mix with a wire whisk until smooth. Add milk, whisking as you pour it in to smoothly incorporate it into flour mixture. Heat until mixture thickens, stirring frequently. (For those of you who don't cook a lot, what you have at this point is a basic white sauce. If you added celery, you could turn it into cream of celery soup, or mushrooms to make cream of mushroom soup.)

3. Add mustard, garlic powder, salt, and pepper to white sauce. Let simmer over medium heat, stirring frequently. Gradually add Cheddar, cream cheese, if using, and ½ cup Parmesan. The sauce is done when cheeses are well combined, smooth, and melted.

4. Add macaroni to sauce and stir until well mixed with sauce. Sprinkle with a little more Parmesan and a bit of paprika for color, if using.

chapter 9

soups, stews & chilis

I can't think of a more economical, more versatile food than soup. If you're not serving soup a couple of times a week, you're probably spending more than you need to at the grocery store. You could just buy it from the store, but you'll see the best money savings if you make your own.

Many of the recipes in this chapter go together in 30 minutes or less. Soup is extremely flexible and very forgiving of substitutions. Don't be afraid to experiment. In the summer, I make lots of tomato-based soups, since we have so many tomatoes. Every fall we get free onions—"seconds"—from a local farmer. That makes fall a perfect time for me to cook Ethiopian food, which depends heavily on onions. In late winter and spring, the chard is coming up in our greenhouse. That's when I make soups with lots of greens in them. As you read the recipes in this chapter, think about what food you have a lot of, or can buy affordably, and develop some of your own recipes that use those ingredients.

· • · •• • •· • ••

This recipe has great flavor and doesn't take much cooking time. It's also a great way to use up those corn tortillas getting stale in your refrigerator.

Chicken Tortilla Soup

serves 6   prep time: 25 minutes

6 cups chicken broth

One 14.5-ounce can diced or crushed
tomatoes, undrained

2 tablespoons vegetable oil

Six 6-inch corn tortillas, cut into strips
½ inch wide and 2 to 3 inches long

2 boneless, skinless chicken breast halves
or 3 thighs, cut into bite-size pieces

1 onion, chopped

2 cloves garlic, finely chopped

2 jalapeños, seeded and minced

½ teaspoon ground cumin

½ teaspoon kosher or sea salt

½ cup shredded Monterey Jack cheese

Chopped fresh cilantro

1 lime, cut into 6 wedges

1. Combine broth and tomatoes in a soup pot, and bring to a boil; reduce heat to medium-low, and let simmer 10 minutes.

2. Meanwhile, heat oil in a medium skillet over medium-high heat until hot. Add tortilla strips in a couple of batches and cook, stirring once or twice, until light brown and crisp, 5 to 7 minutes. Remove fried strips to paper towels to drain.

3. In same skillet, cook chicken 3 to 5 minutes without stirring, until nicely browned on first side. Add onion, garlic, jalapeños, cumin, and salt; cook 5 minutes or so, stirring occasionally, until chicken is cooked through and vegetables are softened.

4. Add contents of skillet to simmering broth; cook 10 minutes.

5. Ladle soup into bowls. Garnish each with tortilla strips, cheese, and cilantro; serve each bowl with a wedge of lime.

This is possibly the easiest soup ever. Every kid over the age of eight at my house can make this without help. If you don't happen to care for cabbage and carrots, or don't have time to chop them, try frozen corn or peas. If you happen to have a cup or two of already-cooked chicken in the freezer, or maybe a leftover piece or two of deli chicken, you can prepare this in 10 minutes.

Quickest Chicken Noodle Soup

serves 6   prep time: 15 to 20 minutes

My kids love the taste of ramen noodles, and I love how quickly they cook. Several of the recipes in this book show you how to jazz up a simple package of ramen to add more nutrition and better flavor. One hint: Never use all the seasoning packets if you're using multiple packages of ramen. You'll probably find that you can get good flavor using half as many of the packets as you have packages of ramen. But don't throw away the unused packets; I set them aside and use them to make broth for other recipes.

8 cups water

2 tablespoons oil (I like to use sesame oil)

2 boneless, skinless chicken breast halves, cut into bite-size pieces

1 carrot, shredded

1 cup thinly slivered cabbage (like for coleslaw)

2 cloves garlic, minced or crushed

1 teaspoon peeled and grated fresh ginger (optional)

4 packages chicken- or oriental-flavor ramen noodles

Soy sauce to taste

1. Bring water to a boil in a soup pot. While water comes to a boil, heat oil in a large skillet over medium-high heat until hot. Sauté chicken until browned on all sides and cooked through.
2. Once water comes to a boil, add sautéed chicken, carrot, cabbage, garlic, and ginger to pot. Cook 2 minutes, then add ramen noodles along with only 2 of the flavor packets that come with the noodles. Cook 3 minutes and not a second longer—ramen is best when not cooked to death. Taste, then add a slosh of soy sauce if you like. (I like.)

I love to add sweet potatoes to recipes that call for regular potatoes. Since sweet potatoes take a little more cooking time, I usually cut the sweet potatoes just a little smaller than the regular ones, so that they get done around the same time.

Chicken, Potato, and Black Bean Soup

serves 6   prep time: 45 minutes

4 cups chicken broth

4 cups water

4 medium-size russet potatoes, peeled and cut into bite-size pieces

1 medium-size sweet potato, peeled and cut into bite-size pieces

1 tablespoon olive oil

2 cups chicken (dark or white meat) cut into bite-size pieces

1 medium-size onion, finely chopped

2 ribs celery, thinly sliced

2 teaspoons dried oregano

2 teaspoons ground cumin

1 teaspoon cayenne pepper

½ teaspoon dried sage

2 tablespoons seeded and diced green chiles (or more, to taste)

One 15-ounce can black beans, undrained

¼ cup fresh lime juice

Salt and black pepper to taste

Sour cream and taco chips, for serving

1. Bring broth and water to a boil in a soup pot; add both potatoes and boil 10 minutes.

2. Meanwhile, heat olive oil in a medium skillet over medium-high heat until hot. Add chicken and cook until it turns opaque. Add onion and celery; cook, stirring a few times, until vegetables are soft. Add oregano, cumin, cayenne, sage, and green chiles. Stir to combine and cook for 1 to 2 minutes longer.

3. Add mixture from skillet into soup pot with boiling potatoes. Reduce heat to medium and add black beans including liquid in the can. Simmer soup until potatoes are tender. If soup gets too thick, you can add another 1 to 2 cups broth later in the cooking time.

4. When potatoes are done, stir in lime juice. Season with salt and pepper. Serve hot with sour cream and taco chips.

Throw this into the slow cooker in the morning before you head off to work, and all day you'll be able to enjoy the satisfaction of knowing exactly what you're going to have for dinner. Using chicken rather than beef in this recipe makes it lower fat than your standard chili. Feel free to amp up the cayenne pepper if you really like the heat.

Slow-Cooker White Chicken Chili

serves 6   prep time: 20 minutes, plus 5 hours on High, or 9 to 10 hours on Low

quick tip

One great way to make it easier to use dried beans is to cook up a bunch ahead of time, and freeze them in 2-cup packages. If you happen to have some already-cooked beans in the freezer (or if you prefer to use canned beans instead of dried beans), this whole recipe can be put together in an hour or less on the stovetop. However, do let the stew simmer for at least 30 minutes, as longer simmering does help develop the flavor of this recipe. And don't be afraid to make the full batch, even if your family won't eat it all in one meal. It freezes well for later.

1 tablespoon olive oil

3 cups chicken (dark or white meat) cut into bite-size pieces

1 onion, chopped

6 cloves garlic, minced or crushed

6 cups water

4 cups chicken broth

One 1-pound package dried Great Northern beans, rinsed and picked over

Two 4.5-ounce cans green chiles, drained and chopped

1 tablespoon chili powder

1 teaspoon ground cumin

1 teaspoon dried oregano

1 teaspoon cayenne pepper

1 cup shredded Monterey Jack cheese

Taco chips for serving

1. Heat oil in a large pot over medium heat. Add chicken, onion, and garlic and cook, stirring, until onion is tender and chicken is cooked through.
2. Transfer mixture to a 4- or 5-quart slow cooker. Add remaining ingredients, except cheese and taco chips. Cook 30 minutes on High.

3. Depending on your schedule, you can either leave the slow cooker set on High and your chili will be ready in 5 hours, or you can switch heat to Low and let it cook 9 to 10 hours.

4. To serve, ladle chili into individual bowls. Top each with cheese and serve with chips on the side.

◆◆◆◆◆◆◆◆◆

My mother-in-law gave me a variation of this soup soon after John and I got married. John is always happy when I make it, especially in colder weather. It's hearty and delicious. In soup, barley keeps soaking up water even after it's done cooking. Stick leftovers of this soup in the fridge and by morning all the liquid will be gone. If this happens to you, just add another cup or two of chicken broth to the soup before you heat it up.

Chicken-Barley Stew

serve 6   prep time: 1 hour 30 minutes

8 cups chicken broth
2 boneless, skinless chicken breast halves
    or 4 boneless, skinless thighs, cut into
    bite-size pieces
1 cup pearl barley
2 ribs celery, chopped
3 medium-size carrots, chopped

1 cup finely slivered green cabbage
1 large onion, chopped
2 cloves garlic, minced
1 teaspoon dried basil
1 teaspoon dried sage
½ teaspoon dried thyme
2 teaspoons minced fresh parsley

1. Bring broth to a boil in a soup pot.

2. When broth is boiling, add all ingredients to the pot, except parsley. Return broth to a boil, then partially cover pot and reduce heat to medium-low. Let stew simmer 1 hour, stirring occasionally.

3. Ladle stew into individual bowls. Garnish each with a sprinkling of parsley before serving.

This spicy stew is traditionally served in Ethiopia at Christmastime. Since this recipe is somewhat labor intensive, be sure to make it in a big batch so you can enjoy it again later in the week or freeze to serve again at a later date. The original recipe calls for chicken thighs, cut in half across the bone. I think this stew is much easier to eat and just as delicious if you don't have to wrestle with bones, so I make mine with boneless chicken thighs. Turmeric gives the stew its authentic flavor, but if you don't have it on hand, the stew will be just as good without it.

Ethiopian Chicken Stew (Doro Wat)

serves 8   prep time: 2 hours

quick tip

Ethiopian recipes tend to require large quantities of onions. This is good from a frugal standpoint—they're affordable and they add lots of flavor. But chopping all those onions can be time consuming. I've found that pureeing them in the food processor speeds prep tremendously. It also makes it less likely that picky children will notice them and spend their mealtime picking them out.

8 large eggs

2 cups water

¼ cup fresh lemon juice

3 pounds boneless, skinless chicken thighs

2 tablespoons olive oil

3 large onions, finely chopped

2 tablespoons butter

1 tablespoon peeled and grated fresh ginger or ½ teaspoon ground

1 tablespoon sweet paprika

1 teaspoon cayenne pepper, or more to taste (to make it authentic, use at least 1 tablespoon)

½ teaspoon black pepper

½ teaspoon ground turmeric

2 cups finely chopped ripe tomatoes or canned crushed tomatoes

2 cups water

1. Hard-boil eggs; drain, let cool, and peel.

2. Meanwhile, combine water and lemon juice in a large bowl. Add chicken to bowl and let soak 10 minutes. Remove chicken from water and let drain. Cut into bite-size pieces.

3. Heat oil in a large heavy skillet over medium-high heat until hot. Add chicken and cook until it is opaque. Remove chicken to a plate.

4. Add onions to skillet. Over medium heat, cook, stirring frequently, until liquid steams off and onions start to look dry and get some browned bits. Add butter. Continue to cook over medium heat, stirring and watching carefully, 7 to 10 minutes or until onions are well browned.

5. Add ginger, paprika, cayenne, black pepper, and turmeric. Add chicken, tomatoes, and water. Stir well. Cover and simmer over medium-low heat, stirring every 10 minutes for half an hour.

6. Five minutes before serving, set whole, peeled, hard-boiled eggs on top of the stew, one for each person. This stew can be served with pita bread, tortillas, or over hot rice.

The original version of this recipe is convenient. However, it uses so many cans and packets and mixes that it's not the most affordable recipe to make. You can make this cheaper by using your own seasoning mixes. If you have a garden, this is a great recipe to try when you've got a lot of corn and tomatoes. To further save time and money, I use my own cooked-ahead-of-time meat and beans. Even some of these modifications will make the meal more affordable. Do them all to save the most money.

Taco Soup

serves 6   prep time: 1 hour

1 large onion, chopped

1 pound lean ground beef or ground turkey

1 packet store-bought or ¼ cup homemade (page 278) Onion Soup Mix

1 packet store-bought or ¼ cup homemade (page 274) Taco Seasoning Mix

Two 14-ounce cans chili-style beans

One 16-ounce can corn kernels, undrained

One 28-ounce can diced or pureed tomatoes or 3 cups fresh pureed tomatoes

4 cups beef broth

Taco chips and sour cream for serving

1. Heat a soup pot over high heat until hot. Add onion to pot; cook for a couple of minutes, stirring occasionally, until onion starts to soften and get some browned bits. Add ground beef and brown, using a spoon to break into small pieces. Drain off any excess fat. Stir in onion soup mix and taco seasoning. Add beans, corn, tomatoes, and broth; bring to a boil. Reduce heat to medium-low and simmer 45 minutes.

2. Serve with taco chips and sour cream.

The other day, lunchtime kind of snuck up on me, and at 1 p.m. I was scrambling to think of something that could be pulled together quickly. The soup that I came up with surprised me with its goodness and brilliant color. Already-cooked brown rice could be substituted for the white rice in this recipe.

Confetti Pepperoni Soup

serves 6   prep time: 30 minutes

1 cup uncooked long-grain white rice

6 cups beef broth

2 cups pureed canned or fresh tomatoes
   or one 14-ounce can crushed tomatoes

2 tablespoons olive oil

1 onion, minced

4 cloves garlic, minced

2 carrots, thinly sliced

1 beet, peeled, quartered, and thinly sliced

½ cup chopped pepperoni

1 cup uncooked shell pasta or elbow
   macaroni

1 tablespoon chopped fresh parsley or
   1 teaspoon dried

1 teaspoon dried thyme

½ teaspoon black pepper

Salt to taste

1. Combine rice, broth, and tomatoes in a soup pot and bring to a boil.

2. While broth comes to a boil, heat oil in a small skillet over medium-high heat until hot. Add onion and cook, stirring, until softened. Add garlic and cook, stirring, for another minute or two. Add sautéed onion and garlic, carrots, beet, pepperoni, pasta, parsley, thyme, and pepper to soup. Cook until vegetables are tender and pasta is cooked al dente, 10 to 15 minutes. Season with salt. Serve with rolls or bread and butter.

This is my "not-100%-authentic" version of a more complicated Vietnamese recipe. But it's a fun twist on your typical beef stew. Kids will like being able to decide which seasonings to add when serving up their own soup. Many grocery stores carry both fish sauce and rice noodles in their ethnic section. These items will be cheaper at an Asian market, if you're fortunate enough to have one in your area. If you can't find these ingredients, you can substitute soy sauce for fish sauce, and ramen noodles for rice noodles, and still get good flavor.

Vietnamese Beef Soup

serves 4 to 6   prep time: 3 hours

Soup:

8 cups beef broth

Beef bones (leg bones are best, but ribs will work, too)

1 tablespoon olive oil

One 1-inch piece peeled fresh ginger

2 onions, cut in half and thinly sliced into half-moons

2 tablespoons fish sauce

1 tablespoon chopped fresh cilantro

1 tablespoon chopped fresh basil

1 teaspoon salt

½ teaspoon ground cinnamon

¼ teaspoon ground cloves

1 bay leaf

12 ounces rice noodles

2 pounds beef rump roast

Juice and zest from 1 lime

For serving:

Hoisin sauce

Sriracha sauce (hot chili sauce)

½ cup chopped fresh cilantro

2 green onions, chopped

1. Place broth and beef bones in a soup pot and bring to a boil. Let boil 10 minutes, skimming any foam from the top.

2. Reduce heat to low. Add oil, ginger, onions, fish sauce, cilantro, basil, salt, cinnamon, cloves, and bay leaf; simmer 2½ hours, uncovered, skimming any foam from the surface as needed.

3. Thirty-five minutes before serving time, set rice noodles in a big bowl of very hot water and let soak for half an hour. Meanwhile, slice beef into ¼-inch-thick strips and toss with lime juice. Let marinate until needed.

4. Five minutes before serving, remove beef bones and bay leaf from broth and discard. Bring broth to a rapid boil. Drain rice noodles; add to the boiling broth along with lime zest and beef strips, including any extra lime juice. Boil 3 minutes and no longer—the meat will continue to cook as it sits in the boiling hot broth. Serve immediately ladled into individual bowls, making sure each bowl contains a good proportion of noodles, beef, and broth. Set out hoisin sauce, Sriracha, cilantro, and green onions so that people can season their own bowl to taste.

Variation: If you like, you can use ramen noodles instead of rice noodles. No presoaking is needed for ramen. Just boil 3 minutes.

super-saver idea

Usually meat is the most expensive portion of a meal. When evaluating a new recipe for affordability, first calculate how much the meat is going to cost. I rarely spend more than a dollar per plate, or $12 for an entire meal. To achieve that goal, most of the recipes in my regular rotation call for only $5 to $7 worth of meat. And remember, that's for 11 to 12 people. No, we don't serve a lot of steak at our house. Even lasagna and meat-loaf are served only occasionally. But remember, a careful attitude about meat frees up money for other things in our life. And eating less meat is better for our health anyway.

If your family consists of only 3 to 5 people, consider trying to get by on $4 of meat or less for most meals. Sure, splurge a little every now and then. But balance that splurge with some vegetarian meals. Keeping an eye on the cost of the meat in a meal will really help lower your food costs.

If you know someone who thinks affordable food can't be filling and delicious, tell them to give this recipe a try. My husband and teenage boys love the satisfying chunks of potato and burger. The fluffy paprika-dusted dumplings lift this comforting stew beyond the ordinary. It can be pulled together in 45 minutes (or less if your kids help peel the veggies).

Hearty Beef Dumpling Stew

serves 6   prep time: 45 minutes

If your day is completely hectic, there's nothing wrong with pulling a loaf of bread out of the freezer and skipping the dumplings. But I think that once you see how easy they are to make and how much yummy goodness they add to this hearty stew, you'll probably opt for them.

Stew:

4 cups beef broth

2 cups pureed canned or fresh tomatoes, or 1 cup tomato sauce and 1 cup water

4 medium-size russet potatoes, peeled and cut into 1-inch cubes

1 pound ground beef or bulk pork sausage

1 tablespoon olive oil

2 carrots, thinly sliced

1 large onion, chopped

2 cloves garlic, minced

¼ cup all-purpose flour

1 tablespoon sweet paprika

½ cup milk

1 cup frozen (thawed) or canned (drained) corn kernels

Salt and black pepper to taste

Dumplings:

3 cups all-purpose flour

1 tablespoon baking powder

1 tablespoon sweet paprika, plus more for serving

1 teaspoon salt

1½ cups milk

2 tablespoons butter

1. In a soup pot, bring broth and tomatoes to a simmer. When broth is simmering, add potatoes and continue to simmer.

2. Heat a large skillet over high heat until hot. Add beef and brown. Be careful not to overstir it; you don't want meat to get too broken up for this stew.

3. Once meat is browned, remove it from pan. Drain off all but 1 tablespoon or so of the rendered fat. Add olive oil to the same skillet, then add carrots, onion, and garlic and cook over medium heat, stirring a few times, until onion is translucent. Sprinkle vegetables with flour and paprika. Stir until combined.

4. Add beef and cooked vegetables to simmering broth. Add milk and corn, and season with salt and pepper. Bring to a simmer and cook 10 minutes or so, while you mix batter for dumplings.

5. To make dumplings, combine flour, baking powder, paprika, and salt in a large bowl. Warm milk and butter together in microwave until butter is just melted. Pour milk mixture over flour mixture and stir together until just barely combined.

6. Spoon dumpling mixture on top of simmering soup by heaping tablespoonfuls. Dumplings will sink down into stew at first, but float back to the surface as they cook. Once dumplings have bobbed back up to the top, take a pinch of paprika and sprinkle it across the tops of the dumplings for a touch of extra color. Cover with a lid and let dumplings simmer over medium-low heat 7 to 8 minutes. When dumplings are fluffy and biscuit-like in the middle, they are done. Serve.

This chili, with its big chunks of hearty beef, is sure to be a guy-pleaser. It can also be made with ground beef if you don't happen to have a roast to chop up. When you cook the ground beef, don't break up the hamburger too much. Make it obvious there's plenty of meat.

Southwest Beef Chili

serves 6   prep time: 30 minutes prep time, plus 1 to 3 hours cooking time

You can avoid the extra cost of buying buttermilk by making your own. In this case, mix 1 tablespoon of plain white vinegar into a scant cup of milk. Let sit a couple of minutes. Presto: a perfect buttermilk substitute.

3 tablespoons vegetable oil

2 pounds beef stew meat, cut into bite-size chunks, or ground beef

2 onions, diced

8 cloves garlic, crushed

One 6-ounce can tomato paste

2 tablespoons store-bought or homemade (page 273) Chili Powder

1 tablespoon unsweetened cocoa powder

2 teaspoons salt

Two 14-ounce cans crushed tomatoes (about 4 cups)

One 15-ounce can red beans (2 cups), drained

1 cup water

1 tablespoon sugar

1 tablespoon Worcestershire sauce

Cornbread Topping (optional):

1½ cups cornmeal

½ cup all-purpose flour

1 tablespoon baking powder

1 teaspoon salt

1 cup buttermilk (or see Super-Saver Idea at left)

¼ cup vegetable oil

2 large eggs

½ cup shredded mozzarella or Cheddar cheese

Sour cream and salsa for serving

1. Heat oil in a large pot over medium-high heat until hot. Brown beef in hot oil in 2 batches. Remove beef from pot and add onions. Cook, stirring, until softened, then return beef to pot. Add garlic, tomato paste, chili powder, cocoa powder, and salt. Stir for a couple of minutes. Add crushed tomatoes, beans, water, sugar, and Worcestershire. Let chili simmer over low heat 1 to 3 hours. The longer you cook it, the better the flavor will be. If you'd like to let it cook unsupervised, stick it in a slow cooker on Low 3 to 5 hours.

2. If making cornmeal topping, preheat oven to 425°F.

3. In a medium-size bowl, combine cornmeal, flour, baking powder, and salt. In a large measuring cup, whisk together buttermilk, oil, and eggs. Add wet ingredients to dry ingredients, stirring until just combined. If chili is not already in an oven-proof pot, transfer it to something that is. Pour cornmeal mixture over chili and bake until golden brown, 20 to 25 minutes.

4. Turn oven to Broil. Sprinkle cornbread topping with cheese and set under broiler for a minute or two. Serve with sour cream and salsa.

super-saver idea

If you're in the mood to do something constructive to help your food budget, skim through The Homemade Pantry chapter (page 266–295) and choose five items that you usually buy. Choices include taco seasoning, pancake syrup, salad dressing, and spaghetti seasoning, among many others. Gather ingredients for the homemade version of these recipes, and spend an hour putting together several different mixes. You can store them in foil packets or in snack-size zip-top plastic bags. Label them clearly, and save the plastic bags after use to refill. Many people are amazed to discover that homemade versions of various convenience foods are actually cheaper and better tasting.

The color of this soup sometimes makes kids suspicious. But the flavor usually wins them over, especially if you make the ham pieces nice and big. This soup is great with cornbread or muffins.

Split Pea Soup with Ham

serves 8   prep time: 1 hour

One 1-pound package dried green split peas, rinsed and picked over

10 cups water

1 ham bone, with some meat still attached, or 2 cups roughly chopped ham

3 tablespoons butter

3 carrots, thinly sliced

2 ribs celery (with leaves), chopped

1 onion, finely chopped

3 cloves garlic, finely minced or crushed

¼ cup chopped fresh parsley or 1 tablespoon dried

½ teaspoon ground turmeric (optional)

Salt and black pepper to taste

1. Combine peas, water, and ham bone in a soup pot, and bring to a boil over high heat. Reduce heat to medium-low and simmer 45 minutes.

2. While peas are cooking, melt butter in a medium skillet over medium heat. Add carrots, celery, and onion; cook, stirring, until softened, about 3 minutes. Add garlic, parsley, and turmeric, if using, and cook, stirring, for a few minutes more. Remove from heat.

3. After peas and ham have been cooking 45 minutes, remove ham bone from pot, picking any meat off the bone and returning it to pot. Discard bone. Add sautéed vegetables to pot and cook until peas are soft, 10 to 15 minutes or so. You may need to add a little more water near the end of cooking time if soup gets too thick. Season with salt and pepper.

My kids are especially fond of the sausage in this soup, which I can usually find for $2/pound. If you're trying to make this recipe lower in fat, you can probably get by with only half a pound of sausage. Or give your kids all your sausages.

Italian Sausage Soup

serves 6   prep time: 40 to 45 minutes

4 slices bacon, chopped

1 pound precooked Italian sausage
    (the kind that looks like a big hot dog),
    sliced into ¼-inch-thick pieces

1 large onion, chopped

1 carrot, thinly sliced

2 cloves garlic, minced

1 teaspoon red pepper flakes (optional)

8 cups chicken broth

4 medium-size russet potatoes, peeled
    and chopped

One 15-ounce can (2 cups) chickpeas
    or white beans, drained

2 cups chopped cabbage or spinach

1. Cook bacon in a soup pot over medium heat until brown and crunchy. Transfer bacon to paper towels and leave bacon drippings in skillet.

2. To the same skillet, add sliced sausage, onion, carrot, garlic, and red pepper, if using; cook, stirring a few times, until onion starts to develop browned bits, 3 to 5 minutes. Press vegetables over to the side of skillet; tilt skillet, and spoon off any excess fat.

3. Add broth to skillet and bring to a boil. Add potatoes, beans, and cabbage. Turn heat down to a simmer, and cook until potatoes and cabbage are soft, 20 to 25 minutes.

4. Just before serving, sprinkle bacon over top of the soup. Serve with rolls or garlic bread.

This comforting recipe is the very first soup I make when the weather turns cold in the fall. If bacon drippings turn you off, feel free to use only a quarter pound of bacon. Just be sure to cook the onion and celery in the drippings. They add a wonderful flavor to this otherwise almost-vegetarian soup.

Cheesy Corn and Potato Chowder

serves 6   prep time: 40 minutes

½ pound sliced bacon, cut into ½-inch pieces

1 onion, minced

2 ribs celery, thinly sliced

2 cloves garlic, minced

2 teaspoons dried thyme

1 teaspoon dried parsley

1 teaspoon salt

½ teaspoon black pepper

⅓ cup all-purpose flour

4 cups chicken broth

4 medium-size russet potatoes, peeled and cut into bite-size cubes

1 cup frozen (thawed) or canned (drained) corn kernels

2 cups milk

1 cup shredded Cheddar cheese

1. Cook bacon in a soup pot until nicely browned. Using a fork or slotted spoon, remove bacon bits from skillet, leaving drippings in pan.

2. Add onion, celery, garlic, thyme, parsley, salt, and pepper; cook, stirring frequently, 2 to 3 minutes. Sprinkle flour into pan; stir well. Gradually whisk in broth. Stir in potatoes; cook 15 minutes over medium to low heat, stirring occasionally.

3. Add corn and milk; simmer 10 more minutes. Add cheese and stir until cheese is melted. Ladle into individual bowls and serve topped with crumbled bacon.

Variation: To make my mom's Christmas Clam Chowder (opposite page), omit corn, substitute half of milk with heavy cream, and add 1 cup canned chopped clams. Yum! Bread bowls are optional but highly recommended!

Christmas Clam Chowder

I am the oldest of eight brothers and sisters. On Christmas Eve we all gather at my mom's to celebrate the holiday. There are about forty of us now, with spouses and children. The long red-clothed dining room table is made even longer with folding tables from church. The star of the dinner is my mom's wonderful clam chowder, a recipe very similar to Cheesy Corn and Potato Chowder (page 192), except it features clams instead of corn. The chowder is always served in bread bowls, smaller ones for the children and larger ones for the adults. The hot, rich soup, eaten in the company of those near and dear to me, and sopped up with torn chunks of pillowy bread, tastes like pure Christmas.

This is great cold-weather comfort food. Serve it with a loaf of garlic bread and a salad.

Slow-Cooker White Bean, Sage, and Sausage Soup

serves 6   prep time: 10 minutes, plus soaking overnight; 7 to 9 hours cooking

One 1-pound package dried white beans, soaked in water to cover overnight

2 cups chopped fresh tomatoes or one 14-ounce can crushed tomatoes

2 cloves garlic, minced

¼ cup chopped fresh sage or 1 tablespoon dried

1 pound Italian sausages, cut into ¼-inch-thick "coins"

1 tablespoon salt

2 tablespoons extra-virgin olive oil

8 cups water

1. Drain beans. Place all ingredients in a 4- or 5-quart slow cooker and stir to combine. Cover, set cooker on Low; cook until beans are soft, 7 to 9 hours.

I first saw this recipe in the "Tightwad Gazette," a newsletter I got every month back in the '90s when John and I were newly married. I adapted it to suit our family and have been making it for a lot of years now. My kids especially love this if I serve it with croutons to sprinkle on top.

Tuna Cheddar Chowder

serves 6   prep time: 30 minutes

Now available in book form, "The Tightwad Gazette" is an excellent resource for families trying to stretch their money to the max. Along with some basic frugal recipes, the book contains frugal tips for almost every aspect of family life.

¼ cup (½ stick) butter
2 carrots, chopped fairly small
1 large onion, minced
1 clove garlic, minced
3 tablespoons all-purpose flour
1 teaspoon celery seeds
6 cups chicken broth
8 ounces egg noodles (a couple of handfuls)
Two 6-ounce cans tuna, undrained
1 cup frozen green peas
2 cups milk
1 cup shredded Cheddar cheese
Salt and black pepper to taste

1. Melt butter in a soup pot over medium heat. Add carrots, onion, and garlic; cook, stirring, until carrots begin to soften, 4 to 6 minutes. Add flour and celery seeds and whisk well. Add broth, whisking well until clumps of flour dissolve, then bring to a boil over high heat.
2. When soup is boiling, add egg noodles, tuna, and peas. When soup comes to a boil again, reduce heat to medium and cook 6 to 7 minutes, stirring often. Add milk and bring to a gentle simmer. Sprinkle with cheese, stirring well. Season with salt and pepper and serve immediately.

This is a simple and comforting winter chowder. It calls for canned salmon, which is an extremely affordable protein. I'm one of those odd people who loves the little crunchy bones that come in canned salmon. If your kids look at the bones cross-eyed, you may want to remove them before adding the salmon to the soup. Or do like I do—eat them yourself! My problem is that some of my kids like them too, so I usually have to share.

Salmon Chowder

serves 4   prep time: 30 minutes

2 tablespoons butter
1 small onion, minced
½ cup chopped celery
¼ cup chopped green bell pepper
1 clove garlic, minced
2 tablespoons all-purpose flour
1 cup peeled and finely diced potato
1 cup thinly sliced carrots
3 cups chicken broth

½ teaspoon dried dillweed
½ teaspoon salt
¼ teaspoon black pepper
2 cups milk
1 cup frozen or canned (drained) corn kernels
One 14-ounce can salmon (buy whichever type is cheapest)
1 cup shredded Cheddar cheese (optional)

1. Melt butter in a soup pot over medium heat and cook onion, celery, and bell pepper, stirring. Add garlic after vegetables start to get soft, 3 to 5 minutes, and cook 1 minute. Add flour and stir until it is evenly dispersed. Add potato, carrots, broth, dill, salt, and black pepper. Stir and bring to a boil over high heat. Reduce heat to medium-low and simmer until potatoes are fork tender, about 20 minutes. **2.** Add milk, corn, and salmon. Heat 5 more minutes. Ladle into bowls and serve with a little grated cheese on top, if using.

I love the exotic flavors in this easy-to-prepare soup. You can find fish sauce in many grocery stores or local Asian markets. A bottle will last a long time in the refrigerator.

Thai Shrimp Noodle Soup

serves 6   prep time: 25 minutes

8 cups water

3 green onions, minced

2 carrots, thinly sliced

2 tablespoons fish sauce or soy sauce

1 tablespoon Thai hot chili sauce

2 cloves garlic, finely minced

2 tablespoons peeled and very thinly slivered fresh ginger

1 teaspoon chopped fresh basil

4 packages oriental- or chicken-flavor ramen noodles, slightly broken

8 ounces medium-size shrimp, peeled and deveined

2 cups coarsely chopped fresh spinach

1 cup sliced mushrooms

Juice and grated zest from 1 lime

1. Bring water to a boil in a soup pot. Add green onions, carrots, fish sauce, chili sauce, garlic, ginger, and basil to pot. Add 2 ramen noodle seasoning packets (if you add all 4 packets, the soup will probably be too salty). Boil 5 minutes.

2. Add shrimp, spinach, mushrooms, and ramen noodles. Cook 5 more minutes. Add lime juice and zest. Stir well and serve.

how to zest if you don't have a zester

Zest is the very thin colored layer on the outside of a lemon, lime, or orange. The easiest way to zest is to use a zester, but not everyone has one. Over the years I've found a couple of ways to get a similar result. One way is to use a cheese grater with very tiny holes. Make sure to apply only very light pressure; if you gouge the fruit too deeply, your zest will contain the white, bitter part of the citrus as well.

Another method is to shave off bits of the rind with a very sharp knife. Cut the trimmings as small as you can julienne-style, turning and chopping them crosswise. This will not result in pieces as tiny as you can get with a fine grater or zester, but using a knife is much better than skipping the zest in a recipe.

I enjoy the way pasta catches lentils in all its creases in this interesting soup. If you don't have sun-dried tomatoes, you can add tomato paste for a similar flavor at a lower cost.

Curly Noodle and Lentil Soup

serves 4 to 6   prep time: 35 minutes

¼ cup (½ stick) butter

2 large cloves garlic, minced or crushed

One 2-inch piece fresh ginger, peeled and grated

½ teaspoon dried sage

1 cup dried lentils, rinsed and picked over

½ cup chopped sun-dried tomatoes or one 6-ounce can tomato paste

4 cups chicken broth

2 cups water

8 ounces uncooked spiral pasta

2 cups firmly packed chopped fresh spinach

Black pepper to taste

1. Melt butter over medium heat in a soup pot. Add garlic and ginger; cook 1 minute, stirring. Add sage, lentils, tomatoes, broth, and water. Bring to a boil over high heat; cover, and reduce heat to medium. Simmer until lentils begin to soften, about 20 minutes.

2. Turn heat up to high. Once soup is boiling, add pasta and boil 5 minutes. Add spinach and season with pepper; stir. Cook 2 more minutes before serving.

My husband is tomato crazy. Every year he plants 100 tomato plants in our garden. Even with our big family, that's a lot of tomatoes to eat. I'm constantly on the lookout for ways to use them up. In the summer I make this with fresh tomatoes, but it's also just as tasty made with either store-bought canned or home-canned tomatoes.

Slow-Cooker Tomato Soup

serves 6   prep time: 15 minutes, plus 6 to 8 hours on Low

1 onion, peeled

Two 14-ounce cans crushed tomatoes

1 cup beef broth

¼ cup firmly packed brown sugar

2 tablespoons chopped fresh basil or
  2 teaspoons dried

1 tablespoon Worcestershire sauce

1 teaspoon unsweetened cocoa powder

One 14-ounce can evaporated milk

2 tablespoons butter

Salt and black pepper to taste

1. Puree onion in a blender or food processor along with enough tomatoes to yield about 4 cups of tomato puree.

2. Pour puree into a 4- to 5-quart slow cooker along with broth, brown sugar, basil, Worcestershire, and cocoa powder. Cover and cook on Low 6 to 8 hours.

3. Ten minutes before serving, stir in evaporated milk and butter; season with salt and pepper. Heat an additional 10 minutes, and serve.

This is a filling and incredibly affordable stew that you can serve with flour tortillas or over hot rice or biscuits. It's very quick to put together, with a flavor twist that is out of the ordinary.

Indian-Style Lentil Stew

serves 6   prep time: 45 minutes

¼ cup (½ stick) butter
2 medium-size onions, minced
2 cloves garlic, minced
One 1-pound package dried lentils, rinsed and
   picked over
2 cups pureed canned or fresh tomatoes
6 cups chicken broth
1 tablespoon ground cumin
1 tablespoon curry powder
One 1-inch piece fresh ginger, peeled and
   grated or finely minced
1 tablespoon minced fresh cilantro (optional)
Salt to taste

1. Melt butter in a soup pot over medium heat; add onions and cook, stirring a few times, until softened. Add garlic and lentils, stirring for a couple of minutes, to thoroughly coat lentils with butter. Add remaining ingredients, except salt, and bring to a boil over high heat.
2. Reduce heat to medium and simmer, uncovered, until lentils are soft, about 40 minutes, stirring occasionally. Season with salt and serve.

Savvy shoppers know that recipes that include shrimp are in general not the most affordable. Ditto for ones with large amounts of red meat. So why include them in a frugal cookbook? Variety. But if your budget is in desperate times, you may need to entirely skip such higher-cost meals.

Most people can fit in a "splurge" recipe now and then. Keep in mind, though, if you consistently choose higher-cost recipes, your grocery bill will not be as low as it could be. Be sure to balance out higher-cost meals with lower-cost ones.

A great goal would be to prepare four vegetarian meals for every meal that includes shrimp, salmon, steak, or other high-cost meat. One way to do this might be to go vegetarian for breakfast or lunch most weekdays, and save the "expensive" meat for Saturday night. Experiment to see what works for your family.

chapter 10

sides & salads

O ne of the ways to save money at mealtime is to offer a variety of choices. I often serve bread and butter, chopped carrots, and sliced oranges or apples along with my main dish. This chapter contains many other simple side dishes that fill out a meal in an affordable way, while also making it more nutritionally balanced.

Lots of people swear they hate Brussels sprouts, but most likely they've only had the boiled type. Until you've tried roasted Brussels sprouts, you haven't had them at their best. Here's a deliciously easy recipe that might succeed at converting a veggie-hater in your life.

Roasted Brussels Sprouts and Carrots

serves 6   prep time: 20 minutes

2 cups Brussels sprouts

3 tablespoons olive oil

2 carrots, thinly sliced

Salt and black pepper to taste

1 tablespoon fresh lemon juice

¼ cup grated Parmesan cheese (optional)

1. Preheat oven to 500°F.

2. Cut bottom off each Brussels sprout, remove any discolored leaves, and cut each sprout in half.

3. Pour oil onto a baking sheet. Place sprouts and carrots on sheet and toss well with oil. Arrange Brussels sprouts, cut sides down, on pan; season vegetables with salt and pepper.

4. Roast until sprouts start to brown in spots, 10 to 15 minutes. Sprinkle with lemon juice and cheese, if using.

Variation: You can also make this with broccoli florets and sliced stems instead of the Brussels sprouts and carrots. Use 2 bunches of broccoli.

I found a recipe somewhat like this in an Ethiopian cookbook, but decided to try it with bacon and a little less heat. If you like spicy food, a jalapeño pepper or more red pepper flakes would make it more authentically Ethiopian, as does the addition of turmeric. If you don't have turmeric on hand, it's fine to leave it out.

Green Beans and Potatoes with Bacon

serves 6   prep time: 40 minutes

4 slices bacon, cut into small pieces
1 onion, chopped
2 cloves garlic, chopped
1 pound green beans, ends trimmed
   and snapped in half
2 cups chicken broth

4 medium-size russet potatoes, peeled
   and cut into 1-inch cubes
1 teaspoon ground turmeric
½ teaspoon salt
½ teaspoon red pepper flakes or to taste
Black pepper to taste

mom to mom

One great way to encourage your kids to eat their vegetables is to set freshly chopped vegetables out as you're preparing dinner. Usually kids have the munchies by then and will tend to eat more carrots, cherry tomatoes, and/or celery at that point than they would be inclined to do during a meal when there are other options available.

1. Cook bacon in a large heavy skillet over medium heat until fully cooked, stirring occasionally. Using a fork or slotted spoon, remove bacon from pan.

2. Add onion and garlic to drippings in pan; cook, stirring, 2 to 3 minutes. Add green beans and cook 1 to 2 more minutes. Add broth, potatoes, turmeric, salt, red pepper, and black pepper. Reduce heat to low and cover, leaving the lid cracked just a little to let steam out. Cook, stirring occasionally, until liquid evaporates and potatoes are cooked through and have some caramelized bits, 20 to 25 minutes. If all liquid evaporates before potatoes are cooked, you may need to add just a little more water.

For years our Sunday noon meal has been barbecued hamburgers and oven-fried potatoes. Rain or shine, my husband turns on the grill, and I toss potatoes with oil and seasonings and bake them in the oven. When we decided to adopt a couple of older girls from Ethiopia, we added berbere to these potatoes, an Ethiopian spice, to make them feel a little more at home. Berbere is composed mostly of red pepper, along with some other herbs and spices. If you don't feel like doing Ethiopian-style seasonings, you can sprinkle these potatoes with barbecue seasoning, paprika, grated Parmesan cheese, or simple salt and pepper.

Ethiopian-Style Home Fries

serves 6   prep time: 25 minutes

5 medium-size russet potatoes
¼ cup olive or vegetable oil
1 to 2 tablespoons store-bought or
    homemade (page 275) Easy Berbere
½ teaspoon salt

1. Preheat oven to 500°F. Coat a large baking sheet with nonstick cooking spray.
2. Slice potatoes thickly, french-fry style. In a plastic bag, toss potatoes with oil, berbere, and salt. Spread fries over baking sheet in a single layer. Bake until browned and tender, 10 to 15 minutes. Serve with lots of ketchup—and plenty of water to drink, especially for those delicate American palates!

super-saver idea

In the early years of our marriage, we often bought tater tots to go with hamburgers. However, one day I crunched the numbers and realized that I could make our own potatoes for one quarter of the cost, spending only 5 minutes of extra time. We've been making our own fries ever since.

Street venders all over Seoul, Korea, sell freshly baked vegetable pancakes made with green onions, grated vegetables, and eggs. Here is my adaptation. These pancakes taste great with soy sauce, wasabi, or even applesauce. I like to offer all these options so that my kids can choose whichever they prefer. We serve this with rice as a vegetarian lunch.

Korean Vegetable Pancakes

serves 6, about 18 small pancakes   prep time: 40 minutes

2 cups peeled and shredded russet
    potatoes, rinsed in a colander under
    cold running water until the water runs
    clear and squeezed out in a towel as
    much as possible
1 onion, minced
1 cup shredded carrot or sweet potato

2 cloves garlic, minced
¼ cup cornmeal
1 cup all-purpose flour
2 large eggs
1 teaspoon peeled and grated fresh
    ginger
Vegetable oil for frying

1. In a large bowl, combine all ingredients, except oil. (You may find it's easiest to do this if you use your hands.)

2. Pour enough oil into a large heavy skillet to coat the bottom and heat over medium heat until oil is hot. Form enough 2- to 3-inch-diameter, ½-inch-thick patties from vegetable mixture to fill the skillet without letting them touch each other. Cook until golden brown and crispy on one side, about 2 minutes, then carefully flip and repeat on the second side. Watch carefully; the second side will cook more quickly. Remove to a paper-towel-covered plate. Repeat with remaining vegetable mixture, adding more oil if needed. Serve hot.

frying tips

When you're frying food, the trickiest part is regulating the temperature of the oil. A thermometer helps, but it's not necessary if you know what to watch for. First of all, wait to add the pancakes until the oil is hot enough. A bit of potato tossed into the pan should sizzle and jump, and turn light brown within 20 seconds or so if it's hot enough. Usually that takes at least a couple of minutes over medium heat.

Once the oil is hot enough, add your first batch of pancakes and watch to see how long they take to cook. Each side should take 1 to 2 minutes to brown. If they brown in less than a minute, turn down the heat. Once you've fried a batch or two, you'll probably need to turn down the heat again. The oil should not smoke—that means the oil is way too hot. If you get to that point, carefully move the skillet off the heat and let it cool for a minute or two. Turn the burner down as well and, after the oil cools a bit, continue to cook at a lower temperature. You may also need to add a little more oil halfway through the cooking, since the pancakes will soak up a little oil while cooking.

Here's a delicious, fast way to prepare zucchini. It has a lot less fat than your typical breaded, deep-fat-fried recipe.

Oven-Baked Breaded Zucchini

serves 4 to 6   prep time: 20 minutes

2 medium-size zucchini
¼ cup saltine or Ritz cracker crumbs
2 tablespoons grated Parmesan cheese

¼ cup store-bought or homemade
    (page 268) Balsamic Vinaigrette
    Dressing

1. Preheat oven to 475°F. Grease a large baking sheet.

2. Peel zucchini; cut in half lengthwise. Cut each half into 8 lengthwise strips.

3. Combine cracker crumbs and cheese on a plate. Pour dressing in a large shallow dish. Dip each zucchini strip into dressing, then dredge in crumbs. Place on prepared baking sheet.

4. Bake 5 minutes, then turn strips over and bake until crumbs are lightly browned, about 5 more minutes.

The day after our older Ethiopian daughter arrived, she spotted a cabbage in the garden, claimed it, and proceeded to make this delicious dish with it. Ethiopian cooking is fearless when it comes to the use of oil. That's part of what makes it so good. But if you prefer lower-fat food, cut the oil in half and substitute a little extra water instead, just enough to keep the cabbage from sticking to the bottom of the pot as you cook.

You can use any kind of cabbage—white, purple, or Napa. I often use both purple and green cabbage, because I think the colors look pretty together.

Serve this as a side dish at any meal. We like it with rice and Ethiopian Chicken Stew (page 180).

Ethiopian Sautéed Cabbage (Gomen)

serves 6   prep time: 45 minutes

1 large onion, peeled
2 ripe tomatoes
1 hot red pepper (optional)
1 head cabbage

¼ cup vegetable oil
2 cloves garlic, minced
1 to 2 teaspoons salt, to taste

1. Mince onion very fine. Chop tomatoes very fine or puree in a food processor. If using, cut hot pepper into very narrow threads, discarding seeds. Core, then chop cabbage into bite-size pieces, an inch or so across.

2. Put onion in a large pot and cook, dry, over medium-high heat, stirring often, until it starts to turn translucent. When onion loses its liquid and starts to stick to the bottom of the pot a bit, add ¼ cup oil and continue to cook over medium heat. Once oil is hot, add tomatoes, red pepper, and garlic; simmer a few minutes over medium-high heat, stirring often. Add cabbage. Don't panic if it looks like a lot—it will cook down.

3. Cover pot and continue to cook over medium-high heat 3 to 5 minutes before stirring. (It seems like you should turn down the heat, but liquid in the cabbage and oil in the pot will keep it from sticking.) Reduce heat to medium; cook, covered, about 20 minutes, stirring often. If cabbage begins to stick, add a little more oil or some water partway through the cooking time. You can also turn the heat down a little if you need to. Season with salt. The end result should be soft, shiny, very tender cabbage.

Spanish rice is a wonderful partner to refried beans, quesadillas, tacos, and almost any other Mexican food.

Rice-Cooker Mexican Rice

serves 6   prep time: 30 minutes

2 tablespoons butter
½ cup minced onion
3 cloves garlic, minced
1½ cups uncooked long-grain rice
2½ cups chicken broth
1 tablespoon chopped fresh cilantro or parsley
2 teaspoons ground cumin

1. Melt butter in a small skillet over medium heat. Add onion and garlic to pan; cook, stirring, until softened, 3 to 5 minutes. Transfer to rice cooker.
2. Add remaining ingredients to cooker; stir to combine with rice. Cook according to manufacturer's directions.
3. When cooking time is finished, stir and let rice sit, uncovered, 5 minutes before serving.

quick tip

If you're in a time crunch, you can dump all the ingredients for this recipe into the rice cooker at once. However, I think the flavor is richer and more developed if you take a couple of minutes to sauté the onion and garlic before combining it with the other ingredients.

Here's an easy recipe for making your own rice-a-roni, proving once again you don't need to rely on those boxes. Serve this alongside chicken or fish.

Homemade Rice-a-Roni

serves 4 to 6   prep time: 30 minutes

mom to mom

Have the kids break the pasta up for you. Even two-year-olds will have a blast helping mom with this project.

super-saver idea

Lots of people gravitate toward boxed mixes for sheer convenience. What they don't realize is that in many cases cooking from scratch takes only a few minutes more. Mixes get even more expensive if your family is large and requires more than one box to make a meal. Learning to cook without mixes will net you big money savings—and better nutrition as well.

¼ cup (½ stick) butter

2 tablespoons oil (olive oil is good but not essential)

2 cups uncooked long-grain white or brown rice

1 cup uncooked vermicelli or spaghetti broken into 1-inch pieces or shorter

5 cups beef broth

2 cloves garlic, minced

¼ cup chopped fresh basil or sage

1 cup frozen mixed vegetables (carrots and peas are good)

2 teaspoons salt

½ teaspoon black pepper or to taste

1. In a wok or cast-iron pan, heat butter and oil over medium heat. When butter begins to melt, add rice and toss to coat well with butter and oil. Cook until some of the rice starts to brown.

2. Add pasta and keep stirring until some of it has browned bits as well. When mixture begins to stick a little, add broth, garlic, basil, and mixed vegetables. Continue to cook until rice is tender, about 15 minutes, stirring occasionally. If rice starts to stick to bottom before it is fully cooked, you may need to turn down the heat a little and add ½ cup water. Total cooking time for white rice will be 20 to 25 minutes. Brown rice will take 40 to 55 minutes. Season with salt and pepper.

I haven't had especially great luck with brown rice in the rice cooker, so I was pleased to find a recipe for this oven-baked brown rice. This recipe takes a little time, but it's mostly hands-off cooking time, which leaves you free to do other things while it bakes. Any leftovers can be used to make Fried Rice (see page 150).

Baked Brown Rice

serves 6   prep time: 1 hour 15 minutes

2 cups water

2 cups beef broth

2 tablespoons butter

2 cups uncooked long-grain brown rice

1. Preheat oven to 375°F. Grease an 8-inch square casserole dish.

2. Bring water and broth to a boil in a small saucepan. Add butter; stir until melted.

3. Place rice in prepared casserole dish. Pour boiling broth mixture over rice; stir. Cover with aluminum foil; bake on center rack until rice is tender, about 1 hour and 10 minutes. Stir before serving.

• • • • • • • • •

I've known for years that my rice cooker is a great tool for cooking rice and oatmeal, but it wasn't until lately that I learned how to cook this savory polenta in the rice cooker as well. Think of polenta as a substitute for pasta. You can ladle anything saucy, sautéed, or fried on top of a bowl of polenta and enjoy.

Rice-Cooker Polenta

serves 4 to 6   prep time: 25 minutes

3 cups chicken broth, cool or at room
   temperature

1 cup cornmeal

2 tablespoons butter

1 teaspoon salt

½ teaspoon dried thyme

1. Combine all ingredients in rice cooker, stirring briskly as you add cornmeal to break up any clumps. Cook 5 minutes with lid on, then lift lid briefly to stir.

2. Close lid and cook according to manufacturer's directions.

3. Remove lid; stir, and let stand 5 more minutes before serving.

My mother-in-law serves this yummy dish at our family's traditional prime rib Christmas dinner. Her recipe includes a handful of slivered almonds, which I don't usually buy since they're fairly expensive. I've discovered that sesame seeds (bought at the Asian market) add a nice affordable crunch.

Grandma's Easy Mushroom Barley

serves 4   prep time: 1 hour 10 minutes

super-saver idea

As I work to keep our food costs affordable, one of the things that adds interest to my life is trying new foods. However, I make sure that new foods aren't extremely expensive. If you're bored with what you're eating, try a new grain, a new vegetable, or a new recipe for bread. There are lots of affordable ways to add interesting food to your diet.

½ cup (1 stick) butter
1½ cups uncooked pearl barley
1 small onion, minced
½ cup chopped mushrooms
2 tablespoons sesame seeds or ¼ cup chopped slivered almonds
3¾ cups beef broth

1. Preheat oven to 350°F. Grease an 8-inch square casserole dish.
2. Melt butter in a medium-size skillet over medium heat. Add barley, onion, mushrooms, and sesame seeds; cook, stirring, until onion softens, about 5 minutes. Stir in broth and bring to a boil.
3. Transfer contents of skillet to prepared casserole dish. Bake 1 hour, stirring once during baking time.

I make this chicken salad almost every time we go camping. I prep the veggies, make the dressing, and cook the meat ahead of time. Then, when it's time for dinner, all I have to do is throw all the ingredients together. I adapted this from a recipe that was in our local newspaper about 10 years ago.

Mexican Chicken Salad

serves 6 to 8 as a main dish   prep time: 40 minutes, plus 1 hour chilling time

¼ cup white vinegar

¼ cup honey

1 tablespoon ground cumin

1 teaspoon salt

½ teaspoon black pepper

2 tablespoons olive oil

2 boneless, skinless chicken breast halves, cut into 1-inch cubes

1 clove garlic, minced

1 cup frozen (thawed) or canned (drained) corn

1 cup chopped ripe tomatoes

One 15-ounce can black beans, drained

2 green onions, chopped

1 red bell pepper, seeded and chopped

One 10-ounce package lettuce mix

2 cups shredded Monterey Jack cheese

2 cups slightly crushed tortilla chips

1 cup sour cream

1 cup thick, chunky salsa

1. In a small jar with a lid, combine vinegar, honey, cumin, salt, and black pepper. Shake vigorously until well mixed. Set aside.

2. Heat oil in a large skillet. Sprinkle chicken cubes with garlic, then cook until no longer pink in the center, about 5 minutes.

3. Place chicken, corn, tomatoes, beans, green onions, and red pepper in a large bowl and stir to combine. Add honey dressing and toss until well coated. Cover with plastic wrap and chill at least 1 hour.

4. When ready to serve, combine chicken mixture with lettuce. Serve with cheese, tortilla chips, sour cream, and salsa in separate bowls.

quick tip

Both Mexican Chicken Salad and Chinese Chicken Salad (page 212) make great easy summer dinners. I often pack the ingredients for one or both of them when we go camping.

Many chicken salad recipes feature almonds, which are so expensive that I rarely buy them. However, peanuts are very reasonably priced at Asian markets. Stock them in your pantry, as they're often a good substitute for more expensive nuts.

Chinese Chicken Salad

serves 6 as a main dish   prep time: 30 minutes, plus marinating and chilling time

Marinade:

½ cup firmly packed brown sugar

½ cup sesame oil

½ cup rice vinegar or ⅓ cup white vinegar

2 ramen noodle seasoning packets (reserved from ramen noodle packages used in salad)

1 tablespoon peeled and minced fresh ginger

½ teaspoon black pepper

2 cups cubed chicken breasts or thighs

Salad:

1 tablespoon sesame oil

1 head Napa cabbage, cut into very thin slivers

4 green onions, thinly sliced

¼ cup chopped fresh cilantro

¼ cup chopped peanuts

2 tablespoons sesame seeds, toasted in a dry skillet over medium heat

Three 3-ounce packages oriental- or chicken-flavored ramen noodles, broken

1. In a 2-cup measuring cup, whisk together first 6 marinade ingredients. In a medium-size bowl, toss chicken with ¼ cup marinade and marinate for 1 hour.
2. Heat sesame oil in a medium-size skillet over medium-high heat. Add chicken and cook, without stirring, until nicely browned on one side, 3 to 5 minutes. Stir and cook until chicken is no longer pink in the center, 5 to 8 more minutes. (If you're short on time, cook chicken immediately after tossing it with marinade.)
3. Transfer cooked chicken to a large bowl, and add remaining salad ingredients; toss to combine. Pour remaining marinade over salad and toss until everything is well coated. Cover with plastic wrap and refrigerate several hours, or overnight, to let the flavors develop.

This recipe isn't the most affordable in the book since it calls for steak. But cutting the meat super thin and arranging it artfully across the salad makes the most of it and offers a nice change from an ordinary salad.

Thai Beef Salad

serves 4 as a main dish   prep time: 30 minutes

1½ pounds sirloin steak (rump or filet),
   trimmed of fat
Sesame or olive oil as needed

Salad:

10 ounces salad greens or spinach
1 onion, cut in half and thinly sliced into half-moons
3 large mild red chiles, seeded and cut into
   very thin threads
¼ cup chopped fresh cilantro or parsley
¼ cup chopped fresh basil

Dressing:

3 tablespoons fresh lime juice
3 tablespoons brown sugar
2 tablespoons fish sauce
1 teaspoon soy sauce

1. Brush beef with a little oil, and grill or broil until cooked to your liking. Set cooked beef aside 5 minutes to let the juices settle, then slice thinly.
2. Combine salad greens, onion, chiles, cilantro, and basil in a salad bowl and toss lightly.
3. In a small bowl, whisk together dressing ingredients until brown sugar dissolves.
4. Arrange sliced beef over greens; pour dressing over top. Serve immediately.

One of the things to consider when you're picking up an item at the grocery store is the number of ingredients in that package. In general, the longer the ingredients list, the more expensive the item will be. Frozen mixed vegetables that also include pasta will cost you more than a bag of frozen peas. A salad containing a mix of 5 lettuces will almost certainly be more expensive than a bag of just spinach. A box of flavored rice will cost more than a bag of plain. Buying packaged foods with shorter ingredient lists every time you shop will help you get home with more money in your pocket.

This easy salad is great with bread as a light lunch, or as a side dish at a barbecue as part of a larger meal.

Mushroom-Bacon-Spinach Salad

serves 6   prep time: 30 minutes

One way to help save money is to extend the refrigerator life of your vegetables. There's no greater waste of money than having to throw away greens and veggies that give up the ghost before you can turn them into a meal. And the solution is as simple as tucking a paper towel into the bag in which you're storing the vegetables. The towel soaks up the extra water that turns vegetables into mush. This tip is most helpful for lettuce, spinach, peppers, broccoli, mushrooms, and cucumbers.

8 cups torn fresh spinach
2 cups sliced mushrooms
3 green onions, thinly sliced
1 medium-size ripe tomato, diced
¼ cup grated Parmesan cheese
6 slices bacon, cooked until crispy and crumbled
½ cup honey
⅓ cup white vinegar
⅓ cup vegetable oil
2 teaspoons yellow or spicy brown mustard
2 teaspoons fresh lemon juice

1. Combine spinach, mushrooms, green onions, tomato, and cheese with two-thirds of the crumbled bacon in a large bowl.
2. In a medium-size bowl, whisk together honey, vinegar, oil, mustard, lemon juice, and remaining crumbled bacon. Pour over salad and toss until well coated. Serve immediately.

This recipe comes together quickly and is full of flavor.

Chickpea Salad

serves 4 to 6   prep time: 15 minutes

Two 15-ounce cans chickpeas
4 tablespoons red wine vinegar, divided
3 teaspoons fresh lemon juice, divided
2 cups diced (½-inch) ripe tomatoes, drained
½ cup pitted ripe olives, sliced into lengthwise slivers
½ cup chopped onion
½ cup chopped fresh basil or 2 tablespoons dried
¼ cup chopped fresh parsley or 1 tablespoon dried
¼ cup extra-virgin olive oil
1 tablespoon sugar
Salt and black pepper to taste

1. Drain chickpeas into a colander and rinse well under cold running water. Drain. Place in a large plastic bowl and toss with 1 tablespoon vinegar and 2 teaspoons lemon juice; marinate 10 minutes.
2. Add drained tomatoes, olives, onion, and herbs to chickpeas and gently combine.
3. Whisk together remaining 3 tablespoons vinegar, 1 teaspoon lemon juice, olive oil, and sugar in a small bowl until well mixed. Gently toss dressing with salad. Season with salt and pepper. The salad can marinate at room temperature 1 to 2 hours before serving. Store any leftovers in fridge 3 to 5 days.

Any bean recipe is made more affordable by cooking your own beans. The trick is to allow enough time for presoaking. Soaking overnight is easiest, but 2 to 3 hours will do for most beans, including chickpeas. Then all you have to do is place them in a pot with enough water to cover by a couple of inches, and simmer until tender (see Bean Cooking Times chart on page 74). Keep in mind that if your beans are old, they'll take a little longer to cook.

Here's a great dish that makes use of garden ingredients on a hot summer evening. If your family isn't thrilled with vegetarian offerings, dice and cook a couple of chicken breasts, then add them to the salad.

Asian Noodle Salad

serves 6   prep time: 30 minutes

Lettuce salads are fine, but over the years I've grown to love cabbage salads. Cabbage is more affordable and more healthful than standard iceberg lettuce. It has a refreshingly crisp taste. And the fridge life of cabbage is much longer than that of lettuce—lettuce sometimes goes bad in as little as four days. Cabbage can last for up to a month. This translates to fewer trips to the grocery store, which will save you even more money.

Salad:

6 to 8 ounces linguine, cooked according to package directions, drained, rinsed under cold running water, and cooled

2 cups loosely packed spinach or Swiss chard, washed well and tough stems removed

1 cup slivered green cabbage

1 cup slivered purple cabbage

1 green bell pepper, seeded and slivered

2 green onions, thinly sliced

1 medium-size cucumber, peeled and thinly sliced

1 tablespoon minced fresh cilantro

1 cup roasted, salted peanuts, lightly toasted in a dry skillet over medium heat

Dressing:

⅓ cup soy sauce

⅓ cup firmly packed brown sugar

⅓ cup olive oil

Juice of 1 lime (about 2 tablespoons)

1 tablespoon sesame oil

1 tablespoon peeled and grated fresh ginger

2 cloves garlic, chopped

1 jalapeño pepper (optional), seeded and finely minced

1. In a large salad bowl, combine salad ingredients.

2. In a 2-cup measuring cup, whisk together dressing ingredients and pour over salad. Toss until everything is well coated. Serve immediately.

· ◦ ◦ ◆ ◦ ◆ ◦ ◆ ◦ ◦

I came up with this recipe one summer when we had lots of apricots and strawberries. The colors of the ingredients make this a beautiful and tasty addition to any meal. If you don't have cabbage, try substituting spinach. For the greens, try using turnip greens, spinach, or chard. You can also add some purple cabbage for more color if you'd like.

Summer Confetti Salad

serves 6   prep time: 20 minutes

Salad:
3 cups very thinly shredded cabbage
1 cup other greens
1 cup hulled and diced strawberries
1 cup pitted and diced apricots

Dressing:
¼ cup fresh lime juice (from about 2 limes)
¼ cup sugar
2 tablespoons vegetable oil

1. Combine salad ingredients in a large bowl.

2. Whisk together dressing ingredients until sugar is dissolved. Pour dressing quickly over salad and toss to coat evenly.

This recipe is often served in the southern United States.

Southern-Style Fresh Cabbage Salad

serves 4 to 6   prep time: 15 minutes

Half of a head green cabbage, cored and
  slivered
1 carrot, shredded

¼ cup white vinegar
¼ cup sugar
2 tablespoons olive oil

1. Combine cabbage and carrot in a medium-size bowl.
2. Whisk together vinegar, sugar, and oil in a small bowl until sugar dissolves.
Pour over salad and toss until well coated. Salad will keep, tightly covered, for
several days in the fridge.

⋄•⋄•⋄•⋄•⋄•

In Korea no meal is complete without *kimchi*, a side dish made from fermented cabbage
and lots and lots of red pepper. This fresh version of the salad skips the fermentation
step. You can use as little or as much red pepper as you like. We have this quite often in
the wintertime.

Fresh Kimchi Salad

serves 4 to 6   prep time: 20 minutes

Salad:
Half of a head Chinese cabbage, cored
  and slivered
2 green onions, minced

Dressing:
2 to 3 cloves garlic, minced
1 tablespoon sesame oil

1 teaspoon sesame seeds
1 tablespoon white or rice vinegar
1 tablespoon sugar
1 tablespoon soy sauce
1 to 2 teaspoons red pepper flakes
  or to taste

1. Combine cabbage and green onions in a medium-size bowl.

2. In a small bowl, whisk together dressing ingredients until sugar dissolves. Pour over salad and toss until well coated. Salad will keep, tightly covered, several days in the fridge, even after dressing has been added.

Cucumber Kimchi: This kimchi can be made with cucumbers if your family prefers them over cabbage. Peel 2 cucumbers and slice in half lengthwise. Use a spoon to scoop out seeds. Now slice each "boat" into little C's by cutting halves crosswise into ¼-inch-thick slices. Mix with green onions and dressing. The cucumber version is best eaten the day it's made, so make only as much as you can eat in 1 meal.

* * * * * * * * * *

This salsa always goes fast at our house. You can vary the vegetables to suit the tastes of your family.

Black Bean Salsa

serves 4   prep time: 20 minutes, plus chilling time

One 15-ounce can black beans,
    rinsed and drained
1 cup fresh or frozen (thawed) corn or
    one 11-ounce can corn kernels, drained
1 jalapeño pepper, seeded and minced
2 medium-size ripe tomatoes, chopped
½ cup minced cabbage
½ red bell pepper, seeded and chopped

½ green bell pepper, seeded and chopped
¼ cup chopped fresh cilantro or
    1 teaspoon dried
1 small red or yellow onion, diced
Juice from 1 lime (about 2 tablespoons)
¼ cup store-bought or homemade
    (page 268) Italian salad dressing
1 to 2 cloves garlic, minced

1. Combine all ingredients in a medium-size bowl. Cover with plastic wrap and chill at least 2 hours to let the flavors develop. Overnight is even better. Serve with chips. Salsa will keep in the fridge for several days.

A Korean friend of mine taught me to make these wonderful egg rolls. If you like spicy food, you can add red pepper flakes to the filling. It's also perfectly fine to steam them instead of frying, if you prefer. I serve these with plain rice and sometimes a light soup. They're best freshly cooked, but can be reheated in the oven or microwave.

Korean Egg Rolls (Mandu)

makes about 20 egg rolls   prep time: 45 minutes

½ pound ground beef

2 cloves garlic, minced

1 tablespoon sesame oil

Half of a head green cabbage, cored and thinly slivered

1 medium-size carrot, shredded

2 green onions, finely chopped

2 tablespoons soy sauce

1 tablespoon cornstarch

1 tablespoon peeled and grated fresh ginger

¼ teaspoon black pepper

1 package 6-inch egg roll wrappers

Vegetable oil for frying

1. Heat a large skillet over medium-high heat until hot. Add ground beef and garlic and cook until beef is no longer pink, breaking up any clumps. Remove beef to a bowl and drain fat from skillet. Wipe skillet with a paper towel to remove beef fat.

2. Add sesame oil to skillet and heat several minutes over medium heat. Add cabbage, carrot, and green onions; cook until soft, 3 to 5 minutes, stirring a few times.

3. In a small bowl, mix together soy sauce and cornstarch. Add ginger and pepper, stirring again.

4. Return beef to skillet. Add soy sauce mixture; stir to combine everything, and cook a few more minutes, until cornstarch thickens any liquid. Remove from heat and cool.

5. Prepare a clean work surface, with a small bowl of water close by. Place 1 egg roll wrapper in front of you, with 1 corner pointing away from you. Imagine the wrapper is a clock face and the point furthest from you represents 12 o' clock. Spoon a couple of tablespoons of filling horizontally across the center of wrapper. Fold the 6 o' clock point up over filling, tucking it under the filling after you cover it to make a little rounded log.

6. Next, fold the 3 o' clock and 9 o' clock points of the wrapper toward the center so that those two points overlap a little. Finally, wet the 12 o' clock point of the wrapper with a little water, and roll up the whole egg roll toward that point until you've formed a tidy little bundle. Gently press the 12 o' clock point so that it adheres well to roll. Repeat with remaining wrappers and filling.

7. Heat enough vegetable oil in a medium-size skillet to immerse egg rolls halfway. The ideal frying temperature is about 350°F. I usually begin over medium-high heat, reducing the temperature a notch every 5 minutes or so as I cook, since the longer you cook, the faster the eggs rolls will brown. Usually it takes no longer than 3 to 4 minutes to cook an egg roll. Cook them a few at a time (you don't want to crowd them) about 3 minutes on the first side, then turn carefully and cook 2 more minutes on the other side. Watch them, because they can burn quickly. Remove to a paper-towel-covered plate to cool before eating. Keep warm in a 200°F oven until all rolls are cooked.

storing ginger to last

I love to cook with fresh ginger—it's so much better than dried. But it doesn't last forever, and can get moldy in the fridge. The best place to keep ginger is in the freezer, stored in a zip-top plastic bag. When you need it, all you have to do is grate the right amount into a bowl, using a regular cheese grater. Then stick the remaining ginger back in the freezer. It will keep for months there.

chapter 11

breads,
muffins &
desserts

When I was a kid I remember reading the Laura Ingalls Wilder book *Farmer Boy* and feeling envious of Almanzo. Anytime he walked into his mother's kitchen, he could be assured of something delicious to eat. Donuts, cakes, pies, cookies, and breads—you name it and chances most likely were his mother baked it at least once a week.

If you're trying to spend less at the grocery store, it might be tempting to decide that baking and desserts are an extravagance. But I believe they have an important place in the frugal lifestyle. Granted, we don't really need chocolate pudding or homemade soft pretzels. But plain and simple, they make life better. And being able to provide our families with affordable treats is an important way to help them feel satisfied with the cutbacks you may have made in other areas of your grocery budget.

As with anything, it's possible to overdo baking, especially if you choose recipes that contain lots of expensive ingredients. But the recipes in this chapter focus on maximum taste at minimal cost. As you thumb through the pages, I hope at least a few of these recipes will inspire you to whip up something delicious for your family.

• • • • • • • • •

This is my daughter Amanda's mouthwateringly decadent biscuit recipe. The butter! The garlic! The cheese! Handle the batter as little as possible to get the lightest biscuits possible.

Amanda's Buttery Garlic-Cheese Biscuits

makes 12 biscuits   prep time: 30 minutes

2 cups all-purpose flour
2 tablespoons sugar
1 tablespoon baking powder
1 teaspoon salt

1 cup milk
¼ cup shredded Cheddar cheese
3 tablespoons butter, melted
3 cloves garlic, minced

1. Preheat oven to 375°F. Grease a 12-cup muffin tin.
2. In a large bowl, mix together flour, sugar, baking powder, and salt. Add milk and cheese; stir just until combined. Divide batter among 12 muffin cups.
3. Here's where it gets really yummy: Mix together melted butter and garlic; drizzle over biscuits. Bake until golden brown, about 15 minutes. Serve hot.

There's nothing like a light, flaky biscuit to add that perfect touch to a winter meal. But when I started cooking, light and flaky wasn't what I was turning out—hockey pucks would be a more appropriate description. After many batches of biscuit failure, I went on a quest for perfect biscuits and these are what I found. They taste delicious and rise hugely, especially if you follow the cardinal rule of biscuit-making: Handle the dough no more than directed in recipe.

Really Big Biscuits

makes 16 big biscuits   prep time: 40 minutes

To get biscuits into the oven faster and avoid overhandling, I simply plop rough clumps of the dough onto the baking sheet. I like their rustic look. If you want yours pretty, feel free to roll them out. Either way, this recipe will give you big, fluffy biscuits.

4 cups all-purpose flour
2 tablespoons baking powder
2 tablespoons sugar
2 teaspoons salt
⅔ cup cold butter
2 cups milk

1. Preheat oven to 425°F.

2. In a large bowl, whisk together flour, baking powder, sugar, and salt. Using a box grater, shred cold butter into mixture and stir to distribute it evenly through dry mixture. Add milk gradually, stirring just until dough pulls away from the side of the bowl.

3. Turn dough out onto a floured surface and knead 15 times. Pat or roll dough out to a 1-inch thickness. Cut biscuits using a large glass dipped in flour. Keep patting remnants of dough together and cutting biscuits until all dough is used.

4. Brush excess flour off biscuits and place them on an ungreased baking sheet. Bake until edges begin to brown, 13 to 15 minutes. Serve hot.

This recipe takes more time than using a store-bought packet of tortillas, but it may just save you a trip to the store.

Homemade Tortillas

makes 12 tortillas   prep time: 40 minutes

3 cups all-purpose flour, plus ¼ cup for rolling
2 teaspoons baking powder
1 teaspoon salt
½ cup vegetable shortening
1 cup warm water

1. Combine 3 cups flour, baking powder, and salt in a large bowl. Work in shortening until mixture is crumbly, using your fingertips, a fork, or a pastry blender. Slowly add warm water to mixture while tossing with a fork. With your hands, knead dough vigorously in the bowl until it forms a nice dough ball, about 2 minutes. Add a little more water if needed to collect any loose flour. Cover bowl with a clean dish towel and let stand at least 15 minutes.

2. Divide dough into 12 balls. Take a dough ball, roll it in flour, then place on a floured surface. Roll out very thin and evenly with a rolling pin.

3. Place a large cast-iron skillet over medium heat until hot. Add a tortilla and cook for 1 to 2 minutes per side, until it gets brown spots and no longer looks doughy. Note: Leftover tortillas can be cooled, then stored in a plastic bag in the refrigerator or freezer until needed. You can also store leftover dough in the fridge a day or two. Let it sit on the counter for half an hour before rolling any leftover dough.

quick tip

Unless you're using those sticks of shortening (which you pay a premium for), measuring shortening is a messy business. Try my method. Put 1 cup of water in a 2- or 4-cup glass measuring cup, depending on how much shortening you need. Add dollops of shortening until the water line in the measuring cup reads 1 cup more than the amount of shortening you need. For example, this tortilla recipe calls for ½ cup shortening, so you'd add shortening until the measuring cup reads 1½ cups. Then simply drain off the water and dump the shortening into your bowl. No sticky, time-consuming cleanup!

I've had varying levels of success with homemade yeast bread—it would probably help if I was better at following recipes. But you'll be happy to know that pizza dough is much more forgiving than bread dough. This recipe can be whipped out in 10 minutes flat. For maximum fluffiness, allow at least 20 minutes of rise time before you spread it onto pizza pans. If your crew is starving, you can skip the rise time. Your results will still be delicious.

This recipe makes 2 baking sheet–size pizzas. If that's too much pizza for your family, cut the recipe in half. Or, better yet, make the whole recipe and freeze what you don't use for another night. Just take the dough out and put it in the fridge the evening before you need it. Or get it out in the morning and let it sit on the counter, covered, all day.

Homemade Pizza Dough

makes 2 pizzas   prep time: 20 to 40 minutes

2 tablespoons active dry yeast

2 tablespoons sugar

4 cups hot tap water (no hotter than 110°F)

¼ cup vegetable or olive oil, plus 1 to
   2 tablespoons for the pans

5 to 7 cups all-purpose flour, as needed

½ cup cornmeal

1. In a large bowl, combine yeast, sugar, and water; let stand for 5 minutes to allow yeast time to start working. If it's active, it should start to foam. (If it doesn't get foamy, you need to purchase new yeast.)

2. Add ¼ cup oil, 4 cups flour, and cornmeal; stir. When mixture gets too heavy to mix effectively with a wooden spoon, sprinkle about 1 cup flour onto a clean counter and oil your hands. (Keep flour bin and a scoop close by, because you will most likely need to add more flour as you knead.) Turn dough out onto the floured counter and begin kneading. Continue to knead, adding more flour as long as dough feels sticky. When dough is smooth, elastic, and maintains a nice mounded-up shape on the counter when you stop kneading, you've probably added enough flour.

3. Rinse out your bowl and lightly oil it. Place dough in bowl, cover it with a clean dish towel, and allow to rise in a warm, draft-free spot 20 to 30 minutes. (An hour or 2 is fine if you have the time.)

4. Preheat oven to 550°F. Oil 2 pans. (You can use baking sheets or round pizza pans, whichever you prefer. Spread dough in larger pans for a thinner crust pizza or use smaller pans for a thick crust.) Sometimes my kids make personal pan pizzas using greased 8-inch pie pans. I give my smaller kids less dough and my bigger kids larger pieces of dough. Using oiled fingers, press dough gently out across pan until it covers the pan. Spread desired toppings over crust.

5. Place pan in oven. Watch carefully and remove pizza when crust is a deep brown at the edges and toppings have some nice deeply browned bits, about 10 to 15 minutes, depending on the size of your pizza and heat of your oven.

Variations: If you like your pizza dough to be whole-grain, substitute whole-wheat flour for 1 cup all-purpose flour. You can also add ½ cup wheat germ if you happen to have that in your pantry. If you prefer your dough to be lower fat, you can skip oiling the pan and instead sprinkle it with cornmeal to keep it from sticking.

pizza topping ideas

Whenever I make spaghetti, I try to set aside a cup or two of sauce in a freezer container to use for pizzas later. If I don't happen to have already-made spaghetti sauce in the freezer, I make my own pizza sauce using canned pureed tomatoes and the spaghetti seasoning on page 274. Most of our pizzas are topped with pepperoni. We also enjoy green peppers and fresh mushrooms. I think mozzarella cheese is best on pizza, but Cheddar is fine if that is all you have. Usually I finish off a pizza with a sprinkle of Parmesan cheese and, when they're in season, sliced fresh tomatoes.

This recipe produces a moist, flavorful loaf. You can make it with or without nuts. For a different taste, try adding 1 cup shredded coconut to the mix. This bread freezes beautifully.

Zucchini Bread

makes two 4 x 8-inch loaves   prep time: 1 hour 20 minutes

2½ cups all-purpose flour

½ cup wheat germ (or substitute ½ cup more flour)

2 teaspoons baking powder

1 teaspoon baking soda

1 teaspoon salt

1 teaspoon ground cinnamon

½ teaspoon ground cloves

3 large eggs

1 cup vegetable oil

1 tablespoon vanilla extract

2¼ cups sugar

2 cups shredded zucchini

1 cup chopped walnuts (optional)

quick tip

In the summertime almost anyone with a gardening friend can lay their hands on more zucchini than they need. If you find yourself with an overabundance of this prolific vegetable, grate your extra zucchini (no need to peel it!) and freeze it in 2-cup amounts so you can make this bread in cold weather or anytime the baking bug hits.

1. Preheat oven to 325°F. Grease and flour two 4 x 8-inch loaf pans.

2. Combine flour, wheat germ (if using), baking powder, baking soda, salt, cinnamon, and cloves in a medium bowl with a fork.

3. Beat eggs, oil, vanilla, and sugar together in a large bowl. Add dry ingredients to creamed mixture and beat well. Stir in zucchini and, if using, nuts until well combined.

4. Pour batter into prepared pans. Bake until a tester inserted in the center comes out clean, 50 to 60 minutes. Let cool in pans on a wire rack for 20 minutes. Remove bread from pans and completely cool before slicing.

If you've always assumed you don't have time to bake, it may be time to change your mind. With this easy recipe, you could be eating fresh bread an hour from now.

Easy Cuban Bread

makes 2 medium loaves   prep time: 1 hour

5 to 6 cups all-purpose flour
2 tablespoons active dry yeast
2 tablespoons sugar
1 tablespoon salt

2 cups hot water (no hotter than 110°F)
1 large egg
1 tablespoon sesame or poppy seeds
   (or a mix of both)

1. Mix 4 cups flour with yeast, sugar, and salt in a large bowl. Add hot water and beat 100 strokes with a wooden spoon or mix with a stand mixer for 3 minutes. (You can do this in a KitchenAid mixer fitted with a dough hook if you have one.) Add remaining flour until dough is no longer sticky. Knead for 8 minutes (again, you can also do this in a stand mixer). Remove dough from bowl.

2. Rinse bowl and oil it lightly. Place dough in bowl, cover with a clean dish towel, and let rise in a warm, draft-free spot 15 minutes.

3. Preheat oven to 400°F.

4. Punch down dough; cut in half and shape into 2 loaves. You can make loaves round and set them side by side on a large greased baking sheet. Or you can grease 2 (4 x 8-inch) loaf pans for rectangular loaves. Once you've formed loaves, beat egg and brush across the tops of both loaves. Sprinkle with sesame seeds. Bake until bread is medium brown and sounds hollow when you thump it, 40 to 50 minutes.

5. Let bread cool before cutting. Once it's completely cool, store in a gallon zip-top plastic bag or wrap in plastic wrap at room temperature. Eat within 3 days.

quick tip

Even if your family is small, making a double batch of bread is a good use of time—just freeze that second loaf for another day. You can even freeze half-loaves or single slices.

I adapted this recipe years ago from one on the back of a can of Libby's pumpkin pie filling. It's a moist bread with a lovely color and flavor, and makes a wonderful home-made Christmas gift.

Using canned pumpkin is easiest. But if you happen to have a pumpkin that you'd like to use, just chop it into large chunks, remove the seeds, and boil in water until soft. Drain; then, once cool, remove skin and puree in a food processor.

Cranberry-Pumpkin Bread with Orange Glaze

makes two 4 x 8-inch loaves   prep time: 1 hour 20 minutes

3⅔ cups all-purpose flour
1½ cups granulated sugar
2 teaspoons baking soda
1 teaspoon baking powder
1 teaspoon ground cinnamon
½ teaspoon ground ginger
½ teaspoon ground nutmeg
¼ teaspoon ground cloves
¾ cup chopped walnuts
One 16-ounce can whole-berry
   cranberry sauce

One 16-ounce can solid-pack pumpkin
⅔ cup vegetable oil
4 large eggs

Orange Glaze:
1 cup confectioners' sugar
¼ cup thawed orange juice concentrate
¼ teaspoon ground cinnamon
1 teaspoon grated orange zest

1. Preheat oven to 350°F. Generously grease two 4 x 8-inch loaf pans.
2. Combine flour, granulated sugar, baking soda, baking powder, and spices in a large bowl. In another large bowl, mix together walnuts, cranberry sauce, pumpkin, oil, and eggs until well combined. Add cranberry-pumpkin mixture to flour mixture and stir until everything is well moistened.
3. Pour batter into prepared loaf pans. Bake until a tester inserted into the center of each comes out clean, 50 to 60 minutes. Let cool in pans on a wire rack for 10 minutes, then remove from pans.
4. In a small bowl mix together glaze ingredients until smooth. Once loaves are totally cool, drizzle glaze over both loaves. Cut and serve. You may freeze the second loaf for later use if you like.

This recipe is a perfect use for over-ripe bananas. My eleven-year-old daughter enjoys making this, so whenever she sees an over-ripe banana, she squirrels it away in the freezer. When she's collected 3 bananas, she happily makes a batch. Frozen bananas will develop a very dark skin, but they're still good for baking once thawed.

Blue Ribbon Banana Bread

makes two 4 x 8-inch loaves   prep time: 1 hour 20 minutes

1 cup (2 sticks) butter, softened at room temperature

2 cups sugar

4 large eggs

3 cups all-purpose flour

2 teaspoons baking soda

1 teaspoon ground nutmeg

1 teaspoon salt

2 cups mashed ripe bananas (about 3 bananas)

1 cup sour cream

2 teaspoons vanilla extract

1 chopped pecans or walnuts (optional)

1. Preheat oven to 350°F. Generously grease two 4 x 8-inch loaf pans.

2. In a large bowl, cream together butter, sugar, and eggs.

3. In a medium bowl, combine flour, baking soda, nutmeg, and salt, using a fork. Add to butter mixture and blend well. Add bananas, sour cream, and vanilla; stir well. Add nuts, if using.

4. Pour batter into prepared pans. Bake until a toothpick inserted into the center of each loaf comes out clean, 50 to 60 minutes. Cool in pans on a wire rack for 10 minutes; remove from pans and cool completely. Once cool, wrap the second loaf and freeze it for later if you like.

super-saver idea

One way to save money is to avoid having to throw out produce that over-ripens before you can eat it. If you would like your bananas to ripen more slowly, store them in a plastic bag on the counter. This will extend the life of your bananas by at least a couple of days. I always bag my bananas right at the grocery store and leave them in the bag at home. I also try to choose one bunch that's ready to eat soon and one bunch that's very green. By doing this and by bagging my bananas, I can make my bananas last for a week after a trip to the store. That is, if the kids don't eat them all.

If your family eats a lot of packaged granola bars, try this recipe for a homemade—and much more economical—substitute. As soon as they've cooled, I wrap the bars individually in plastic wrap so they're ready to grab and throw into a lunch bag, backpack, or my purse.

Honey-Granola Bars

makes 18 bars   prep time: 40 minutes

1½ cups granola cereal (any brand)

1½ cups quick-cooking oats

1¼ cups all-purpose flour

2 teaspoons ground cinnamon

1 teaspoon baking powder

½ cup (1 stick) butter, softened at room temperature

½ cup honey

1 cup firmly packed brown sugar

3 large eggs

1 teaspoon vanilla extract

½ cup raisins

1. Preheat oven to 350°F. Grease a 9 x 13-inch baking pan.

2. Combine granola, oats, flour, cinnamon, and baking powder in a large bowl. Beat butter, honey, brown sugar, eggs, and vanilla together in a medium bowl. Fold butter mixture into flour mixture just until combined. Mix in raisins.

3. Press dough firmly into prepared baking pan and bake until medium brown, 25 to 30 minutes. Cool in pan on a wire rack for 10 minutes. The bars will firm up as they cool. Carefully cut into 18 rectangular bars. Cool completely. Wrap individually (if desired) and store at room temperature.

I was given this recipe by a neighbor not long after my husband and I bought our first home. It's a delicious use for pumpkin, and the streusel topping makes it extra special. But if you're short on time, just spoon a little brown sugar on top of each muffin before baking.

Pumpkin Muffins with Streusel Topping

makes 18 muffins   prep time: 45 minutes

2 cups all-purpose flour
¾ cup granulated sugar
1½ teaspoons baking powder
½ teaspoon salt
½ teaspoon ground cinnamon
½ teaspoon ground nutmeg
½ cup (1 stick) butter
½ cup raisins

One 16-ounce can solid-pack pumpkin
2 large eggs
¾ cup milk

Streusel Topping:
½ cup all-purpose flour
½ cup firmly packed brown sugar
¼ cup (½ stick) cold butter

1. Preheat oven to 400°F. Grease and flour a 12-cup muffin tin.

2. Combine flour, granulated sugar, baking powder, salt, cinnamon, and nutmeg in a large bowl. Cut in butter with a fork or pastry blender until butter is evenly dispersed and mixture looks crumbly. Stir in raisins.

3. In another large bowl, whisk together pumpkin, eggs, and milk until well combined. Add to flour mixture and mix lightly just until combined. Spoon into prepared muffin cups, filling each three-quarters full.

4. Combine streusel topping ingredients in a small bowl. With clean hands, rub butter into other ingredients until mixture is crumbly. Sprinkle each muffin with about 1 tablespoon streusel topping. Bake until set when touched, 20 to 25 minutes. Repeat with remaining batter and streusel.

These moist muffins are delicious and easy to make. For additional blueberry flavor, try adding ½ cup of fresh or frozen berries to the batter when you add the yogurt.

Blueberry–Poppy Seed Muffins

makes 18 muffins   prep time: 40 minutes

2 cups all-purpose flour
1 tablespoon poppy seeds
½ teaspoon salt
½ teaspoon baking soda
1 cup sugar, divided
½ cup (1 stick) butter, softened at room
    temperature

2 large eggs
½ cup blueberry yogurt
¼ cup milk
1 teaspoon vanilla extract

super-saver idea

In my opinion, muffins should be a staple in any frugal kitchen. They make for an extremely affordable and portable snack or breakfast. I make them in big batches and freeze them, individually wrapped, for later use. Let muffins thaw at room temperature or in the microwave. Any meal, however simple, feels like a treat when you have fresh bread to eat.

1. Preheat oven to 400°F. Grease and flour a 12-cup muffin tin.

2. In a medium-size bowl, combine flour, poppy seeds, salt, and baking soda.

3. In a large bowl, cream together ¾ cup sugar and butter. Beat in eggs, 1 at a time. Add yogurt, milk, and vanilla; mix until smooth. Stir in flour mixture until just moistened.

4. Spoon batter into prepared muffin cups, filling each three-quarters full. Evenly sprinkle top of each muffin with remaining ¼ cup sugar, reserving some sugar for remaining batter. Bake until edges of muffins are lightly browned and a tester inserted into the center comes out clean, 20 to 25 minutes. Let cool a couple of minutes. Run a knife around the edge of each cup to loosen muffins, and invert tin. Repeat with remaining batter. Serve warm or let cool on a wire rack.

Here's my adaptation of another recipe my mom used to make regularly. Instead of baking these all at once, you make a big batch of batter, then bake only as many muffins as you need at one time. As the recipe implies, you can keep the batter in the fridge, tightly covered, for up to 6 weeks. It never lasts that long at our house, though.

You can add raisins to the batter just before you bake the muffins, if you like, as well as give them a sprinkle of sugar to coax suspicious kids into taking the first bite. (Once they taste 'em, they'll love them!)

6-Week Bran Muffins

makes 6 dozen muffins   prep time: 30 minutes

1 cup boiling water

3 cups bran cereal (like All-Bran or Raisin Bran), divided

½ cup vegetable shortening, melted, or vegetable oil

1½ cups sugar

2 large eggs, beaten

2 cups buttermilk (or make your own; see Super-Saver Idea on page 188)

2½ cups all-purpose flour

1 tablespoon baking soda

1 tablespoon salt

1. Pour boiling water over 1 cup bran cereal in the largest bowl you've got, and let stand until water is absorbed. Stir in melted shortening until well combined.
2. In a large bowl, combine remaining 2 cups cereal, sugar, eggs, and buttermilk; set aside. In another bowl, sift together flour, baking soda, and salt. Add buttermilk mixture to the cereal mixture in first bowl, stirring until combined. Then add flour mixture, stirring again until just combined. Store batter in refrigerator, tightly covered, up to 6 weeks.
3. To make muffins, preheat oven to 400°F. Grease and flour a muffin tin. Spoon batter into muffin cups, filling each three-quarters full. Bake until tops of muffins feel set when touched, 20 to 25 minutes.

My ten-year-old son likes to make this recipe for our family. The donuts have a crispy outside and a lovely soft interior. I do help him with the frying of the donuts. If you've never made homemade donuts, give this recipe a try. You may be surprised at how easy it is!

Orange-Glazed Homemade Donuts

makes 1 dozen donuts   prep time: about 2 hours, including 1 hour to rise

1 tablespoon active dry yeast

½ cup warm water (not hotter than 110°F)

3 cups all-purpose flour

¼ cup granulated sugar

1 tablespoon baking powder

1 teaspoon salt

½ cup buttermilk (or make your own; see Super-Saver Idea on page 188)

3 tablespoons vegetable shortening, melted

Glaze:

2½ cups confectioners' sugar

¼ cup milk

1 teaspoon grated orange zest

Vegetable oil for frying (at least 2 to 3 cups)

1. Combine yeast and warm water in a large bowl and let stand 5 minutes. If yeast is good, it will start to foam.

2. Measure 2 cups flour into a large bowl and mix in granulated sugar, baking powder, and salt. Add buttermilk, yeast mixture, and melted shortening; mix well. Add enough of remaining flour to make a soft dough.

3. Turn dough onto a floured work surface and knead for a minute or two. Roll dough out until ½ inch thick and cut with a donut cutter. If you don't have one, use a large glass tumbler to cut the outside of donuts and a small lid (like on the top of a bottle of cooking oil) to cut hole in center.

4. Place donuts on wax paper or on a lightly floured counter. Cover with a light cloth or another piece of wax paper. Let rise about an hour. (The donuts will puff even more during cooking.)

5. To make glaze, combine confectioners' sugar, milk, and orange zest in a medium-size bowl, stirring until smooth. Set aside.

6. Fill a deep medium-size pot with 2 to 3 inches oil. (I use a pot that fits just

3 donuts at once so I don't have to use so much oil.) Heat oil over medium heat to 325° or 350°F. If you don't have a thermometer, heat oil 3 to 4 minutes; check temperature by frying one donut. The first side of the donut should get a nice medium brown in about a minute, at which point you should carefully flip it over and cook for another minute on the other side. If donut gets dark brown in under a minute, the oil is too hot; adjust the temperature as necessary. Also, oil will get hotter the longer it heats. After your first batch, you'll need to turn the burner down a little so donuts don't cook too fast. You can also add a bit more oil to the hot oil to cool the temperature down even more. However, don't let oil cool too much or donuts will cook too slowly and be overly greasy. Using tongs, remove donuts to paper towels to drain.

7. While donuts are still hot, using a knife, spread glaze over the tops, allowing excess to drip off. Let donuts cool completely, or serve them warm. Or make a double batch so you can eat half warm and half later!

* ◆ ◆ ◆ ◆ ◆ ◆ ◆ ◆ ◆

Enlist your kids to help you peel and slice the apples for this yummy dessert.

Easy Apple Turnovers

makes 6 to 8 turnovers   prep time: 30 minutes

2 tablespoons butter, divided
6 apples (any kind is fine), peeled, cored, and thinly sliced
¼ cup sugar (or to taste)

⅛ teaspoon ground cinnamon
⅛ teaspoon ground nutmeg
Six to eight 8-inch flour tortillas
Maple syrup and chopped nuts for serving

1. Melt 1 tablespoon butter in a large skillet over medium heat. Add apples and cook until tender, 6 to 8 minutes, stirring a few times. Add sugar, cinnamon, and nutmeg; cook for aout 2 more minutes, stirring to combine.
2. Place tortillas on a clean work surface. Divide sautéed apples evenly among tortillas. In a large skillet over medium-high heat, melt remaining 1 tablespoon butter. Fold tortillas, then brown for a couple of minutes on each side in hot butter.
3. To serve, drizzle each turnover with a little maple syrup and sprinkle with chopped nuts. Serve hot.

Last year my mother spent a month volunteering in a rural hospital in Ethiopia. One morning when she had a class to teach, she brought these donuts for the nurses to eat. The nurses prayed over the food—and then ate every bite. Apparently this recipe tastes good anywhere in the world.

Baked Apple "Donuts"

makes 2 dozen donuts   prep time: 45 minutes

3 cups all-purpose flour

1 cup sugar

1 tablespoon baking powder

1 teaspoon salt

1 teaspoon ground nutmeg

½ cup vegetable shortening

2 large eggs, beaten

1 cup milk

2 cups cored and finely diced apples

Topping:

½ cup (1 stick) butter

1 cup sugar

2 teaspoons ground cinnamon

super-saver idea

Lots of people think that paper liners for muffin tins are essential. I've found that a little shortening and flour work every bit as well—maybe better, since muffins often don't want to release from those papers anyway.

1. Preheat oven to 350°F. Grease and flour a 12-cup muffin tin.

2. In a large bowl, combine flour, sugar, baking powder, salt, and nutmeg using a fork. Add shortening and work into mixture using a fork or pastry blender until mixture looks like coarse crumbs.

3. Combine eggs, milk, and apples. Add to flour mixture; stir just until blended. Spoon batter into prepared muffin cups, filling each cup three-quarters full. Bake until donuts are light to medium brown, about 20 to 25 minutes.

4. While donuts bake, melt butter for topping. Set aside. In a small bowl, combine sugar and cinnamon. When donuts are done and before they have a chance to cool, remove from pan and dip in butter then in sugar. Repeat with remaining batter and topping. Any leftover donuts can be frozen for an easy breakfast later.

With a cookie base and chocolate–peanut butter top, these taste just like Reese's Peanut Butter Cups.

Chocolate–Peanut Butter Cookie Bars

makes one 9 x 13-inch pan, about 18 bars   prep time: 40 minutes

1 cup (2 sticks) butter, softened at
   room temperature
1 cup firmly packed brown sugar
1 large egg
1½ teaspoons vanilla extract

½ teaspoon salt
2 cups all-purpose flour
8 ounces semisweet chocolate chips
¼ cup peanut butter
¾ cup salted roasted peanuts, chopped

1. Preheat oven to 350°F. Line a 9 x 13-inch baking pan with parchment paper.

2. In a large bowl, cream together butter and brown sugar until light and fluffy. Add egg and vanilla; mix. Add salt and flour slowly until everything is well mixed.

3. Spread batter evenly across bottom of prepared baking pan. Bake on center rack of oven until edges begin to pull away from sides of pan, about 15 minutes.

4. Meanwhile, combine chocolate chips and peanut butter in a microwave-safe bowl; microwave on High 20 seconds at a time, stirring each time and repeating until chocolate is just melted and blended with peanut butter.

5. When cookie layer is completely ready, remove it from oven and cool 5 minutes. Spread chocolate–peanut butter mixture over the surface. Sprinkle peanuts evenly over the top. Cover with plastic wrap and chill until chocolate is firm. Cool completely in pan before cutting into squares and enjoying.

quick tip

Many recipes call for softened butter, but if you're like me, when you decide to bake you don't want to wait. The good news is that you can soften butter in the microwave. But remember, you're aiming for soft, not liquid. Many cakes and cookies will not turn out right if you liquefy the butter. In my microwave, I can soften 2 sticks of butter in 20 to 30 seconds, turning once during the heating time.

egg-free cooking

If you're looking to adapt a cookie recipe to be egg free, first try substituting 2 tablespoons water for each egg called for in the recipe. Without the egg, the cookies will be a little denser and more brownie-like, but many people prefer their cookies that way. If you're having issues with the cookie dough not holding together, try whisking 1 tablespoon cornstarch into 2 tablespoons water and adding that mixture in place of each egg in the recipe. If you would like to make an egg-free cake, try substituting half a banana for each egg in the recipe.

These cookies were adapted by my daughter when we were looking for a good egg-free cookie recipe. It's so good you won't even miss the eggs!

Choco-Choco-Chip Cookies

makes 3 dozen cookies   prep time: 45 minutes

1 cup (2 sticks) butter, softened at
   room temperature
1 tablespoon molasses
1 tablespoon vanilla extract
⅓ cup water
¾ cup granulated sugar
¾ cup firmly packed brown sugar

2½ cups all-purpose flour
½ cup unsweetened cocoa powder
1 teaspoon baking powder
½ teaspoon baking soda
½ teaspoon salt
2 cups semisweet chocolate chips

1. Preheat oven to 375°F.
2. In a large bowl, cream together butter, molasses, vanilla, and water. Add sugars and mix well.
3. In a medium-size bowl, mix together flour, cocoa powder, baking powder, baking soda, and salt. Add flour mixture to sugar mixture and stir well to combine thoroughly. Stir in chocolate chips until well mixed.
4. Shape dough into 1-inch balls and place 1 inch apart on an ungreased baking

sheet. Bake until edges are firm but centers are still soft, about 8 minutes. These cookies can be stored in a tightly covered container at room temperature for 3 to 4 days, and they freeze beautifully. In fact, some people at our house prefer to eat them frozen.

◆ ◆ ◆ ◆ ◆ ◆ ◆ ◆ ◆ ◆

Let your kids help you roll out the balls when you make this egg-free, no-bake recipe.

Peanut Butter Balls

makes 30 pieces   prep time: 1 hour 45 minutes

¼ cup semisweet chocolate chips
1 cup sifted confectioners' sugar
½ cup creamy peanut butter
3 tablespoons butter, softened at room
    temperature
1 pound chocolate or almond bark
    (found near chocolate chips in the baking
    section of the grocery store)

1. Whiz chocolate chips in a food processor a few seconds or chop into small bits with a knife.
2. In a medium-size bowl, cream together chocolate bits, confectioners' sugar, peanut butter, and butter until well mixed. Shape dough into 1-inch balls and place on a baking sheet lined with wax paper. Refrigerate for about 30 minutes.
3. Melt chocolate or almond bark per package directions. Drop balls 1 at a time into melted bark. Using a fork, remove balls from chocolate, letting the excess drip off. Place balls back on wax paper. Let stand until dry, about an hour. Store tightly covered in a cool, dry place for up to a week.

mom to mom

Cookies are a great way to introduce your children to cooking. As soon as they can read reliably, usually by the age of eight or nine, they can be taught to measure ingredients and follow a simple recipe. Sure, there may be a flop or two, especially the first time you hand them the cookbook and let them make something from start to finish by themselves. But the pride they have in the final product and the life skills they learn as they practice are well worth the occasional mishap.

If you like your brownies rich and fudgelike, this recipe is for you! Melting butter and sugar on the stovetop before stirring it into the batter is one thing that makes this recipe extra yummy.

Soft Rich Brownies

makes one 9 x 13-inch pan, about 18 brownies   prep time: 45 minutes

I like cookies as well as anyone, and I'm delighted that my kids love to make them. But as a busy mom, I tend to gravitate towards bar recipes when I'm making dessert. Bar recipes get me in and out of the kitchen more quickly, and save me the time of fussing over batch after batch of cookies.

1 cup (2 sticks) butter
2 cups firmly packed brown sugar
2 cups semisweet or dark chocolate chips
2 cups all-purpose flour
¼ cup good-quality unsweetened cocoa powder
½ teaspoon salt
4 large eggs
1 teaspoon vanilla extract

1. Preheat oven to 350°F. Grease a 9 x 13-inch baking pan.
2. Combine butter and brown sugar in a medium pan over medium heat until simmering but not quite boiling, stirring to combine. Sugar crystals should be dissolved. Remove from heat and add chocolate chips, stirring until melted. Cool a few minutes.
3. In a large bowl, combine flour, cocoa powder, and salt. Add eggs, 1 at a time, and vanilla; mix until combined. Add chocolate mixture and mix well. Pour batter into prepared pan. Bake for 28 to 30 minutes (you want this gooey, but set). Let cool completely in pan on a wire rack, then cut into squares and enjoy!

Years ago I was given a recipe for a dump cake that called for a boxed cake mix as well as canned cherry pie filling, neither of which I keep in the pantry. I adapted the recipe using what I had and discovered that many kinds of canned fruit work just as well. Yes, this recipe calls for a lot of butter. But remember, it's a dessert! Don't eat it every day and don't eat a whole pan yourself, and you'll be fine.

No-Mix Dump Cake

makes one 9 x 13-inch pan   prep time: 35 minutes

2 quarts canned peaches or apricots
 in juice
2 cups all-purpose flour
1 cup granulated sugar

½ cup firmly packed brown sugar
1 teaspoon baking powder
½ teaspoon baking soda
¾ cup (1½ sticks) cold butter, cut into pats

1. Preheat oven to 400°F.
2. Drain juice from 1 quart of fruit; set aside juice for a different purpose, such as mixing it with tomorrow's breakfast orange juice. Pour remaining fruit with juice plus drained fruit into a 9 x 13-inch pan.
3. In a medium-size bowl, combine flour, sugars, baking powder, and baking soda. Sprinkle mixture evenly over fruit. Arrange butter pats evenly over the top.
4. Bake until cake is browned, with crispy bits and little bubbles of juice filling popping up through the crust here and there, about 30 minutes. Spoon into bowls while still warm, and serve with ice cream, if you like.

Variations: If you don't happen to have home-canned fruit, store-bought is fine. You'll need about 8 cups drained fruit with about 2 cups liquid. A variety of canned fruit will work well, including fruit cocktail, apples, peaches, and pineapple. Experiment and see what your family enjoys the most.

I adapted this recipe from one I found in *Taste of Home* magazine. Making your own press-in pie crust is almost as quick as using a store-bought crust, and a lot cheaper. You can make this recipe with apples if you like, baking an additional 10 minutes.

Cheddar-Pear Pie

makes one 8- or 9-inch pie   prep time: 50 minutes

1 Push-in Pie Crust (recipe follows)
4 large ripe pears, peeled, cored, and
  thinly sliced
⅓ cup sugar
1 tablespoon cornstarch
¼ teaspoon salt

Topping:
½ cup shredded Cheddar cheese
½ cup all-purpose flour
¼ cup (½ stick) butter, melted
¼ cup sugar
¼ teaspoon salt

1. Preheat oven to 400°F.

2. Press crust into an 8- or 9-inch pie pan.

3. In a large bowl, combine pears, sugar, cornstarch, and salt. Pour into pie crust. In a medium-size bowl, combine topping ingredients until crumbly. Sprinkle evenly over filling.

4. Bake until crust is golden and cheese is melted, 25 to 35 minutes. Let cool on a wire rack for 10 minutes. Serve warm. Store any leftovers in the refrigerator.

Many people choose not to make pie because they're intimidated by pie crust. This incredibly easy recipe is my go-to pie crust. I don't have the time or patience to roll out, then coax a crust into a pan. This crust works well for pumpkin pie or a fruit pie with a crumble topping. If you would like to use this when making a quiche, decrease the sugar to 1 teaspoon. I often have my children help out with pushing the dough into the pans.

Push-in Pie Crust

makes one 8- or 9-inch pie crust   prep time: 5 minutes

1½ cups all-purpose flour
2 tablespoons sugar
1 teaspoon salt

½ cup vegetable oil
2 tablespoons milk

1. Place flour, sugar, and salt in an 8- or 9-inch pie pan. Mix with a fork. Add oil and milk. Mix again, until all ingredients are combined.

2. Press dough into the bottom and against the sides of pan with your fingertips. If you like, you can make a scalloped edge on the crust, pinching dough between your thumb and index finger.

3. If you are using this crust for a pudding-type pie, bake empty pie shell in a preheated 425°F oven for 10 to 12 minutes. Otherwise, bake for the amount of time recommended in your pie recipe.

The most time-consuming part of this recipe is slicing the apples.

Apple Crisp with Crunchy Oat and Brown Sugar Topping

makes one 9 x 13-inch or two 8-inch square casserole dishes   prep time: 1 hour

8 apples (any kind but tart apples are best)
½ cup (1 stick) butter
½ cup all-purpose flour
1 cup quick-cooking oats

1 cup firmly packed brown sugar
1 tablespoon ground cinnamon
1 teaspoon ground cloves (optional)
1 teaspoon salt

things I love!

apple peelers

An apple peeler is a great gadget to have around, especially if you like to make pies. My children may love this gadget even more than I do. A good hand-cranked apple peeler can peel, core, and slice one apple in less than a min- ute. You'd have to be pretty fast with a knife to do that by hand! You can find apple peelers at kitchen supply stores, hardware stores, and sometimes at yard sales, so keep an eye out.

1. Preheat oven to 375°F.

2. Peel, core, and thinly slice apples. Spread slices over the bottom of a 9 x 13-inch or two 8-inch square casserole dish(es).

3. In a small bowl, soften butter until a little melted but not totally liquid. In most microwaves, you can do this by cooking on High 15 seconds, turning butter over, and zapping for another 10 seconds. Combine flour, oats, brown sugar, cinnamon, cloves (if using), and salt in a medium- size bowl. Add butter and mix with a spoon or your hands until dry ingredients start to clump together and butter is dispersed. Sprinkle crumb topping over apples. If you used 2 smaller dishes, at this point you can cover and freeze 1 of the pans to bake later.

4. Bake crisp until the topping is light to medium brown and you can see a little bubbly juice at the edges of pan, 25 to 30 minutes. Serve warm or cool, with whipped topping or ice cream if you like.

Your family probably won't even know that this delicious chocolate cake contains zucchini. This is a great recipe to make when your garden is exploding with them. You can sprinkle it with a little confectioners' sugar once it has cooled or top it with your favorite frosting.

Chocolate-Zucchini Cake

makes one 9 x 13-inch pan   prep time: 1 hour 20 minutes

2 cups all-purpose flour
¼ cup wheat germ (optional)
2 cups sugar
¾ cup unsweetened cocoa powder
2 teaspoons baking soda
1 teaspoon baking powder

1 teaspoon ground cinnamon
½ teaspoon salt
4 large eggs
1½ cups vegetable oil
3 cups shredded zucchini
¾ cup chopped walnuts

1. Preheat oven to 350°F. Grease and flour a 9 x 13-inch baking pan, tapping out any excess flour.

2. Combine flour, wheat germ (if using), sugar, cocoa powder, baking soda, baking powder, cinnamon, and salt in a medium-size bowl. Add eggs and beat for 1 minute, then add oil and mix well. Fold in zucchini and nuts until evenly distributed. Pour batter into prepared pan.

3. Bake until a knife inserted into the center comes out clean, 50 to 60 minutes. Cool cake completely in pan on a wire rack.

If you're partial to boxed pudding, give this recipe a try. You may be surprised at how easy it is to make your own pudding from scratch.

Homemade Vanilla Pudding

serves 4   prep time: 20 minutes, plus 1 hour chilling time

mom to mom

Occasionally when I'm making pudding, I get sidetracked by a needy child and end up scalding a bit of the pudding on the bottom of the pan. If this ever happens to you and your pudding is only a little scorched, you may still be able to save it by very quickly dumping the pudding mixture into a different pot and continuing to cook it over low heat. Be sure not to scrape the burned bits off the bottom of the first pan, as that tends to be where most of the "burned" flavor will be. Incidentally, you can also save a mildly scorched pot of soup or chili this way. In an ideal world, you wouldn't need this trick. But most of us don't live there!

⅓ cup sugar

1½ tablespoons cornstarch

⅛ teaspoon salt

2 cups milk

2 teaspoons vanilla extract

1 tablespoon butter

1. Combine sugar, cornstarch, and salt in a medium-size saucepan. Whisk in about 1 cup milk, stirring until smooth. Whisk in remaining 1 cup milk until well combined. Cook over medium heat, stirring constantly and gently, until mixture begins to thicken. Reduce heat to low and continue to cook 2 to 3 more minutes, stirring gently.
2. Remove from heat and add vanilla and butter, stirring until butter is melted. Pour pudding into serving dishes. Cover with plastic wrap, laying the plastic right on the surface of the pudding to keep a skin from developing. Chill until cool and set, about 1 hour.

Chocolate Pudding: Increase cornstarch to ¼ cup, decrease vanilla to 1 teaspoon, and add ¼ cup unsweetened cocoa powder along with sugar, cornstarch, and salt.

chapter 12

entertaining
on a
budget

Just because you're on a budget doesn't mean you can't have a good time. This chapter contains menus for when you want to entertain in style without breaking the bank or spending your guests' entire visit in the kitchen. The main-course recipes in this chapter are going to cost you a little more than those elsewhere in this book, but they'll still be considerably cheaper than going out to dinner.

Each menu contains a "Game Plan." This is my take on how to time your prep and cooking for the greatest efficiency.

Elegant Make-Ahead Chicken Dinner

Baked Chicken Kiev
Easy Scalloped Potatoes • Strawberry-Spinach Salad
Cheddar-Pear Pie (page 244)

game plan..

Here's a great menu for the hostess who doesn't want to be scurrying around doing last-minute prep before a dinner party. All four recipes can be made ahead of time. The potatoes and chicken can be cooked in the same oven. The potatoes take a few minutes longer than the chicken, so you'll want to put them in first.

For our daughter's eighteenth birthday, we had a big dinner party at church, to which we invited about 30 people. This wonderful recipe was what we chose to serve as the main dish. It can be made ahead of time, looks beautiful on the dinner plate, and (most importantly) is simply delicious. You can make it with chicken breasts if you're serving a bunch of big eaters, but I prefer to use thighs. For the average person, one thigh is a reasonable serving, and you can always prepare an extra piece or two for seconds for the more enthusiastic diners in your group.

Baked Chicken Kiev

serves 8   prep time: 1 hour, plus 4 hours chilling time

8 boneless, skinless chicken thighs
1 cup Ritz or saltine cracker crumbs
½ cup grated Parmesan cheese
1½ teaspoons dried oregano, divided
2 teaspoons garlic powder

½ teaspoon black pepper
¼ cup (½ stick) butter, softened
1 tablespoon chopped fresh parsley
1 cup Monterey Jack cheese
¼ cup (½ stick) butter, melted

1. Place chicken thighs, 1 at a time, between wax paper or plastic wrap and gently pound with a meat mallet until about ½ inch thick. Set aside.

2. Get out 2 flat bowls or pie pans. In bowl #1, place cracker crumbs, Parmesan, 1 teaspoon oregano, garlic powder, and pepper; stir to combine. In bowl #2, stir together softened butter, parsley, and remaining ½ teaspoon oregano.

3. Cut Jack cheese into strips about 2 inches long and ½ inch wide. Spread about ½ tablespoon herb butter mixture across the inside of each flattened chicken thigh. Lay a strip of cheese across butter mixture. Fold the edge of the chicken over filling and roll up cutlet, egg-roll style, tucking in sides to enclose filling.

4. Dip each bundle in melted butter and let any excess drip off briefly. Roll in cracker crumb mixture until evenly coated. Place chicken bundles in a large casserole dish, seam sides down, so they don't touch each other. Drizzle with any remaining melted butter. Cover and refrigerate at least 4 hours, or until the next day.

5. Preheat oven to 375°F. Bake, uncovered, until chicken is lightly browned and the largest piece of chicken is no longer pink when lightly slashed, 35 to 45 minutes.

company's coming!

When I am having company over, I usually assign one or two of my children the job of setting the table nicely. I try to have them begin this task several hours ahead of time if possible. This allows the children enough time to shine the glasses, gather together matching silverware, and fold the napkins in an unusual way if they desire. (Try googling napkin folding if you need inspiration.) For an occasion like Thanksgiving, sometimes the children will even decide to make place cards so that guests will know where they can sit. Place cards can be written by hand, or if your children are computer savvy, they may enjoy using a computer to design and print out place cards.

This is my go-to recipe when I'm asked to contribute something to a holiday dinner. These potatoes are easy to make and a big hit with kids.

Easy Scalloped Potatoes

serves 8   prep time: 1 hour

32 ounces frozen shredded hash brown potatoes, thawed
1 medium-size onion, peeled
1 chicken bouillon cube
1 cup hot water
¼ cup (½ stick) butter

¼ cup all-purpose flour
1 cup milk
1 cup sour cream
½ teaspoon garlic salt
1 cup shredded Cheddar cheese
1 cup crushed corn flakes

super-saver idea

To make this recipe even more affordable, shred your own potatoes in the food processor instead of using frozen hash browns. You'll need about 12 medium-size peeled russet potatoes, or enough to make 10 cups of shredded potatoes.

1. Preheat oven to 375°F.
2. Squeeze out excess water from thawed hash brown potatoes. Mince onion very fine. (If your kids dislike onion, try chopping it in the food processor and chances are they won't even know it's there.) Dissolve bouillon cube in hot water.
3. Melt butter in a medium-size skillet over medium heat. Add onion and cook until softened, 2 to 3 minutes, stirring a few times. Add flour and stir well. Add milk and whisk briskly. Heat until milk is warm. Add chicken bouillon, increase heat to medium-high, and continue to heat, stirring occasionally, until bubbly.
4. Remove skillet from heat. Stir in sour cream and garlic salt. Combine creamed mixture with thawed hash browns in a 9 x 13-inch casserole dish. Sprinkle with cheese, then corn flakes. (You can make this casserole up to 2 days ahead of time and keep refrigerated.)
5. Bake until hot and bubbly, 40 to 50 minutes.

My sister-in-law brings this salad to family gatherings, where it always gets rave reviews. You can serve it immediately if you wish. But it's also wonderful after the dressing has marinated the strawberries a while and the spinach becomes limp.

Strawberry-Spinach Salad

serves 8   prep time: 20 minutes

Dressing:
½ cup sugar
3 tablespoons fresh lemon juice
3 tablespoons white wine vinegar
2 tablespoons vegetable oil
1½ teaspoons poppy seeds

Salad:
2 cups fresh strawberries (½ pound)
1 small red or Vidalia onion
1 medium-size cucumber
One 10-ounce package baby spinach
⅓ cup chopped almonds or peanuts

1. Combine dressing ingredients in a small bowl. Whisk until well blended and sugar has dissolved. Cover; refrigerate until ready to use.

2. Hull, then slice strawberries. Slice onion very thinly. Peel cucumber; cut it in half lengthwise, then slice crosswise.

3. Put spinach in a large serving bowl; add strawberries, onion, and cucumber. Whisk dressing vigorously; pour over salad, gently tossing to coat. Sprinkle with chopped nuts.

Christmas Morning Breakfast

Stuffed French Toast Strata
Homemade "Eggnog" or Hot Mulled Cider
Honeyed Fruit Salad

game plan

This breakfast can be made almost entirely the night before. In the morning all you have to do is stick the French toast strata in the oven and set the table! On a morning that you have breakfast guests, what could be easier or more delicious?

This is our traditional Christmas morning breakfast. I love that we can make it the night before and just pop it in the oven in the morning. Also, it can be made egg-free: just add a little more milk instead of eggs. We make a tiny casserole dish of this egg-free for our egg-allergic child. Any leftovers can easily be warmed in the microwave. You could also make this in two 8-inch pans and freeze one pan for later.

Stuffed French Toast Strata

serves 6 to 8   prep time: 1 hour, plus at least 2 hours chilling time

One 1-pound loaf French bread
One 8-ounce package cold cream cheese
8 large eggs
2½ cups milk
6 tablespoons (¾ stick) butter, melted

½ cup store-bought or homemade (page 272) pancake syrup
1 teaspoon ground cinnamon
1 teaspoon vanilla extract

1. Cut French bread loaf roughly into ¾-inch cubes (about 12 cups bread cubes). Cut cream cheese into small cubes. Grease a 9 x 13-inch baking pan. Place half of bread cubes in prepared pan. Top with cream cheese cubes, then remaining bread cubes.

2. Whisk together eggs, milk, melted butter, pancake syrup, cinnamon, and vanilla until well combined. Pour egg mixture evenly over bread and cheese cubes. Using a metal spatula, slightly press down layers to moisten all bread.

3. Cover pan with plastic wrap and refrigerate at least 2 hours and up to 24 hours.

4. Preheat oven to 325°F.

5. Remove plastic from pan and bake strata until the center appears to be set and eggs are golden, 40 to 45 minutes. Let stand 10 minutes before slicing.

Variation: Try sprinkling 2 cups blueberries in with the layer of cream cheese and serving the strata with blueberry syrup.

◦ ◦ ◦ ◦ ◦ ◦ ◦ ◦ ◦

Eggnog is ridiculously expensive in the grocery store. Even with the instant pudding mix, this delicious recipe is very affordable. It's also lower in fat than the store version and egg-free. It tastes best if you refrigerate it for a couple of hours before serving. To disperse the spices evenly, remember to stir each time you pour a portion.

Homemade "Eggnog"

serves 6 to 8   prep time: 10 minutes, plus chilling time

One 3-ounce package instant French
   vanilla pudding mix
½ gallon milk (2% or whole milk will
   give the richest flavor)

½ cup sugar
1 tablespoon vanilla extract
½ teaspoon ground cinnamon
½ teaspoon ground nutmeg

1. Whisk together pudding mix and about 1 cup milk. When it's all blended and dissolved, add sugar, vanilla, and spices. Pour into a 2-quart pitcher, add remaining milk, and stir well.

If eggnog is too rich for you, try this hot fruit drink.

Hot Mulled Cider

serves 8   prep time: 25 minutes

½ teaspoon allspice berries

1 cinnamon stick

½ teaspoon whole cloves

4 cups apple cider

½ cup sugar

1 cup orange juice

1 cup pineapple juice

¼ cup lemon juice

2 cups ginger ale, at room temperature

1. Tie allspice, cinnamon, and cloves in a cheesecloth bag. If you don't have cheesecloth, bundle them into a coffee filter and tie with string.

2. Pour cider into a large pot, add spice bag, and turn heat to medium. As cider begins to warm, add sugar and orange, pineapple, and lemon juices, stirring until sugar is dissolved. Bring to a simmer, but do not boil.

3. Remove spice bag. Add ginger ale just before serving. Ladle into cups.

◆ ◆ ◆ ◆ ◆ ◆ ◆ ◆ ◆

This easy salad can be adapted to any fruit you happen to have around. Be sure to toss the apples well with the lemon juice to prevent browning.

Honeyed Fruit Salad

serves 8   prep time: 15 minutes, plus at least 8 hours chilling time

3 apples, left unpeeled, cored and
   cut into bite-size pieces

¼ cup lemon juice

Two 11-ounce cans mandarin oranges,
   drained

1½ cups raisins

One 14-ounce can sliced peaches,
   or 2 cups sliced ripe peaches

¾ cup orange juice

⅓ cup honey

1 teaspoon ground cinnamon

1. Toss apples with lemon juice in a bowl. Add oranges, raisins, and peaches.

2. In a 2-cup measuring cup, combine orange juice, honey, and cinnamon until well combined and pour over fruit. Gently toss to coat fruit with mixture.

3. Cover with plastic wrap and chill at least 8 hours or overnight.

company's coming!

My mother in law is one of the most gracious hostesses that I know. One of the things that she does when having a slew of company over is to give various guests simple prep tasks. One of the guys usually gets to cut the meat. Someone else helps make punch. A few of the children get to bring up the children's table and set it up. Someone else stirs gravy. Sometimes hostesses hesitate to get help from guests, but guests almost always appreciate being included in the happy hubbub of preparing for a holiday meal.

Spectacular Holiday Dinner

Pork Crown Roast with Cranberry Stuffing

Doctored-Up Cranberry Sauce • **Garlic Mashed Potatoes**

Ginger- and Orange-Glazed Baby Carrots

Soft Rich Brownies (page 242)

game plan

This menu is a little more time consuming than some, but the wow factor makes it worth it. The nice thing is that you can get the pork into the oven within a few minutes, then use the first part of the cooking time to put together the stuffing. Once you have the stuffing done, work on the potatoes. Half an hour before the meat is done, you can make the carrots and cranberry sauce. Total cooking time will be 3 to 4 hours, but if you approach the meal in an organized fashion, you won't need to be in the kitchen the whole time.

My brother-in-law gave me this recipe for a really amazing-looking company dinner. In my area, pork rib roasts can be bought on sale for $2/pound or less, which makes this a fairly affordable meat. You'll need to request a crown pork roast from your butcher.

The butcher will "French" the ribs (slice the tops of the ribs apart and clean them, so you can put those frilly white booties on them if you want) and tie it into the "crown" shape. Many butchers will do this for free (though you need to supply the booties!).

Pork Crown Roast with Cranberry Stuffing

serves 10 to 12   prep time: 4 hours

One 8- to 10-pound bone-in pork roast

Rub:
2 tablespoons olive oil
4 cloves garlic, minced
2 tablespoons sugar
1 teaspoon sweet paprika
½ teaspoon black pepper
½ teaspoon salt
½ teaspoon ground sage
½ teaspoon ground rosemary

Stuffing:
½ cup (1 stick) butter
1 medium-size carrot, minced

1 medium-size onion, minced
1 cup minced celery
2 cloves garlic, minced
1 cup chopped mushrooms
1 cup canned whole-berry cranberry sauce
  or 1 cup raisins
5 cups dried cubed bread
1 tablespoon dried sage or 2 tablespoons
  chopped fresh
1 teaspoon dried parsley
1 teaspoon salt
½ teaspoon black pepper
1 cup chicken broth

1. Preheat oven to 350°F.

2. Tie roast into a crown and place in a wide shallow roasting pan. Combine olive oil and garlic. Rub mixture all over the inside and outside of crown roast. Mix together remaining rub ingredients, and rub all over meat. Cover all bone ends with small pieces of aluminum foil to keep from burning. Bake 2 hours.

3. To prepare stuffing, melt butter in a large skillet over medium heat. Add carrot, onion, celery, and garlic; cook until softened, 4 to 5 minutes, stirring a few times. Add mushrooms and cranberry sauce; cook until mushrooms soften, 3 to 4 minutes, stirring occasionally.

4. Place bread cubes in a large bowl and add sage, parsley, salt, and pepper. Heat broth in a small saucepan until hot and pour over seasoned bread cubes. Mix until soft. Add sautéed vegetables and mix thoroughly.

5. Remove roast from oven. Spoon stuffing into the center of roast. Return roast to oven; cook until a meat thermometer inserted into the thickest part of roast (away from bone) reads 150°F to 155°F and juices run clear, another 1 to 1½ hours.

6. Remove roast from oven and let rest for 15 minutes. Remove foil from bones and discard. Remove stuffing to a serving dish and slice pork between ribs. Reserve roasting pan juices for Doctored-Up Cranberry Sauce (recipe follows).

Variation: If you want a true "crown" roast, you need to order 12 to 14 ribs so the butcher will have enough to work with. However, if you would like to make this recipe for 6 people, half all the ingredients, then lay ribs flat in a casserole dish to bake for about 1½ hours. The ribs are done when the internal temperature of the meat reaches 150°F. Bake the stuffing for 30 minutes in a separate dish.

* * * * * * * * * *

This lovely sauce adds a sweet-and-sour note that really brings out the wonderful flavor of the crown roast.

Doctored-Up Cranberry Sauce

serves 12   prep time: 25 minutes

One 15-ounce can whole-berry cranberry sauce
½ cup sugar

½ cup reserved roasting pan juices (from recipe above) or chicken broth
½ cup water

1. In a medium-size heavy saucepan, combine cranberry sauce, sugar, and water. Simmer over low heat 15 to 20 minutes.

2. When roast is done, add ½ cup roasting pan juices to cranberry sauce. Bring to a boil, reduce heat to low, and simmer until sauce is somewhat reduced. It will be like a thin gravy. Serve with sliced chops.

This wonderful, filling side dish is made extra special with garlic and sour cream.

Garlic Mashed Potatoes

serves 12   prep time: 30 minutes

12 medium-size russet potatoes
½ cup (1 stick) butter
8 cloves garlic
1 cup sour cream

2 teaspoons salt
1 teaspoon white or black pepper
1 cup milk, or more as needed

To easily remove the peel from multiple cloves of garlic, separate the individual cloves, set them in a small bowl, and microwave for 10 to 15 seconds. After cooking, they'll practically fall out of their peels.

1. Fill a large pot halfway with water and bring to a boil. While water is coming to a boil, peel potatoes and cut each one into 6 to 8 pieces. Put potatoes in boiling water; boil until fork-tender, 15 to 18 minutes.

2. Meanwhile, melt butter in a small saucepan or microwave. Remove from heat. Peel garlic and mash cloves; add to melted butter and mix well. Let stand for a few minutes.

3. Once potatoes are cooked, drain, but leave them in the same pot. Add garlic-butter mixture, sour cream, salt, and pepper. With a hand mixer, mix thoroughly until potatoes are smooth, adding milk until potatoes reach your desired consistency. Scoop into a pretty serving dish, and serve nice and hot.

This fast and easy carrot recipe is a colorful and delicious addition to any meal. It's especially nice paired with a main dish that is somewhat time consuming, like the crown roast.

Ginger- and Orange-Glazed Baby Carrots

serves 12   prep time: 15 minutes

2 pounds baby carrots

½ cup orange juice

¼ cup (½ stick) butter

¼ cup firmly packed brown sugar

2 tablespoons lemon juice

2 teaspoons peeled and grated fresh ginger

2 teaspoons grated orange zest

2 teaspoons dried parsley

2 teaspoons powdered chicken bouillon

1 teaspoon salt

½ teaspoon black pepper

1. Rinse carrots under cold running water and place in a 2-quart microwave-safe casserole dish. Cover and microwave on High 5 to 6 minutes, or until crisp-tender, stirring halfway through. Drain any water that accumulates during cooking.

2. In a medium-size saucepan, combine remaining ingredients and mix well. Add carrots. Bring to a boil and cook, stirring often, until liquid has evaporated and carrots are lightly glazed, 3 to 5 minutes. Serve hot.

super-saver idea

This dish goes together very quickly when using baby carrots. However, regular carrots can be used instead. Simply peel and cut them into pieces similar in size to baby carrots. I like to cut the thick end of the carrot into lengthwise halves or quarters before cutting crosswise into 2-inch pieces. The narrow end of the carrot can be cut crosswise. The object is to get pieces that are roughly similar in size so that they'll cook evenly.

Dill Salmon Dinner

Salmon Roasted in Butter
Rosemary-Roasted Root Vegetables • Cottage Cheese–Dill Rolls
Homemade Chocolate Pudding (page 248)

game plan

For this menu, you'll want to start your preparation by mixing the rolls. While the dough rises, chop the root vegetables. Then shape the rolls and let them rise a little longer. You can bake the rolls and vegetables in the same 375°F oven. The vegetables will take 5 to 10 minutes longer to cook than the rolls. When the rolls are done, place them in a covered bowl to stay warm. At that point you can turn the oven temperature up to 475°F for the salmon. The high temperature at which the salmon cooks will caramelize the root vegetables nicely and finish their cooking.

When I serve salmon, I almost always buy single-serving frozen fillets. In my area I can buy 4 to 6 servings in a package for about $7. You can buy fresh salmon if you wish, but it will cost more. Try seasonings other than the parsley or dill.

Salmon Roasted in Butter

serves 4 to 6   prep time: 15 minutes

2 tablespoons butter

1 tablespoon olive oil

3 tablespoons minced fresh parsley or dill, divided

1 salmon fillet (1½ to 2 pounds), cut into 6 servings

Salt and black pepper to taste

5 or 7 lemon wedges

1. Preheat oven to 475°F.

2. Place butter, olive oil, and 2 tablespoons parsley in a roasting pan that is just big enough to hold salmon in a single layer. Place roasting pan in oven; heat for 5 minutes.

3. Place salmon pieces in hot pan, skin side up. Roast for 5 minutes. Season with salt and pepper. Turn each piece of salmon over; salt and pepper again.

4. Roast 3 to 4 minutes more, depending on thickness of fillet and degree of doneness you prefer. Remove from oven. Spoon a little of the melted butter in the pan over the salmon. Sprinkle with a squeeze of lemon and remaining 1 tablespoon parsley. Serve with lemon wedges.

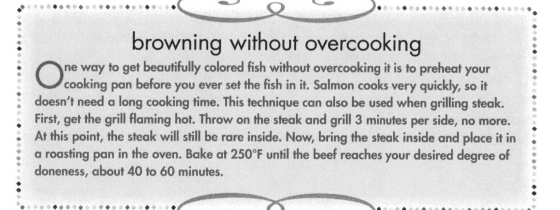

browning without overcooking

One way to get beautifully colored fish without overcooking it is to preheat your cooking pan before you ever set the fish in it. Salmon cooks very quickly, so it doesn't need a long cooking time. This technique can also be used when grilling steak. First, get the grill flaming hot. Throw on the steak and grill 3 minutes per side, no more. At this point, the steak will still be rare inside. Now, bring the steak inside and place it in a roasting pan in the oven. Bake at 250°F until the beef reaches your desired degree of doneness, about 40 to 60 minutes.

Roasting adds an appealing color and a wonderful flavor to affordable root vegetables.

Rosemary-Roasted Root Vegetables

serves 4 to 6   prep time: 30 minutes

1 medium-size sweet potato
3 medium-size russet potatoes
2 medium-size carrots
¼ cup olive oil

2 teaspoons dried rosemary
Salt and black pepper to taste
½ cup grated Parmesan cheese, divided

1. Preheat oven to 375°F. Line a baking sheet with aluminum foil.

2. Peel vegetables; cut them into 1 x 2-inch pieces. (A medium-size potato should be cut into 4 to 6 pieces.) Place potatoes and carrots in a large bowl. Add oil and rosemary, and season generously with salt and pepper. Stir well to thoroughly coat vegetables. Stir in two-thirds of the cheese.

3. Spread vegetables onto prepared baking sheet in a single layer. Sprinkle with remaining cheese. Bake until vegetables are fork-tender and have some nicely browned spots, 20 to 30 minutes. As mentioned in the Game Plan, you can cook them at 475°F the last 10 minutes of cooking time. (Do keep an eye on them to make sure they don't get too dark.)

Remember the cardinal rule of wonderful dinners: Fresh bread makes any meal better. The cottage cheese in these rolls makes them extra rich and delicious.

Cottage Cheese–Dill Rolls

makes 12 rolls   prep time: 1 hour 40 minutes (mostly rising time)

1 tablespoon active dry yeast

½ cup warm water (not hotter than 110°F)

1 tablespoon sugar

3 cups all-purpose flour

1 tablespoon dried minced onion

1 tablespoon dried dillweed

1 teaspoon salt

½ teaspoon baking powder

1 cup cottage cheese

1 large egg

1. Combine yeast, warm water, and sugar in a small bowl. Let stand 5 minutes. If yeast is good, it will begin to foam.

2. In a large bowl, mix together 2 cups flour, onion, dill, salt, and baking powder. Add cottage cheese, egg, and yeast mixture. Mix with a heavy spoon until a soft dough forms. Place dough on a floured counter and knead for 3 to 5 minutes, adding flour as needed until dough feels smooth and elastic and is no longer sticky. Place in a greased bowl, cover with a clean dish towel, and let rise in a warm place for at least 30 minutes.

3. Divide dough into 12 pieces, rolling each into a ball before placing on a greased baking sheet. (Your kids may enjoy helping you with this.) Cover and let rise 20 to 30 minutes.

4. Preheat oven to 375°F.

5. Bake rolls until golden brown on top, 20 to 25 minutes.

chapter 13

the homemade pantry

One simple way to save at the store is to have fewer items on your grocery list. This chapter can help you greatly with that goal. In many cases, it's possible to save several dollars with 10 minutes of work. You probably won't choose to make every item in this chapter, but even choosing one or two recipes a week could add up to several hundred dollars of savings. Plus, it's fun! I always feel good when I can whip up something from ingredients I have on hand instead of always depending on stores to supply my cooking needs with convenience items.

This dressing is one of my family's favorites.

Greek Dressing

makes about 1¼ cups   prep time: 10 minutes

½ cup olive oil

¼ cup water

1 tablespoon Dijon mustard

1 tablespoon sugar

1½ teaspoons garlic powder

1 teaspoon dried oregano

1 teaspoon dried basil

1 teaspoon black pepper

1 teaspoon salt

1 teaspoon onion powder

2 cloves garlic, minced

½ cup red wine vinegar

1. Combine all ingredients in a pint-size container with a tight-fitting lid. Shake well. Store, tightly covered, in refrigerator up to 2 months.

super-saver idea

When you're looking for good storage containers, don't forget to check the dollar store. You can also wash out empty bottles from store-bought dressing and use those. Homemade dressing separates a little faster than store-bought, so choose a container that has a tight-fitting cap and that you can shake easily, without it leaking.

how long does it last?

Most salad dressings have a high vinegar content and will easily last in the fridge for 2 months. Since ranch dressing contains dairy products, as well as a lower proportion of vinegar, you should use it within 2 weeks. You can always cut a recipe in half if you're not sure you'll use it soon enough.

This dressing tastes similar to store-bought Italian dressing.

Balsamic Vinaigrette Dressing

makes about 1¼ cups   prep time: 10 minutes

½ cup vegetable oil

¼ cup water

¼ cup balsamic or cider vinegar

2 tablespoons grated Parmesan cheese

1 clove garlic, crushed

1 teaspoon dry mustard, like Colman's

1 teaspoon salt

1 teaspoon sugar

1 teaspoon dried parsley

1. Combine all ingredients in a pint-size container with a tight-fitting lid. Shake well. Store, tightly covered, in refrigerator up to 2 months.

• ◆ ✦ ✦ ◆ ◆ ✦ ◆ ✦ •

I love to have this dressing ready-made in my fridge. It's the perfect topping for a crisp cabbage salad and a lightning-fast seasoning for a stir-fry. One-quarter cup poured over almost-cooked vegetables in a wok imparts a wonderful Asian flavor.

Asian Ginger Dressing

makes about 1½ cups   prep time: 15 minutes

3 cloves garlic, minced

⅓ cup white vinegar

⅓ cup water

¼ cup vegetable oil

¼ cup soy sauce

3 tablespoons honey

2 tablespoons sesame oil

1 tablespoon peeled and minced fresh
   ginger

½ teaspoon salt

1. Combine all ingredients in a pint-size container with a tight-fitting lid. Shake well.
2. Remove lid and heat jar in microwave on High 1 minute just to dissolve honey. Cool and shake well before serving. Store, tightly covered, in refrigerator up to 2 months.

French dressing has always been a favorite of mine. This recipe is miles better than most store-bought French dressings, and is so quick and easy to make!

Easy French Dressing

makes about 1¾ cups   prep time: 5 minutes

½ cup ketchup

½ cup vegetable oil

½ cup firmly packed brown sugar

⅓ cup red wine vinegar

1 tablespoon dried minced onion

1 teaspoon sweet paprika

1. Combine all ingredients in a pint-size container with a tight-fitting lid. Shake well. Chill at least 1 hour before serving. Store, tightly covered, in refrigerator up to 2 months.

◦ ◆ ◦ ◆ ◦ ◆ ◦ ◆ ◦ ◆

This ranch dressing doesn't require one of those store-bought seasoning packets, but it's every bit as good.

Ranch Dressing

makes about ¾ cup   prep time: 5 minutes

⅓ cup mayonnaise

¼ cup low-fat sour cream

¼ cup milk (or a little more, for a thinner dressing)

1 tablespoon white vinegar

½ teaspoon dried parsley

½ teaspoon garlic powder

½ teaspoon onion powder

½ teaspoon vegetable oil

½ teaspoon salt, or to taste

¼ teaspoon dried dillweed

1. In a small bowl, whisk together all ingredients. If you like your dressing a little thinner, add more milk until you get the desired consistency.

2. Pour into a pint-size container with a tight-fitting lid. Cover and refrigerate at least 30 minutes to meld flavors together before serving. Store, tightly covered, in refrigerator up to 2 weeks.

basting without burning

When you're using barbecue sauce on the grill, keep in mind that the sugar in the sauce can cause the outside of the meat to burn more quickly. It's best to cook one side of your meat before adding any barbecue sauce. Then turn the meat, brushing the sauce over the already-cooked side. Once the second side is adequately cooked, you can turn the meat again, baste the other side with sauce, and cook for just a minute or two longer. This will let the sauce caramelize without burning.

Since we barbecue every weekend, rain or shine, barbecue sauce is a particularly nice thing to have handy. It's good brushed on almost any meat, whether you cook it on the grill or in the oven.

Honey Barbecue Sauce

makes about 3 cups   prep time: 15 minutes

1½ cups ketchup
½ cup firmly packed brown sugar
½ cup white vinegar
½ cup honey
2 tablespoons soy sauce
1 tablespoon vegetable oil

1 tablespoon dried minced onion
1 teaspoon ground ginger
1 teaspoon salt
1 teaspoon dry mustard, like Colman's
1 teaspoon garlic powder
1 teaspoon black pepper

1. Combine all ingredients in a medium-size saucepan and simmer over medium heat 15 minutes.

2. Cool and store, tightly covered, in refrigerator up to 2 months.

Teriyaki sauce has many uses. Use it to flavor meatloaf or meatballs, add some when barbecuing salmon or chicken, toss it with vegetables in a stir-fry, or come up with your own ideas.

Teriyaki Sauce

makes about 2 cups   prep time: 15 minutes

¼ cup cornstarch

¼ cup cold water

2 cups water

½ cup soy sauce

½ cup firmly packed brown sugar

1 tablespoon honey

1 teaspoon ground ginger or 1 tablespoon
   peeled and grated fresh ginger

1 clove garlic, minced

1. Whisk together cornstarch and ¼ cup cold water in a medium-size saucepan. Whisk in remaining ingredients and cook over medium heat, stirring frequently, until sauce thickens. Cool and store, tightly covered, in refrigerator up to 2 weeks. Reheat in the microwave, adding a little water to thin it when reheating.

• • • • • • • • •

This recipe is every bit as good as the honey-mustard you'd get in a restaurant. Of course, it makes a great salad topping, but you'll also love it on chicken, hot dogs, or even fish sticks.

Sweet Honey-Mustard Sauce

makes about 1 cup   prep time: 5 minutes

½ cup mayonnaise

¼ cup prepared mustard

¼ cup honey

2 tablespoons fresh lemon juice

1. In a small bowl, whisk together all ingredients until smooth. Store, tightly covered, in refrigerator up to 2 months.

This simple syrup cooks up in minutes. Chances are you already have most of the needed ingredients sitting in your cupboard. If you don't happen to have maple flavoring, don't sweat it. Believe it or not, this recipe tastes great without the maple.

Homemade Pancake Syrup

makes 3 cups   prep time: 30 minutes

1½ cups firmly packed brown sugar
½ cup granulated sugar
1½ cups water
¾ cup light corn syrup

1 teaspoon salt
1 teaspoon vanilla extract
1 teaspoon maple flavoring (optional)

1. In a medium-size saucepan, combine sugars, water, and corn syrup; bring to a boil over medium heat. Boil until slightly thickened, about 7 minutes.

2. Remove from heat; stir in salt, vanilla, and maple flavoring, if using. Cool for 15 minutes before using, or cool entirely before storing in a tightly covered bottle in the cupboard just as you would with any syrup. Serve over pancakes, waffles, or French toast.

* ◆ ◆ ◆ ◆ ◆ ◆ ◆ ◆

This sauce is a real treat. When poured hot over ice cream, it makes a nice shell, and is incredibly chocolaty and delicious.

Hot Fudge Sauce

makes about 3 cups   prep time: 15 minutes

½ cup (1 stick) butter
¾ cup unsweetened cocoa powder
¾ cup sugar
½ cup light corn syrup

¼ cup water
¼ teaspoon salt
1 teaspoon vanilla extract

1. Melt butter in a medium-size saucepan over low heat. Add cocoa powder, sugar, corn syrup, water, and salt; heat slowly, stirring frequently, until sugar crystals have dissolved and mixture is smooth.

2. Remove from heat and stir in vanilla. Serve it immediately over ice cream or let it cool, then refrigerate, tightly covered, up to 3 months. It will thicken even more once it cools, and can be warmed in the microwave if you would like to serve it hot another day.

◦ • ◦ • ◦ ◆ • ◦ • ◦ ◦

This is a fairly spicy chili powder. If you tend towards caution in seasoning, try halving the cayenne pepper, which is the hottest component of the recipe.

Chili Powder

makes about ½ cup   prep time: 5 minutes

¼ cup sweet paprika

1 tablespoon garlic powder

1 tablespoon cayenne pepper

1 tablespoon onion powder

1 tablespoon dried oregano

2 teaspoons ground cumin

1. Place all ingredients in a small container with a tight-fitting lid and shake to combine well. Store in a cool, dark place.

don't skip the paprika!

Several of these recipes call for sweet paprika. If your paprika doesn't specify whether it's sweet or hot, it's most likely sweet. Sweet paprika is made from red bell peppers and adds lots of color to recipes, but very little heat. So don't be afraid when it shows up in large quantities in recipes.

I love taco seasoning for all sorts of things. I even add a little to spaghetti to provide a bit of heat.

Taco Seasoning Mix

makes about 1½ cups or 6 seasoning "packets"   prep time: 10 minutes

½ cup dried minced onion

¼ cup sweet paprika

¼ cup cornstarch

3 tablespoons chili powder

2 tablespoons salt

2 tablespoons garlic powder

1 tablespoon ground cumin

1 tablespoon dried oregano

1 teaspoon cayenne pepper

1. Place all ingredients in a medium-size container with a tight-fitting lid; shake well to combine. You can divide mixture evenly among 6 snack-size zip-top plastic bags, or store it in the jar and scoop out a scant ¼ cup for every 1 pound ground beef you cook.

◆●◆●◆◆●◆◆●

This seasoning mix adds body as well as classic Italian seasoning to pureed tomatoes.

Spaghetti Seasoning Mix

makes about 2 cups or 6 seasoning "packets"   prep time: 10 minutes

¾ cup cornstarch

¼ cup onion powder

¼ cup dried parsley

¼ cup garlic powder

3 tablespoons salt

2 tablespoons sugar

2 tablespoons dried basil

1 tablespoon dried oregano

2 teaspoons ground sage

1. Place all ingredients in a medium-size container with a tight-fitting lid; shake well until combined. Divide equally among 6 snack-size zip-top plastic bags, or store in the jar and scoop out ⅓ cup for every quart of crushed tomatoes that you use.

Since I've included several Ethiopian recipes in this cookbook, I wanted to offer you an easy substitute for *berbere*, an essential spice in Ethiopian cooking. It's not an exact replica of what you would buy in an Ethiopian market, but it will give you an idea of the taste.

Easy Berbere

makes about ¼ cup   prep time: 5 minutes

¼ cup cayenne pepper
1 teaspoon ground ginger
½ teaspoon ground cloves

½ teaspoon ground cinnamon
½ teaspoon ground turmeric

1. Place all ingredients in a small container with a tight-fitting lid and shake well until combined.

＊＊＊＊＊＊＊＊＊

Besides its most obvious use on chicken, this seasoning adds a wonderful flavor to stir-fried fresh or frozen green beans.

Poultry Seasoning

makes about ¼ cup   prep time: 5 minutes

1 tablespoon dried rosemary, crumbled
1 tablespoon dried oregano
1 tablespoon dried thyme

2 teaspoons ground sage
2 teaspoons ground ginger
1 teaspoon black pepper

1. Place all ingredients in a small container with a tight-fitting lid and shake well until combined.

This dressing mix is a delicious substitute for Hidden Valley Ranch seasoning packets.

Ranch Dressing Mix

makes about 2 cups mix   prep time: 10 minutes

10 saltines, finely crushed
¾ cup dried parsley flakes, crushed
¼ cup dried minced onion

¼ cup onion powder
¼ cup garlic powder
1 tablespoon dried dillweed

1. Combine all ingredients in a medium-size container and shake well. Store in an airtight container at room temperature up to 6 months.

To make ranch dressing: Combine 1 tablespoon mix with 2 cups sour cream.

⋅✦⋅✦⋅✦⋅✦⋅✦⋅

I tend to splurge on convenience food when we go camping. After all, who wants to spend vacation time cooking? One of my indulgences has always been instant oatmeal—the flavored kind in the individual packets. But that was before I learned how to make my own.

Ready-to-Make Instant Oatmeal

makes 8 single servings   prep time: 10 minutes

7 cups quick-cooking oats, divided
1 teaspoon salt

16 snack-size zip-top plastic bags

1. In a food processor, blend 3 cups oats and salt until powdery.
2. Place ¼ cup unpowdered oats and 2 tablespoons powdered oats into each zip-top plastic bag.

To make Instant Oatmeal: Empty 1 oatmeal packet into a bowl. Add ¾ cup boiling water. Stir and let stand 2 minutes. For thicker oatmeal, use less water. For thinner oatmeal, use more water. To make this even more affordable, save the zip-top bags to use again.

We've tried a lot of pancake recipes over the years, but this version creates the fluffiest, most tender pancakes we've tried. Make up a batch of this mix, and you'll have quick and easy pancakes and waffles at your fingertips any day of the week. If you would like to boost the nutrition of this a little more, you can add ½ cup wheat germ.

Blue Ribbon Pancake/Waffle Mix

makes five 2½-cup batches   prep time: 5 minutes

8 cups all-purpose flour

2 cups powdered milk

1 cup sugar

¼ cup baking powder

1 tablespoon salt

1. Mix all ingredients together and store in an airtight container at room temperature up to 1 year.

To make pancakes, see the recipe on page 84.

◦ ◦ ◦ ◦ ◦ ◦ ◦ ◦ ◦

My kids love coming in from a cold day outdoors to find that I've made hot cocoa. This recipe can be made for about one-third the cost of Swiss Miss, making cocoa a more affordable indulgence.

Homemade Cocoa Mix

makes about 8 cups mix or 24 servings   prep time: 5 minutes

3½ cups powdered milk

2½ cups confectioners' sugar

1 cup powdered coffee creamer

1 cup unsweetened cocoa powder

1. Place all ingredients in a large bowl. Stir until thoroughly combined. Store in an airtight container at room temperature up to 1 year.

For 1 serving of hot cocoa: Place ⅓ cup cocoa mix in a coffee cup or mug and add ¾ cup boiling water. Stir to dissolve. Top with a dollop of whipped cream or a few marshmallows if you like.

This is a great mix for coating chicken or pork chops before frying or baking. I usually dip the meat in an egg and milk mixture first, then dredge it in the shake-and-bake.

DIY Shake-and-Bake

makes about 4½ cups, enough for 2 meals   prep time: 10 minutes

One really great thing about making your own mixes is that they don't have as many artificial flavorings and preservatives as the store-bought mixes do.

2 cups all-purpose flour
2 cups cracker crumbs (I use saltines crushed in the food processor)
¼ cup vegetable oil
3 tablespoons sweet paprika
2 tablespoons salt
1 tablespoon sugar
1 tablespoon garlic powder
1 teaspoon onion powder

1. Mix all ingredients well in a large bowl. Store, tightly covered, in refrigerator in an airtight container up to 3 months.

This easy recipe is extremely flavorful. I use it most often mixed into sour cream as a chip dip. However, it is also a nice seasoning for a roast or added to scalloped potatoes or a green bean casserole. If you like, you can substitute celery seeds for the dill.

Onion Soup Mix

makes about 1 cup (equivalent of 4 packets of onion soup mix)   prep time: 5 minutes

¾ cup dried minced onion
¼ cup beef bouillon powder
4 teaspoons onion powder

½ teaspoon dried dillweed
1 teaspoon sugar

1. Place all the ingredients in a medium-size jar with a tight-fitting lid and shake to combine well. Store in an airtight container at room temperature for up to a year.

To make onion dip: Mix ¼ cup of the onion soup mix with one 16-ounce container sour cream. Store in the fridge, tightly covered, for up to 2 weeks.

◆ ◦ ◆ ◦ ◆ ◆ ◦ ◦ ◆ ◦

Lots of people use canned soups to speed up the preparation of various meals, especially casseroles. A can here or there won't break the budget. But if you're interested in keeping your grocery budget at its very lowest level, give this cream soup recipe a try. It consists of a dry base, to which you add various ingredients, depending on the type of flavor you need in the recipe you're making.

Cream of Anything Soup Mix

makes about 5 cups dry mix (equivalent to twelve 10.75-ounce cans condensed soup)
prep time: 10 minutes

3 cups powdered milk
1 cup cornstarch
1 cup powdered chicken bouillon
2 tablespoons onion powder

1 teaspoon dried thyme
½ teaspoon dried basil
½ teaspoon black pepper

1. Combine all ingredients in a large bowl. Store, tightly covered, in an airtight container at room temperature up to 1 year.

To make soup: In a medium-size saucepan, combine ½ cup dry soup mix with 1¼ cups water, 1 tablespoon butter, and the following flavorings to make the specific soup you need. Blend well and bring to a boil, cooking 2 to 3 minutes. This mixture will thicken as it cools.

Condensed Cream of Chicken Soup: Prepare as directed above.

Condensed Cream of Mushroom Soup: Add ½ cup minced mushrooms.

Condensed Cream of Celery Soup: Add ½ cup minced celery. You can puree soup when it cools if you prefer a totally smooth soup.

You can make this ready-made biscuit mix in 10 minutes for a fraction of the cost of the biscuit mix you buy in the store (and it's a whole lot cheaper than the ready-to-bake biscuits in the refrigerator case). You can also use it as pancake mix simply by adding an egg and enough additional milk to reach the right consistency for pancakes.

Biscuit Mix

makes about 10 cups mix or 5 batches of 8 biscuits each   prep time: 10 minutes

8 cups all-purpose flour

1½ cups powdered milk

¼ cup baking powder

1 tablespoon salt

1½ cups vegetable shortening

1. Combine dry ingredients. Add shortening and mix by hand or with a pastry blender until well combined. Store, tightly covered, in an airtight container in refrigerator up to 3 months.

To make biscuits: Combine 2 cups biscuit mix with ⅓ cup milk and 1 tablespoon white vinegar to make a soft but not sticky dough. If dough is too sticky, add a little additional flour until dough has a good texture. Turn out on a floured counter. Roll out about ¾ inch thick. Cut with a large glass or biscuit cutter. Place on an ungreased baking sheet. Bake in a preheated 400°F oven until biscuits are golden, 12 to 15 minutes. Each batch makes about eight 3-inch biscuits.

Your kids will think you're awesome if you let them help you make these wonderful marshmallows. They're like store-bought, but better, especially if you use good vanilla.

Homemade Marshmallows

makes 40 marshmallows   prep time: 15 minutes, plus at least 4 hours stand time

3 packets (about 3 tablespoons) unflavored gelatin

½ cup cold water

1½ cups granulated sugar

1 cup light corn syrup

½ teaspoon salt

⅓ cup water

2 tablespoons vanilla extract

Confectioners' sugar for dusting

1. Combine gelatin and ½ cup cold water in a medium-size heat-proof bowl. Let stand for 20 minutes.

2. Combine granulated sugar, corn syrup, salt, and ⅓ cup water in a medium-size heavy saucepan. Stir over low heat until sugar has dissolved. Increase heat to high; heat until mixture comes to a very brisk boil, stirring occasionally. Boil about 2 minutes, stirring frequently. If you have a candy thermometer, the temperature should reach about 240°F.

3. Remove pan from heat, and very carefully pour contents into bowl containing gelatin. Add vanilla. Set a timer for 10 minutes. Using an electric mixer, beat mixture on high speed for at least 10 minutes. When mixture becomes very thick and white and has doubled in size, it is done.

4. Using a rubber spatula, scoop mixture into a 9 x 13-inch casserole dish that has been generously dusted with confectioners' sugar. Smooth the top with a rubber spatula. Let marshmallows sit at room temperature, uncovered, at least 4 hours, or overnight.

5. Using a pizza cutter sprayed with cooking spray, cut marshmallows into squares, dusting cut edges with more confectioners' sugar to prevent sticking. Store, tightly covered, in an airtight container at room temperature up to 3 months.

Variation: For marshmallows with different colors and flavors, add a small amount of unsweetened Kool-Aid powder to mixture on stove as you're heating it.

A friend of mine makes a recipe like this using almonds. Since almonds are rather expensive, I decided to try peanuts. I can get peanuts very affordably at Asian markets in my area. Wrapped in pretty cello bags, these little sweeties make a delicious and very welcome Christmas gift.

Candied Peanuts

makes about 6 cups   prep time: 1½ hours

2 teaspoons water
2 large egg whites
6 cups unsalted shelled peanuts
2 cups sugar

1 teaspoon ground cinnamon
1 teaspoon salt (omit if peanuts are already salted)

1. Preheat oven to 225°F.

2. In a small bowl, beat water and egg whites together until white and frothy. You can do this by hand, but an electric mixer is easiest.

3. On a rimmed baking sheet, toss egg white mixture with peanuts until well coated. Combine sugar, cinnamon, and salt (if using). Pour over nuts and toss until nuts are thoroughly coated. Bake 1 hour, stirring halfway through cooking time.

4. Remove pan from oven; stir nuts once more. Let nuts cool on pan. Fair warning, though: These are so yummy that if you leave them on the pan for long, they'll disappear.

Variation: You can also make this recipe using raw, unroasted peanuts, but you'll need to bake them an extra 15 minutes or so. It's also a good idea to separate peanut halves before coating them with egg, as this allows peanuts to get crunchier while baking. Rubbing handfuls of peanuts briskly between your hands will cause the majority of them to break apart.

You may not use this recipe often, but I was fascinated to learn that making cheese could be this simple. This recipe uses a lot of milk to make a small amount of cheese, but if you use the leftover whey in soup, you won't waste a thing. The cheese can be added to lasagna, tossed in a salad, or used in any recipe that calls for feta cheese.

Soft Cheese (Paneer)

makes about ½ pound cheese   prep time: 40 minutes, including time to drain

6 cups milk
¼ cup white vinegar

1 teaspoon salt

1. Bring milk to a boil in a large pot. Add vinegar and salt. The whey will separate immediately.
2. Line a colander with a thin, smooth (flour sack) dish towel or a piece of cheesecloth. Place colander over a large bowl. Carefully pour contents of pot into colander. Liquid (whey) will drain down into the bowl, leaving cheese curds in colander. (You can save whey to make a milk-based soup such as Cheesy Corn and Potato Chowder on page 192.)
3. Once you've let the majority of liquid drain into bowl, twist together cloth so that you are compressing cheese curds, and fasten it together with a rubber band. At this point, you will have a little bundle of cheese curds about the size of two decks of cards.
4. Weight bundle down with something heavy like a stack of bowls or several dinner plates. Let sit for 30 minutes, letting remainder of whey dribble out and curds bind together into a solid lump. Your final result will be a lump of cheese about the consistency of firm tofu. It is best if used quickly, but can be tighly wrapped and stored in the refrigerator up to 1 week.

I like to save bread heels in the freezer to use for this recipe, or to make the Stuffed French Toast Strata recipe on page 254.

Crispy Croutons

makes 2 cups   prep time: 30 minutes

4 slices bread of your choice
2 tablespoons butter
2 tablespoons olive oil

½ teaspoon dried basil
½ teaspoon dried oregano
½ teaspoon garlic powder

1. Preheat oven to 425°F.

2. Cut bread into 1-inch cubes, leaving crusts on.

3. Melt butter and oil in a medium-size skillet over medium-high heat. Toss in bread cubes and sprinkle with all seasonings. Stir well to coat bread.

4. Remove mixture to a baking sheet and bake until croutons are crisp and evenly brown, 10 to 15 minutes. Remove from pan. Let cool and serve over soup or salad. Store any remaining croutons in an airtight container at room temperature up to 1 month.

Canning and Food Preservation

Lots of people think canning is a tremendously finicky and difficult process. That just isn't true. It does take a little time, but it's one of the few jobs I do where I can admire the fruits of my labor several months down the road. You'll find that the recipes in this section are a little longer than elsewhere in the book. That isn't because they're hard, but simply because I wanted to go through the steps carefully so you can approach canning with confidence.

Canning isn't an art that everyone chooses to learn. However, it can be a real money-saver, especially if you have a good source of reasonably priced produce or if you have your own garden. For the best, most up-to-date information on canning safety, visit the National Center for Home Food Preservation Web site at *www.uga.edu/nchfp/index.html*. It's up to you to make sure you follow safety guidelines. By following processing directions carefully, you can store food for your family safely and with confidence.

equipment you'll need for canning

1
Large pot, deep enough to fully submerge quart-size jars

2
Quart- and pint-size canning jars

3
Canning rings and new lids

4
Canning tongs

5
Hot mitts

6
Canning funnel (optional)

We have a huge garden. Every year my husband plants 100 tomato plants—yes, 100. Really. This means that we spend a lot of time in August and September putting up tomatoes for winter use. I've developed a streamlined way of dealing with large quantities of tomatoes that I hope you'll find helpful.

Home-Canned Tomatoes

yield depends on how many tomatoes you have   prep time: 2 hours

White vinegar

For every quart of tomatoes:
6 to 8 large ripe tomatoes
1 tablespoon fresh lemon juice
1 teaspoon salt

1. Fill canning pot halfway with water and place it on the stove over medium heat. Add a slosh of vinegar to water to avoid hard water spots on your jars.
2. Next, thoroughly wash the quart jars, lids, and rings you intend to use with hot water and soap. Once they're clean, place them in the canner to simmer 2 to 3 minutes. Remove jars from water using tongs and set on a clean towel to drain. Always use new canning lids. Once a lid has been used, the wax seal compresses, which makes it unsafe to use again for a different jar. It's fine to re-use rings, as long as they're not rusty.
3. Next, thoroughly wash your tomatoes. Cut them into quarters, removing stems and any discolored spots. Puree tomatoes in a blender or food processor. If you are using a blender, you may need to add a bit of water to help tomatoes move freely enough to come into contact with the blades.
4. Once you have some of the tomatoes pureed, pour into a large pot and set over medium heat. Continue to puree tomatoes, adding them to the soon-to-be simmering pot of tomatoes until you have enough to make a canner full of tomatoes. Most canners hold 6 or 7 quarts, and to make 6 quarts of tomatoes, you will probably need about 40 large tomatoes. If you don't have a big enough pot to handle all of the tomato puree at once, divide it between a couple of pots.

5. When tomato puree has reached a simmer, if you like, you can let it simmer for an hour or more to reduce some of the water. This step makes for a thicker puree, but it is not essential. To be safe, the puree simply needs to reach a simmer.

6. Once all your puree is simmering, add 1 tablespoon lemon juice and 1 teaspoon salt to each jar. Pour puree into jars. Wipe any spilled puree from rim of each jar. Place lid and ring on each jar, screwing lid on firmly.

WARNING: At this point, it is important the water in the canning pot and tomato puree in the jars be approximately the same temperature. If the temperatures are significantly different, you may lose some jars to breakage, as a large heat differential will cause jars to crack. You don't have to put a thermometer in the water—just hold your hand over it and compare heat coming off the water to temperature of the jars. When you are canning multiple batches, some jars may cool before you can get them into the canner. If that happens, simply add enough cool water to your canning pot to match the temperature of the jars, and remember that your processing time doesn't start until canning water has come to a boil.

7. Set filled jars carefully into canning pot, making sure there is enough water in pot to cover jars by at least ½ inch. Use your canning tongs to do this; DON'T drop jars into water. If you need to add water, make sure it is very hot water and pour it in very slowly, again to avoid breakage of jars due to temperature differences. Turn the burner on high and bring water to a boil. Once water reaches a boil, begin counting processing time. Quart jars of tomatoes will need to process 45 minutes. Pints take only 35 minutes.

8. Once processing is done, using canning tongs, remove jars to a clean, thick towel on the counter. Within half an hour or so, you should hear lovely "pinging" sounds, which mean your jar lids are sealing properly. Before you put jars away into the cupboard, test to make sure they have sealed by pressing your finger in the center of lid. If it is properly sealed, it will feel tight and won't pop down and up when you press on it. If any of your jars don't seal, simply store in fridge and use within 2 weeks.

9. Let the jars sit until they are cool before placing in the cupboard. And always remember to write the year on the jars!

This applesauce recipe takes a little time, but it's very easy. Any type of apple will work. Soft apples will process more quickly. If you choose a tart variety, you may want to add a little more sugar.

Easy Canned Applesauce

makes 4 to 5 quarts or 8 to 10 pints   prep time: 2 hours

White vinegar

4 cups water

2 cups sugar (or up to 3 cups if you have very tart apples)

2 tablespoons ground cinnamon

1 teaspoon ground nutmeg

30 medium-size apples (about 10 pounds)

1. Fill canning pot halfway with water and place it on the stove over medium heat. Add a slosh of vinegar to water to avoid hard water spots on your jars.

2. Next, thoroughly wash quart or pint jars, lids, and rings you intend to use with hot water and soap. Once they're clean, place in the canner to simmer 2 to 3 minutes. Remove jars from water with tongs and set on a clean towel to drain. Always use new canning lids. Once a lid has been used, the wax seal compresses, which makes it unsafe to use again for a different jar. It is fine to re-use rings, as long as they are not rusty.

3. In a large pot, combine water, sugar, cinnamon, and nutmeg.

4. Start peeling, coring, and cutting the apples. This job goes much faster if you have a peeler/slicer/corer gadget, but, really, the apples only need to be peeled, cored, and quartered. Once you have half a dozen apples cut, place them in the pot with water, sugar, and spices; turn heat to medium. Stir occasionally, turning heat down once apples start to simmer.

5. If apples start to stick to the bottom of pot, add a little more water and turn heat down a bit. As apples cook down, they will break up and soften and make space for more apples. Keep adding apples as you cut them. You'll be amazed at how many apples it takes to fill a pot, and you'd be wise to enlist the help of anyone over the age of six who can wield a peeler.

6. Depending on how firm your apples are, it will take 30 to 60 minutes to cook them down into sauce. The final apples into the pot obviously won't get quite as much cooking time as the first ones, so cook them long enough so that they start to break up.

7. If you prefer a very smooth sauce, or are too impatient to cook until apples are completely soft, run part or all of sauce through the blender.

8. Spoon hot applesauce into prepared jars. Wipe any applesauce from rim of each jar. Place lid and ring on each jar, screwing lid on firmly.

WARNING: At this point, it is important that the water in the canning pot and applesauce in the jars be approximately the same temperature. If temperatures are significantly different, you may lose some jars to breakage, as a large heat differential will cause the jars to crack. You don't have to put a thermometer in the water—just hold your hand over it and compare heat coming off the water to temperature of the jars. When you are canning multiple batches, you may have some jars cool before you can get them into the canner. If that happens, simply add enough cool water to your canning pot to match the temperature of the jars, and remember that your processing time doesn't start until canning water has come to a boil.

9. Set filled jars carefully into canning pot, making sure there is enough water in pot to cover jars by at least ½ inch. Use your canning tongs to do this; DON'T drop jars into water. If you need to add water, make sure it is very hot water and pour it in very slowly, again to avoid breakage of jars due to temperature differences. Turn the burner on high and bring water to a boil. Once water reaches a boil, begin counting processing time. Quart jars of applesauce will need to process for 35 minutes. Pints take only 25 minutes.

10. Once processing is done, using canning tongs, remove jars to a clean, thick towel on the counter. Within half an hour or so, you should hear lovely "pinging" sounds, which mean your jar lids are sealing properly. Before you put jars away into the cupboard, test to make sure they have sealed by pressing your finger in the center of the lid. If it is properly sealed, it will feel tight and won't pop down and up when you press on it. If any of your jars don't seal, simply store in fridge and use within 2 weeks.

11. Let jars sit until they are cool before placing in the cupboard. And always remember to write the year on the jars!

I make my own grape juice, using Concord grapes we've grown and a charming old juicer that I borrow from my parents every September. If you're making your own juice and want your jelly to be totally sediment-free, you can strain the juice through a coffee filter set in a wire strainer. I don't bother with this step, as my family isn't that finicky about their jelly. It's perfectly okay to make jelly with grape juice you buy in the store.

Grape Jelly

makes 7 half-pints   prep time: 45 minutes

White vinegar
3½ cups grape juice
¼ cup lemon juice

One 2-ounce box pectin
5½ cups sugar (about 2½ pounds)

1. Fill canning pot halfway with water and place it on the stove over medium heat. Add a slosh of vinegar to water to avoid hard water spots on your jars.
2. Next, thoroughly wash the pint or half-pint jars, lids, and rings you intend to use with hot water and soap. Once they're clean, set in the canner to simmer 2 to 3 minutes. Remove jars from water with tongs and set on a clean towel to drain. Always use new canning lids. Once a lid has been used, the wax seal compresses, which makes it unsafe to use again for a different jar. It is fine to re-use rings, as long as they are not rusty.
3. Get out a second large pot and put it on the stove. Pour in grape juice, lemon juice, and pectin; stir until pectin is dissolved. Heat mixture until it gets to a full rolling boil that cannot be stirred down.
4. Quickly add all sugar, stirring briskly to mix well. Return to a full rolling boil; boil for 2 minutes.
5. Pour jelly into prepared jars, filling to within ½ inch of rim, without overfilling. I find this easiest to do by using a 2-cup glass measuring cup that I dip into the pot. Wipe rims of jars with a clean damp cloth so that no jelly residue remains. Put lids on jars; add rings, screwing on firmly.

   WARNING: At this point, it is important that the water in the canning pot and jelly in the jars be approximately the same temperature. If temperatures are significantly different, you may lose some jars to breakage, as a large heat differential will cause the jars to crack. You don't have to put a thermometer in the water—just hold your hand over it and compare heat coming off the water to temperature of the jars. When you are canning multiple batches, you may have some jars cool before you can get them into the canner. If that happens, simply add enough cool water to your canning pot to match the temperature of the jars, and remember that your processing time doesn't start until canning water has come to a boil.

6. Using canning tongs, carefully place filled jars in boiling water bath, making sure there is enough water to cover jars with ½ to 1 inch of water. DON'T drop jars into water. Bring water to a boil again; boil for 10 minutes.

7. Using canning tongs, remove jars to a clean, thick towel on the counter and let cool undisturbed until the next day. Within half an hour or so, you should hear lovely "pinging" sounds, which means your jar lids are sealing properly. Before you put jars away in the cupboard, test to make sure they have sealed by pressing your finger in the center of the lid. If it is properly sealed, it will feel tight and won't pop down and up when you press on it. If any of your jars don't seal, simply store in fridge and use within a couple of weeks.

8. Remember to write the year on the jars before putting them away!

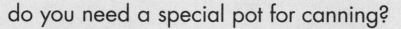

do you need a special pot for canning?

If you'd like to try your hand at canning, but don't have an official canning pot, no problem. Any heavy pot that allows you to totally submerge your jars in water will work. There should be at least ½ inch of water covering the top of every jar. Try pint jars if your pot isn't big enough to submerge quarts. Just be sure to use new canning lids and very clean jars, either dipping them in boiling water for a few minutes before you fill them or running them through the dishwasher.

This recipe makes the most of a moderate quantity of strawberries.

Strawberry-Rhubarb Jam

makes 12 half-pints or 6 pints   prep time: 1 hour

White vinegar

4 cups thinly sliced rhubarb stems (completely cut away and discard the leaves)

4 cups hulled and sliced strawberries

2 tablespoons fresh or bottled lemon juice

Two 2-ounce packages pectin

½ teaspoon butter (keeps the jam from getting too foamy)

10 cups sugar (about 5 pounds)

1. Fill canning pot halfway with water and place it on the stove over medium heat. Add a slosh of vinegar to water to avoid hard water spots on your jars.

2. Next, thoroughly wash the pint or half-pint jars, lids, and rings you intend to use with hot water and soap. Once they're clean, place in canner to simmer 2 to 3 minutes. Remove jars from water with tongs and set on a clean towel to drain. Always use new canning lids. Once a lid has been used, the wax seal compresses, which makes it unsafe to use again for a different jar. It is fine to re-use rings, as long as they're not rusty.

3. In a large pot, combine rhubarb, strawberries, lemon juice, pectin, and butter; bring to a full boil. Add sugar and keep stirring until it is fully dissolved. Return mixture to a boil; boil for 1 minute, stirring. Remove pot from the burner and skim off foam with a spoon.

4. Spoon hot jam into prepared jars. I like to pour the jam into a glass 4-cup glass measuring cup first, then into the jars; it's just easier. Leave ½ inch of space at the top. Wipe jar rims clean and screw lids on firmly.

WARNING: At this point, it is important that the water in the canning pot and jam in the jars be approximately the same temperature. If temperatures are significantly different, you may lose some jars to breakage, as a large heat differential will cause the jars to crack. You don't have to put a thermometer in the water—just hold your hand over it and compare heat coming off the water to temperature of the jars. When you are canning multiple batches, you may have some jars cool before you can get them into the canner. If that happens, simply add enough cool water to your canning pot to match the temperature of the jars, and remember that your processing time doesn't start until the canning water has come to a boil.

5. Using canning tongs, carefully place filled jars in boiling water bath, making sure there is enough water to cover jars with ½ to 1 inch of water. DON'T drop jars into water. Bring water to a boil again; boil for 5 minutes for half-pints and 10 minutes for pints.

6. Using canning tongs, remove jars to a clean, thick towel on the counter. Let jars cool undisturbed until the next day. Within half an hour or so, you should hear lovely "pinging" sounds, which means your jar lids are sealing properly. Before you put jars away in the cupboard, test to make sure they have sealed by pressing your finger in the center of the lid. If it is properly sealed, it will feel tight and won't pop down and up when you press on it. If any of your jars don't seal, simply store in fridge and use within a couple of weeks.

7. Remember to write the year on the jars before putting them away!

will canning really save you money?

Canning will most likely be an economical option for your family if you have a low-cost source of fruits or vegetables. Examples might include a farm stand out in the country, a relative's overly productive fruit tree, a U-pick orchard, or your own back-yard garden. The Colorado State University Web site *(www.ext.colostate.edu/PUBS/ FOODNUT/08704.html)* does a great job of discussing the various factors to consider when thinking about home-canning food.

Apricot Jam

makes 5 pints   prep time: 1 hour

White vinegar

4 pounds apricots

¼ cup fresh lemon juice or white vinegar

One 2-ounce box pectin

6 cups sugar (about 3 pounds)

1. Fill canning pot halfway with water and place it on the stove over medium heat. Add a slosh of vinegar to water to avoid hard water spots on your jars.

2. Next, thoroughly wash the pint jars, lids, and rings you intend to use with hot water and soap. Once they're clean, place in canner to simmer 2 to 3 minutes. Remove jars from water with tongs and set on a clean towel to drain. Always use new canning lids. Once a lid has been used, the wax seal compresses, which makes it unsafe to use again for a different jar. It is fine to re-use rings, as long as they are not rusty.

3. Wash and sort apricots. It is OK to use apricots with small soft spots as long as they aren't discolored or moldy. Tear apricots into halves to remove pits. Fill the food processor with apricot chunks and puree for a minute or so. Repeat until you have enough puree (you'll need 4½ cups).

4. Measure your puree carefully and pour into a big pot along with lemon juice. Immediately mix in pectin using a wire whisk. Heat mixture to a full rolling boil, first stirring occasionally and then more frequently as the mixture heats up. Once it has reached a full rolling boil, add sugar a couple of cups at a time, stirring continuously. When all sugar is added and mixture has returned to a full rolling boil, cook for 1 minute, stirring.

5. Pour mixture quickly into prepared jars, leaving ½ inch of headspace at the top of jar. Wipe edges of jars clean and screw lids on tightly.

   WARNING: At this point, it is important that the water in the canning pot and jam in the jars be approximately the same temperature. If temperatures are significantly different, you may lose some jars to breakage, as a large heat differential will cause the jars to crack. You don't have to put a thermometer in the water—just hold your hand over it and compare heat coming off the water to temperature of the jars. When you're canning multiple batches, you may have some jars cool before you can get them into the canner. If that happens, simply add enough cool water to your canning pot to match the temperature of the jars, and remember that your processing time doesn't start until the canning water has come to a boil.

6. Using canning tongs, carefully place filled jars in boiling water bath, making sure there is enough water to cover the jars with ½ to 1 inch of water. DON'T drop jars into water. Bring water to a boil again; boil for 15 minutes.

7. Using canning tongs, remove jars to a clean, thick towel on the counter. Let jars cool undisturbed until the next day. Within half an hour or so, you should hear lovely "pinging" sounds, which means your jar lids are sealing properly. Before you put jars away in the cupboard, test to make sure they have sealed by pressing your finger in the center of the lid. If it is properly sealed, it will feel tight and won't pop down and up when you press on it. If any of your jars don't seal, simply store in fridge and use within a couple of weeks.

8. Remember to write the year on the jars before storing them!

metric charts

The recipes that appear in this cookbook use the standard U.S. method for measuring liquid and dry or solid ingredients (teaspoons, tablespoons, and cups). The information in the following charts is provided to help cooks outside the United States successfully use these recipes. All equivalents are approximate.

Metric Equivalents for Different Types of Ingredients

A standard cup measure of a dry or solid ingredient will vary in weight depending on the type of ingredient. A standard cup of liquid is the same volume for any type of liquid. Use the following chart when converting standard cup measures to grams (weight) or to milliliters (volume).

Standard Cup	Fine Powder (ex. flour)	Grain (ex. rice)	Granular (ex. sugar)	Liquid Solids (ex. butter)	Liquid (ex. milk)
1	140 g	150 g	190 g	200 g	240 ml
¾	105 g	113 g	143 g	150 g	180 ml
⅔	93 g	100 g	125 g	133 g	160 ml
½	70 g	75 g	95 g	100 g	120 ml
⅓	47 g	50 g	63 g	67 g	80 ml
¼	35 g	38 g	48 g	50 g	60 ml
⅛	18 g	19 g	24 g	25 g	30 ml

Useful Equivalents for Liquid Ingredients by Volume

¼ tsp					=	1 ml	
½ tsp					=	2 ml	
1 tsp					=	5 ml	
3 tsp	=	1 Tbsp		=	½ fl oz =	15 ml	
		2 Tbsp	= ⅛ cup	=	1 fl oz =	30 ml	
		4 Tbsp	= ¼ cup	=	2 fl oz =	60 ml	
		5⅓ Tbsp	= ⅓ cup	=	3 fl oz =	80 ml	
		8 Tbsp	= ½ cup	=	4 fl oz =	120 ml	
		10⅔ Tbsp	= ⅔ cup	=	5 fl oz =	160 ml	
		12 Tbsp	= ¾ cup	=	6 fl oz =	180 ml	
		16 Tbsp	= 1 cup	=	8 fl oz =	240 ml	
		1 pt	= 2 cups	=	16 fl oz =	480 ml	
		1 qt	= 4 cups	=	32 fl oz =	960 ml	
					33 fl oz =	1000 ml	= 1 l

Useful Equivalents for Dry Ingredients by Weight

(To convert ounces to grams, multiply the number of ounces by 30.)

1 oz	=	¹⁄₁₆ lb	=	30 g
4 oz	=	¼ lb	=	120 g
8 oz	=	½ lb	=	240 g
12 oz	=	¾ lb	=	360 g
16 oz	=	1 lb	=	480 g

Useful Equivalents for Length

(To convert inches to centimeters, multiply the number of inches by 2.5.)

1 in					=	2.5 cm	
6 in	=	½ ft			=	15 cm	
12 in	=	1 ft			=	30 cm	
36 in	=	3 ft	=	1 yd	=	90 cm	
40 in					=	100 cm	= 1 m

Useful Equivalents for Cooking/Oven Temperatures

	Fahrenheit	Celsius	Gas Mark
Freeze water	32° F	0° C	
Room temperature	68° F	20° C	
Boil water	212° F	100° C	
Bake	325° F	160° C	3
	350° F	180° C	4
	375° F	190° C	5
	400° F	200° C	6
	425° F	220° C	7
	450° F	230° C	8
Broil			Grill

recipe index

subject index